Advance Praise for

Building Multispecies Resistance Against Exploitation

"Building Multispecies Resistance Against Exploitation: Stories from the Frontlines of Labor and Animal Rights edited by Zane McNeill is a powerful captivating read from authors from around the world. This beautiful engaging collection of insightful writings from emerging international public intellectuals on animal and economic justice needs to be read by anyone interested in the state of agriculture and union organizing."

—Dr. Anthony J. Nocella II, Associate Professor, Department of Criminal Justice, Salt Lake Community College

"This timely volume brings together a select group of committed activist-scholars to address what is perhaps the central question facing the pro-animal movement today: How should we think about violent discrimination against animals in conjunction with other forms of social injustice? The essays highlight not only the entangled forms of oppression at work in slaughterhouses and related institutions, but also uncover subtle forms of marginalization and exploitation at the very heart of the animal rights movement itself. The authors collectively aim to do nothing less than bring these interconnected forms of oppression to the surface and find means for eliminating them. The book deserves to be widely read and its suggestions for change widely implemented."

—Matthew Calarco is a Professor of Philosophy, California State University at Fullerton

"McNeill's collection reveals, in important ways, how the 'necropolitical' animal-industrial complex endangers the lives and interests of society's most vulnerable human and non-human actors in problematic, intersectional, and illegal patterns. This collection forefronts stories and theories of resistance in the face of violence and oppression experienced by human and non-human laborers. It fleshes out a growing recognition of farmed animals as laborers, and their suffering as intersecting with those other human bodies that are rendered killable through white supremacy and racial capitalism. The scholar-activist authors provide brave personal accounts and inspirational tactics for multi-issue activism and total liberation which have interspecies solidarity at their heart. This is a vital and insightful contribution that will help readers locate the animal advocacy movement critically within its challenging social contexts."

—Iyan Offor is a Senior Lecturer in Law at the School of Law, Birmingham, and author of Global Animal Law from the Margins: International Trade in Animals and their Bodies

"Zane McNeill's Building Multispecies Resistance Against Exploitation is a pivotal collection illuminating the intersections of human and nonhuman labor within the necropolitical landscape of racial and carceral capitalism. From spotlighting the often-overlooked resistance of animals to scrutinizing practices in the animal advocacy nonprofit sector that reinforce systemic oppression, the activist-scholar contributors offer crucial insights for forging multispecies solidarity. Essential reading for social justice advocates, interdisciplinary scholars, and animal activists, this work provokes critical thought while charting a transformative path towards total liberation."

—Sarat Colling, Author of Animal Resistance in the Global Capitalist Era

"Building Multispecies Resistance Against Exploitation is a necessary, timely collection. As the North American labor movement is finally building momentum again after decades of neoliberal divestment, the authors here persuasively argue that the animal liberation movement should embrace a truly intersectional, labor-focused theory of change. From theorizing the labor and resistance of individual animals to urging advocates to incorporate strategies from deep organizing, this thought-provoking collection will be a motivator for anyone interested in building a more just and equitable world."

—Michael Swistara, Animal Protection lawyer, scholar, and activist

"This collection of profound and poignant works illuminates the monstrous entangled oppression inherent in the slaughterhouse industry. It highlights the organizational and alliance-building work necessary for transcending the current oppressive social system. Brilliant, timely, and required reading for all pursuing a just and nonviolent future."

—David Nibert, Author of Animal Oppression and Human Violence: Domesecration, Capitalism and Global Conflict

"Relying on contemporary vegan, feminist, and critical race theories, Building Multispecies Resistance Against Exploitation examines the multispecies consequences that result from capitalist control over living (and dying). Emerging scholars specializing in social science, philosophy, and law consider how work and labor politics impact humans and other animals in co-occupied "work" spaces such as slaughterhouses, but also anthropocentric grassroots and professionalized workspaces that engage in rescue work and collective action. Constructions of race, class, gender, and species have historically been manufactured for the reproduction of oppression, but they can also be engaged for strategic resistance. Readers will be encouraged to question the utility of single-issue campaigning, the possibility of "ethical" consumption, and how to build bridges to adjacent human rights movements. With critical and theoretically informed analyses of everyday quandaries in anti-speciesist efforts, this is a book meant to be used and applied for multispecies emancipation and greater quality of life for all."

—Dr Corey Lee Wrenn is a Lecturer in Sociology, University of Kent

"This anthology examines different ways power, oppression, and injustice affect both human and nonhuman animals, unfurling a rich tapestry of narratives to advocate for multispecies resistance. From community organizers to academics, these diverse perspectives represent a broad spectrum of lived experiences and professional backgrounds, uniting around the urgent need for change and creating avenues for genuine liberation for all."

—Amber E. George is a Assistant professor of philosophy and diversity, equity, and inclusion, Galen College

"Amidst a national renaissance of labor activism and rising class consciousness, this timely and necessary collection of essays calls the entire animal advocacy movement into the broader conversation about the disastrous effects of racialized capitalism. Incisive contributions from a diverse array of scholar-activists spotlight the dire need for animal advocacy organizations to recognize and respond to the inextricably linked hierarchies of oppression — including class, species, race, gender, and ability, among others — that form the foundations of capitalist exploitation. A vital intervention in the self-defeating politics and strategies of contemporary animal activism!"

—Elan Abrell is an Instructor in Anthropology and Animal Studies, New York University

"Building Multispecies Resistance Against Exploitation draws on the work of some of the most important activist-scholars in the field at present. In foregrounding the violent landscapes of animal work, labor, and (resistance to) death, the book deepens our understanding of the interconnectedness of human and non-huma animal oppression in highly original and significant ways. Most importantly, these insights are drawn on to provoke new imaginaries into being - ones that might yet inform new approaches to interspecies solidarity that have potential to move us closer toward the liberation of all animals, humans included. It is an excellent, rigorous, and accessible publication, and one that deserves to be read widely."

—Richard J. White is a Co-Editor of Vegan Geographies: Spaces beyond Violence, Ethics Beyond Speciesism

Building Multispecies Resistance Against Exploitation

RADICAL ANIMAL STUDIES
AND TOTAL LIBERATION

Anthony J. Nocella II
Series Editor

Vol. 13

Building Multispecies Resistance Against Exploitation

Stories from the Frontlines of Labor and Animal Rights

Edited by Zane McNeill

PETER LANG

New York · Berlin · Bruxelles · Chennai · Lausanne · Oxford

Library of Congress Cataloging-in-Publication Data

Names: McNeill, Zane, editor.
Title: Building multispecies resistance against exploitation: stories from the frontlines of labor and animal rights / edited by Zane McNeill.
Description: New York: Peter Lang, 2024. | Series: Radical animal studies and total liberation, 2469-3065; vol. 13 | Includes bibliographical references.
Identifiers: LCCN 2024000972 (print) | LCCN 2024000973 (ebook) | ISBN 9781636675602 (paperback) | ISBN 9781636675619 (pdf) | ISBN 9781636675626 (epub)
Subjects: LCSH: Animal rights. | Working animals—Moral and ethical aspects. | Animal industry—Moral and ethical aspects.
Classification: LCC HV4708. B85 2024 (print) | LCC HV4708 (ebook) | DDC 179/.3—dc23/eng/20240307
LC record available at https://lccn.loc.gov/2024000972
LC ebook record available at https://lccn.loc.gov/2024000973
DOI 10.3726/ b21657

Bibliographic information published by the Deutsche Nationalbibliothek.
The German National Library lists this publication in the German
National Bibliography; detailed bibliographic data is available
on the Internet at http://dnb.d-nb.de.

Cover design by Peter Lang Group AG

ISSN 2469-3065 (print)
ISBN 9781636675602 (paperback)
ISBN 9781636675619 (ebook)
ISBN 9781636675626 (epub)
DOI 10.3726/b21657

© 2024 Peter Lang Group AG, Lausanne
Published by Peter Lang Publishing Inc., New York, USA
info@peterlang.com - www.peterlang.com

This publication has been peer reviewed.

Contents

Acknowledgments

Thank you to Dani Green for believing in the vision for this project and Laura Schleifer and Riley Clare Valentine for their feedback on the introduction of this collection. I also want to hold space for my current mentors, Z Williams, Erika Unger, Sandy Freeman, and Jenipher Bonino, who are supporting me as I navigate the intersections of legal, animal, and labor advocacy spaces. Thank you all for working towards total liberation. Lastly, I want to thank VegFund for providing this project with a grant and supporting my work.

Introduction[1]

ZANE MCNEILL

In July 2023 at least three children died from on-the-job injuries at industrial nonhuman animal slaughter facilities in the United States. One such case, Duvan Tomas Perez, 16, died at a Mississippi poultry plant after becoming trapped in equipment on a conveyor belt. Perez was entering ninth grade and was hired in violation of federal child labor laws, which prohibit employers from hiring anyone under eighteen to work in slaughtering, processing, and packing facilities.[2] Perez's death prompted the Occupational Safety and Health Administration (OSHA) and the U.S. Department of Labor (DOL) to open investigations into the fatal incident, which was the plant's second death in two years.[3]

An investigation by the DOL Wage and Hour Division in February 2023 found that more than one hundred children were illegally employed in hazardous jobs.[4] Packers Sanitation Services Inc., one of the country's largest food safety sanitation services, was found to have employed children at 13

1 This chapter includes sections from previous pieces I wrote that were published in *Truthout*.
2 Golgowski, Nina. "Third Teen Worker Killed in Industrial Accident as States Try to Loosen Child Labor Laws." *HuffPost*, July 20, 2023. https://www.huffpost.com/entry/teen-poultry-factory-child-worker-deaths_n_64b7ecbce4b0ad7b75f67af7.
3 Stancil, Kenny. "GOP Assault on Child Labor Laws Under Fresh Scrutiny After 16-Year-Old Dies at Poultry Plant." *Common Dreams*, July 19, 2023. https://www.commondreams.org/news/mississippi-poultry-plant-teen-dies.
4 "More than 100 Children Illegally Employed in Hazardous Jobs, Federal Investigation Finds; Food Sanitation Contractor Pays $1.5m in Penalties." *DOL*, February 17, 2023. https://www.dol.gov/newsroom/releases/whd/whd20230217-1.

meat processing facilities in eight states. The facilities included those of Tyson Food Inc., JBS Foods, and Cargill Inc. Many of the minors were working in hazardous occupations and were routinely forced to work overnight shifts. The DOL fined Packers Sanitation Services Inc. more than $1.5 million for violating the Fair Labor Standards Act (FLSA) by illegally employing children.

Seemingly in response to the federal crackdown on child labor violations in the meatpacking sector, states including Arkansas, Iowa, Ohio, Minnesota, New Hampshire and Wisconsin introduced legislation that would loosen child labor laws and encourage companies to hire children to work in hazardous workplaces.[5] On March 7, 2023, Governor Sarah Huckabee Sanders (R-Arkansas) signed reactionary House Bill 1410 into law, which labor and child advocates hypothesize will make it easier for companies to employ children. A week before Governor Sanders signed the bill, Tyson's Green Forest plant in Arkansas was implicated in the DOL investigation for employing at least six children and was fined $90,828.[6]

The so-called meat barons who own the means, or literally meat, of production, extract wealth by "processing its racialized workers and the carcasses they dismember under dangerous and exploitative conditions to squeeze every last cent from their drooping limbs," in the words of historian William Horne.[7] This system, Horne contends, is built upon the "evolution of the racial state," and its entanglement with capitalism, surveillance, and circularity. Horne asserts that "The racial capitalism that animates American food production [...] remains the central driving force facilitating poor wages and treatment in the rest of the economy."[8] This extractive industry, which milks all of its profit from the human and nonhuman animal bodies within its reach, depends on the commodification and precarity of its laborers.

The lives of children employed at slaughterhouses, like the lives of the nonhuman animals slaughtered and dismembered in the facilities in which they work, are rendered killable by the necropolitical animal agriculture

5 McMenamin, Lexi. "Republicans Are Trying to Roll Back Child Labor Regulations." *Teen Vogue*, March 10, 2023. https://www.teenvogue.com/story/child-labor-repu blicans-are-passing-regulatory-rollbacks.

6 Souza, Kim. "Tyson Foods' Green Forest Plant Implicated in Child Labor Investigation." *Talk Business & Politics*, March 1, 2023. https://talkbusiness.net/ 2023/03/tyson-foods-green-forest-plant-implicated-in-child-labor-investigation/.

7 Horne, William. "The Vampire's Bacon: Meat Work, Empire, and Abolition." Essay. In Z. Zane McNeill (ed.), *Vegan Entanglements: Dismantling Racial and Carceral Capitalism*. New York: Lantern Publishing & Media, 2022, 28.

8 Horne, 21.

industry. The term "necropolitics" refers to the politics—that is, the use of social and political power—to decide who lives, who dies, and how someone should live or die.[9] As described by Marek Muller, who builds on the work of political theorist Achille Mbembe, "The necropolitical refers to the state's potential to make certain bodies killable, such as naming enslaved bodies 'chattel' to deny them of their personhood and subsequently of their legal rights to life and liberty."[10]

While Mbembe describes the necropolitical subject as being kept in a state of unending injury, Muller uses the term zombification to express the social process in which one "becomes socially dead physically, psychologically, and culturally."[11] Muller uses this frame to explore how the nonhuman animal agriculture industry not only "places animals in the role of the ideal socially dead subject (the chattel slave)," but also animalizes and dehumanizes the human workers. "Slaughterhouse subjects, human and animal, exist in uncomfortably close proximity to one another, thus contaminating each other with the particularities of their liminalities and further reifying a colonial sliding scale of humanity," Muller explains.[12] In other words, under racial and carceral capitalism, necropolitics renders not only nonhuman animals as "slaughter-able," but also humans who are animalized. Racism's "ontological plasticity," as posited by Zakkiyah Jackson, "render[s] one's humanity provisional," in which "black(ened) people are not so much as dehumanized as nonhumans or cast as liminal humans nor are black(ened) people framed as animal-like or machine-like but are cast as sub, supra, and human *simultaneously* and in a manner that puts being in peril."[13] In other words, white supremacy constructs and relies on a social malleability of racialized people, and its entanglements with surveillance, control, and carcerality, in order to extract capital from its laborers.

Specifically, the meat-processing industry depends on carcerality in tandem with racial capitalism which evolved out of the convict leasing of the Jim Crow era, which itself evolved out of chattel slavery.[14] This system

9 Muller, S. Marek, and Z. Zane McNeill. "Toppling the Temple of Grandin: Autistic-Animal Analogies and the Ableist-Speciesist Nexus." *Rhetoric, Politics & Culture* 1, no. 2 (2021), 207.

10 Muller, S. Marek. "Zombification, Social Death, and the Slaughterhouse: U.S. Industrial Practices of Livestock Slaughter." *American Studies* 57, no. 3 (2018), 86.

11 Ibid., 87.

12 Ibid., 97.

13 Jackson, Zakiyyah Iman. *Becoming Human: Matter and Meaning in an Antiblack World*. New York, NY: New York University Press, 2020, 16 and 35.

14 Horne, 22.

transforms human and nonhuman bodies into commodities whose labor is consumed and capitalized upon by the elite class. Thus, this collection asserts that there is a shared exploitation between laborers—human and nonhuman alike—which is designed within and by a system built on carceral and racial capitalism.

Embedded deeply within this necropolitical racial and carceral capitalist system is speciesism, or the assumption that individuals deemed (fully or solidly) "human" are superior to other(ed) individuals, human and nonhuman alike, who are deemed "animals." Speciesism is inherently hierarchical and simultaneously justifies the exploitation of nonhuman animals and animalized humans as relatively invisible and unquestioned. "This system of normalized harm forms the foundation of so much economic activity and is impossible to ignore when thinking about animals and organizations," as Coulter explains.[15]

Industrial agriculture depends on speciesism's entanglement with white supremacy and racial capitalism depends on this hierarchized relationship between race, animality and humanity. As Syl Ko explores, humanness is a "certain way of being, especially exemplified by how one looks or behaves, what practices are associated with one's community, and so on...this means that the conceptions of 'humanity/human' and 'animality/animal' have been constructed along *racial* line." In this racial capitalist landscape, meatpacking workers, through ontological plasticity, are simultaneously both human and nonhuman: human as legal "employees" of a company and at the same time rendered nonhuman, "killable" commodities.[16]

Speciesism renders the idea of nonhuman animals as laborers perplexing. Blattner, Coulter, and Kymlicka explain that "On the one hand, exploiting animal labour is one of the paradigmatic ways in which humans use animals.... Animal labour has been a site of intense instrumentalization, exploitation, and degradation."[17] While nonhuman animals are rendered property as

---

15 Coulter, Kendra, 'From Interesting to Influential: Looking Forward with Multispecies Organization Studies'. In Linda Tallberg and Lindsay Hamilton (eds.), *The Oxford Handbook of Animal Organization Studies*, Oxford Handbooks (Oxford Academic, 2022; online edn., 20 Oct. 2022), https://doi-org.du.idm.oclc.org/10.1093/oxfordhb/9780192848185.013.1, accessed 10 Aug. 2023, 21.

16 Ko, Syl. "By 'Human' Everybody Just Means 'White.'" Essay. In Aph Ko and Syl Ko (eds.), *Aphro-Ism: Essays on Pop Culture, Feminism, and Black Veganism from Two Sisters*, 20–27. Brooklyn, NY: Lantern Publishing & Media, 2017, 23.

17 Blattner, Charlotte, Kendra Coulter, and Will Kymlicka, 'Introduction: Animal Labour and the Quest for Interspecies Justice', in Charlotte E. Blattner, Kendra Coulter, and Will Kymlicka (eds.), *Animal Labour: A New Frontier of Interspecies Justice?* (Oxford: Oxford Academic, 2019; online edn., 23 Jan. 2020), https://

objects owned by the industry, they are also autonomous individuals who suffer compulsory labor. As suggested by Blattner, "recognizing animals as workers does not mean endorsing their exploitation or stripping them of rights to refuse work. Rather, we should recognize animals as exploited workers"[18] For example, as explored by Carol Adams in her groundbreaking text, the *Sexual Politics of Meat: A Feminist-Vegetarian Critical Theory* billions of animals are exploited for breeding to literally reproduce the violent structures of which they were born.[19] Millions of other animals, as Catherine Oliver explains in her chapter, experience metabolic labor, or are born to grow and to die. This necropolitical labor saturates the experiences of nonhuman animals rendered "killable."

Both human and nonhuman laborers are exploited for capital accumulation. "If some do not work—those who possess the power and means of production—it is because others do the work for them," Porcher and Estabanez explain. "Work seems therefore to be a world of competition and individualism, but also an essential motor of inequality and discrimination, in particular in the building of socio-professional hierarchies."[20]

Animal activists have alleged that their labor too has been exploited within the animal advocacy nonprofit sector (AANS).[21] Activists have alleged that white goals and interests are centered in the missions of many of these organizations, reifying the hierarchies which the animal agriculture sector is similarly predicated on because of the predominantly white racial makeup of management and funders. This racial dynamic leads to organizational cultures that overwork, alienate, and marginalize Black, Indigenous, People of the Global Majority (BIPGM) animal advocates. There is an embedded

doi-org.du.idm.oclc.org/10.1093/oso/9780198846192.003.0001, accessed 8 Aug. 2023, 4.

18 Blattner, Charlotte E., 'Animal Labour: Toward a Prohibition of Forced Labour and a Right to Freely Choose One's Work', in Charlotte E. Blattner, Kendra Coulter, and Will Kymlicka (eds.), *Animal Labour: A New Frontier of Interspecies Justice?* (Oxford: Oxford Academic, 2019; online edn., 23 Jan. 2020), https://doi-org. du.idm.oclc.org/10.1093/oso/9780198846192.003.0005, accessed 10 Aug. 2023, 92.

19 Adams, Carol J., *The Sexual Politics of Meat: A Feminist-Vegetarian Critical Theory.* New York, NY: Continuum International Publishing Group, 1990.

20 Porcher, Jocelyne and Jean Estebanez. 2019. *Animal Labor: A New Perspective on Human-Animal Relations.* Human-Animal Studies. Bielefeld: transcript Verlag. https://search-ebscohost-com.du.idm.oclc.org/login.aspx?direct=true&db=e025 xna&AN=2245356&site=ehost-live&scope=site, 19.

21 The animal advocacy nonprofit sector has had a long record of racial and sex-based discrimination, sexual harassment, exploitative and toxic work environments, and retaliatory management practices at some of the movement's largest organizations.

neoliberal capitalist culture, or roots in the nonprofit industrial complex, which has led to incidents of sexual harassment and sexual and racial discrimination in the sector. These problems lead to issues of sustaining diversity in the workforce.[22] As Tiffany Lethabo King and Ewuare Osayande explain, the nonprofit industrial complex has been used to by elite to maintain racial hierarchies, capture and undermine social movements, and shield models of capitalist extraction:

> On the surface, progressive philanthropy is an attempt by the Left to advance the movement forward by bolstering it with more resources. But rather than putting more money into the hands of non-profits that address the needs of the marginalized, the results have been little more than a few cosmetic adjustments to make capitalist foundations appear progressive and the Left complicit in supporting systems of oppression, exploitation, and domination.[23]

This collection posits not that the AANS has similarly been constructed to constrain movements for human and nonhuman animal liberation and that, because of this, the AANS reproduces such hierarchies internally. Workers in the AANS have voiced concerns regarding workplace bullying, the silencing of worker-activists' voices, and retaliation against worker-activists who raise concerns about labor practices in the sector. Particularly concerning is that researchers have found that 48.6% of paid AANS workers have experienced discrimination, unfair treatment, harassment, bullying, or abuse in their previous five years of employment.[24] This seems to lead to attrition and efficacy issues, as 40% of advocates leave organizations in the AANS because of problems with leadership and 22.8% of advocates left previous roles because of burnout and traumatic stress. "The mainstream animal movement, as well as 'good food' movement's most influential leaders and frameworks, are simply used as an extension of [sic] empire," Dr. Breeze Harper explains. "Neoliberal-capitalist-whiteness sold to the average untrained mind as 'green' or 'social impact' when the outcomes will still be concentration of power

---

22 "Read Testimonials." CANHAD. Accessed November 6, 2022. https://www.can had.org/read-testimonials/ and "Diversity, Equity, Inclusion, and Justice Progress Report." Mercy For Animals. Accessed November 6, 2022. https://mercyforanim als.org/deij-report/.

23 King, Tiffany Lethabo, and Ewuare Osayande. "The Filth on Philanthropy: Progressive Philanthropy's Agenda to Misdirect Social Justice Movements." Essay. In INCITE! (ed.), *The Revolution Will Not Be Funded: Beyond the Non-profit Industrial Complex*, 79–89. Durham, NC: Duke University Press, 2017, 80.

24 Anderson, Jo. "The State of Animal Advocacy in the U.S. & Canada: Experiences & Turnover." *Faunalytics*, September 17, 2020. https://faunalytics.org/advocate-retention/.

amongst those (mostly white men, but there are also those who may not be white men but uphold [sic] the power structure) who have held, maintain, and created power for centuries."[25]

For example, in the summer of 2020, staff of the Animal Legal Defense Fund (ALDF) who had the intent to unionize, the initiative of which was primarily initiated by dissatisfaction with the organization's lack of response and public solidarity with the Black Lives Matter movement after the murder of George Floyd, was met with classic union-busting tactics.[26] On December 14, a supermajority of ALDF's staffers signed cards to form a union[27]—the first at an animal protection organization. ALDF management's response was to refuse to voluntarily recognize the union[28] and to hire notorious union-busting firm, Ogletree Deakins, to advise management on how to proceed.[29] Staff members reported being forced to attend rolling union-busting and captive-audience meetings to discourage unionization.[30] This response to the unionization effort led reporter Hamilton Nolan to describe the Animal

25 Harper has argued that the FAPM's white executives and funders have profited off of the perceived social impact of their work while not actually targeting or dismantling the structures that uphold and sustain speciesism, white supremacy, and other -isms. Instead of funding the work of BIPGM who are vocal about the interconnections of oppression and the importance of troubling neoliberal capitalism and the state, Simon says that the white leaders of the animal protection movement have accumulated social, cultural, and economic capital by selling consumers the concept of "good food."

26 Nolan, Hamilton. "The Animal Legal Defense Fund Is Busting Its Union with a Smile." *In These Times*, January 13, 2021. https://inthesetimes.com/article/animal-legal-defense-fund-busting-union-labor.

27 NPEU. "Animal Legal Defense Fund Staff Form Union." *Nonprofit Professional Employees Union*, December 14, 2020. https://npeu.org/news/2020/12/14/animal-legal-defense-fund-staff-form-union.

28 NPEU, "Animal Legal Defense Fund Staff Union Files for NLRB Election after Management Refuses to Recognize." *Nonprofit Professional Employees Union*, December 28, 2021. https://npeu.org/news/2020/12/28/animal-legal-defense-fund-staff-union-files-for-nlrb-election-after-management-refuses-to-recognize.

29 Kalmbacher, Colin. "ACLU Accused of 'Union Busting' by Hiring Ogletree Deakins." *Law & Crime*, July 3, 2020. https://lawandcrime.com/civil-rights/aclu-accused-of-union-busting-by-hiring-anti-union-law-firm-over-labor-dispute/.

30 McNeill, Z. Zane, and Riley Valentine. "The Problem with Precarity in the Animal Advocacy Movement: The Non-Profit Industrial Complex and Union Busting." *Animals in Society*, April 6, 2021. https://animalsinsocietygroup.wordpress.com/2021/04/06/the-problem-with-precarity-in-the-animal-advocacy-movement-the-non-profit-industrial-complex-and-union-busting/?fbclid=IwAR1yfvI_fPSA1CDt-Jfj4gOPoQnG7UXhjJEN5GKhcMW5imGUJ_7C0fxhn3as.

Legal Defense Fund as "busting its union with a smile."[31] As of the writing of this introduction (summer 2023), ALDF has not yet finalized their union contract negotiations—three years later.[32]

ALDF's refusal to challenge the carceral State and condemn white supremacy is not isolated. In fact, the AANS has also historically vilified meat-packing and slaughterhouse workers and directly worked with the carceral State to imprison BIPGM. Many of the most prominent organizations in the AANS have been critiqued for engaging in this *carceral veganism*, a philosophy which, as defined by political scientist Riley Clare Valentine, does not "question the normalized violence that is behind prisons and jails...[and] supports white supremacist ideas of *who* is the enemy and from *whom* society needs [to] be protected."[33]

The children as well as adults who are laboring and dying in meatpacking plants, the labor of nonhuman animals themselves and the work done with and for animals by animal activists are all exploited and oppressed by the same interconnected systems of oppression which are subcategories of what Kendra Coulter calls "animal work."[34] If the AANS relies on carceral logic which "reinforces systematic violence against humans and nonhumans," the reinforcing systems of speciesism, necropolitics and racial and carceral capitalism will continue to harm all animal workers.[35]

The present collection, *Building Multispecies Resistance Against Exploitation: Stories from the Frontlines of Labor and Animal Rights*, troubles the relationship between these subcategories of animal work and interrogates the politics that undermines efforts to achieve interspecies solidarity, namely racial and carceral capitalism and the necropolitics embedded within it. To do so, this book centers activist-scholars who have worked in the movement for animal liberation and who question the ways in which the AANS has reified racial and carceral capitalism, not only undermining its potential to achieve

31 Nolan, Hamilton. "The Animal Legal Defense Fund Is Busting Its Union with a Smile." *In These Times*, January 13, 2021. https://inthesetimes.com/article/animal-legal-defense-fund-busting-union-labor.

32 Martinez, Alexandra. "Animal Rights Workers Allege Transphobia, Racism, Union-Busting." *Prism*, June 26, 2023. https://prismreports.org/2023/06/26/animal-legal-defense-fund-toxic-workplace/.

33 Valentine, Riley Clare. "When Care Is Ordinary: A Care Ethics Critique of Carceral Veganism." Essay. In Z. Zane McNeill (ed.), *Vegan Entanglements: Dismantling Racial and Carceral Capitalism*. New York: Lantern Publishing & Media, 2022, 131.

34 Coulter, K. "Introducing Animal Work." In *Animals, Work, and the Promise of Interspecies Solidarity*. New York: Palgrave Macmillan, 2016. https://doi-org.du.idm.oclc.org/10.1057/9781137558800_1

35 Valentine, 131.

interspecies solidarity and animal liberation, but also weaponizing oppressive structures against other animal workers, such as meatpacking and slaughterhouse workers, as well as animal activists in the sector.

This collection posits three questions. (1) What structures of violence and oppression are experienced and shared by human and nonhuman laborers working and dying in these necropolitical facilities? (2) If there is an intersection between class and species, which, in turn incorporates race, gender, abilities, and other categories of oppression, in which ways is the contemporary animal advocacy nonprofit sector reifying or disrupting these hierarchies in its mission towards animal liberation? (3) If there are classist and racist biases in AANS, how can the AANS incorporate social class in dialogue with the liberation of nonhuman animals in order to build strategic alliances and coalitions between social movements and political subjects? To answer these questions, this collection brings together scholarly works by various scholar-activists on the interconnectedness of human and nonhuman labor, the differences and similarities of human/nonhuman oppression, the possibilities of alliances and coalition-building for total liberation, and the challenges and opportunities of incorporating a critical class perspective into animal liberation work.

The first section, "The Necropolitics of Laboring in the Abattoir," examines the labor landscape of animal work—specifically the labor of, and resistance to, killing and being killed in the slaughterhouse. The chapters in this section, "Unfulfilled Resistance: The Labor of Not Surviving" by Catherine Oliver and "Violence Begets Violence: The Necessity of Solidarity with U.S. Slaughterhouse Workers," by Marek Muller explore the entanglements of class, labor, and resistance in human and nonhuman animal communities exploited by the industrial agriculture sector. Specifically, these chapters disrupt expectations about *what* constitutes labor and *who* has choice, autonomy, and recognition of rights under racial capitalism. These chapters posit, as described by Oliver, that "labor and work aren't exclusively human, and the concept of animal rights has existed in some form for centuries, and nor is resistance solely a human activity."

The second section, "The Animal Advocacy Nonprofit Sector and the Reification of Carceral and Racial Capitalism," examines whether, and in which ways, the animal advocacy movement has upheld the systems embedded in and entangled with speciesism, white supremacy, carcerality, and racial capitalism. "Undercover Investigations and Carceral Veganism: The Limitations of 'Removing the Veil'," by Ellyse Winter and "Death or Deportation: A Nebraska-Based Study of the Exploitation of Immigrant Workers in Meatpacking Facilities and the Immigration Consequences of the Animal

Protection Movement," by Kelly Shanahan examine the ways in which the AANS has embedded itself in the prison- and immigration-industrial complexes and harmed migrant and low-wage workers by doing so."

"Laboring for Nonhumans: An Autoethnography of an Animal Rights Non-Government Organization," by Drew Robert Winter and "Horses of a Different Color: Reckoning with Race in the March for Animal Rights," by Raj Reddy examine the ways in which the AANS harms its own workers by perpetuating racial capitalist logics by platforming the lived experiences of activists who have labored in the AANS. These autoethnographies detail the effect of neoliberalism on social movements and how the AANS will not be able to achieve its mission of animal liberation without disentangling itself from the logics of racial capitalism.

The final section, "Moving Towards Multispecies Liberation," offers recommendations for building strategic alliances and coalitions between social movements to dismantle the necropolitical abattoir and its roots in racial and carceral capitalism. "Abolish the Meat Industry: A roadmap for Transforming Animal Liberation from a Single-Issue Cause into a Mass Movement," by Hailey Huget, "Animal Liberation, Class and Direct Action for Total Liberation," by Will Boisseau and "An Essay on Total Liberation: Marcusean Insights for Catalyzing Transformation," by Dan Fischer posit that in order to achieve liberation for one marginalized political subject, we must liberate all political subjects oppressed by these entangled hierarchies. These chapters not only envision a world without these hierarchies but offer tangible steps the AANS can take to achieve liberation for human and nonhuman animals.

Works Cited

"More than 100 Children Illegally Employed in Hazardous Jobs, Federal Investigation Finds; Food Sanitation Contractor Pays $1.5m in Penalties." *DOL*, February 17, 2023. https://www.dol.gov/newsroom/releases/whd/whd20230217-1.

Adams, Carol J. *The Sexual Politics of Meat: A Feminist-Vegetarian Critical Theory*. New York, NY: Continuum International Publishing Group, 1990.

Anderson, Jo. "The State of Animal Advocacy in the U.S. & Canada: Experiences & Turnover." *Faunalytics*, July 22, 2020. https://faunalytics.org/advocate-retention/.

Blattner, Charlotte E. "Animal Labour: Toward a Prohibition of Forced Labour and a Right to Freely Choose One's Work." In Charlotte E. Blattner, Kendra Coulter, and Will Kymlicka (eds.), *Animal Labour: A New Frontier of Interspecies Justice?*. Oxford: Oxford Academic, 2019; online edn., 23 January, 2020. Accessed August 10, 2023.

Blattner, Charlotte, Kendra Coulter, and Will Kymlicka. "Introduction: Animal Labour and the Quest for Interspecies Justice." In Charlotte E. Blattner, Kendra Coulter, and Will Kymlicka (eds.), *Animal Labour: A New Frontier of Interspecies Justice?*. Oxford: Oxford Academic, 2019; online edn., 23 Jan. 2020. Accessed August 8, 2023.

Coulter, K. "Introducing Animal Work." In *Animals, Work, and the Promise of Interspecies Solidarity*. New York: Palgrave Macmillan, 2016.

Coulter, K. "From Interesting to Influential: Looking Forward with Multispecies Organization Studies". In Linda Tallberg and Lindsay Hamilton (eds.), *The Oxford Handbook of Animal Organization Studies*, Oxford Handbooks. Oxford Academic, 2022; online edn., 20 Oct. 2022. https://doi-org.du.idm.oclc.org/10.1093/oxfordhb/9780192848185.013.1, accessed 10 Aug. 2023.

Golgowski, Nina. "Third Teen Worker Killed in Industrial Accident as States Try to Loosen Child Labor Laws." *HuffPost*, July 20, 2023. https://www.huffpost.com/entry/teen-poultry-factory-child-worker-deaths_n_64b7ecbce4b0ad7b75f67af7.

Horne, William. "The Vampire's Bacon: Meat Work, Empire, and Abolition." Essay. In Z. Zane McNeill (ed.), *Vegan Entanglements: Dismantling Racial and Carceral Capitalism*. New York: Lantern Publishing & Media, 2022.

Jackson, Zakiyyah Iman. *Becoming Human: Matter and Meaning in an Antiblack World*. New York, NY: New York University Press, 2020.

Kalmbacher, Colin. "ACLU Accused of 'Union Busting' by Hiring Ogletree Deakins." *Law & Crime*, July 3, 2020. https://lawandcrime.com/civil-rights/aclu-accused-of-union-busting-by-hiring-anti-union-law-firm-over-labor-dispute/.

King, Tiffany Lethabo, and Ewuare Osayande. "The Filth on Philanthropy: Progressive Philanthropy's Agenda to Misdirect Social Justice Movements." Essay. In INCITE! (ed.), *The Revolution Will Not Be Funded: Beyond the Non-profit Industrial Complex*, 79–89. Durham, NC: Duke University Press, 2017.

Ko, Syl. "By 'Human' Everybody Just Means 'White.'" Essay. In Aph Ko and Syl Ko (eds.), *Aphro-Ism: Essays on Pop Culture, Feminism, and Black Veganism from Two Sisters*, 20–27. Brooklyn, NY: Lantern Publishing & Media, 2017.

Martinez, Alexandra. "Animal Rights Workers Allege Transphobia, Racism, Union-Busting." *Prism*, June 26, 2023. https://prismreports.org/2023/06/26/animal-legal-defense-fund-toxic-workplace/.

McMenamin, Lexi. "Republicans Are Trying to Roll Back Child Labor Regulations." *Teen Vogue*, March 10, 2023. https://www.teenvogue.com/story/child-labor-republicans-are-passing-regulatory-rollbacks.

McNeill, Zane. "Animal Protection Movement Struggles to Reckon with Deep-Seated Inequalities," *RARA*, July 17, 2023. https://www.rightsforadvocates.com/rara-blog/animal-protection-movement-struggles-to-reckon-with-deep-seated-inequalities.

McNeill, Zane. "Kids Found to Be Working Overnight Shifts at Minnesota Meat Processing Plant." *Truthout*, March 23, 2023. https://truthout.org/articles/kids-found-to-be-working-overnight-shifts-at-minnesota-meat-processing-plant/.

McNeill, Z. Zane, and Riley Valentine. "The Problem with Precarity in the Animal Advocacy Movement: The Non-profit Industrial Complex and Union Busting." *Animals in Society*, April 6, 2021. https://animalsinsocietygroup.wordpress.com/2021/04/06/the-problem-with-precarity-in-the-animal-advocacy-movement-the-non-profit-industrial-complex-and-unionbusting/?fbclid=IwAR1yfvI_fPSA1CDt-Jfj4gOPoQnG7UXhjJEN5GKhcMW5imGUJ_7C0fxhn3as.

Muller, S. Marek. "Zombification, Social Death, and the Slaughterhouse: U.S. Industrial Practices of Livestock Slaughter." *American Studies* 57, no. 3 (2018): 81–101. https://doi.org/10.1353/ams.2018.0048.

Muller, S. Marek, and Z. Zane McNeill. "Toppling the Temple of Grandin: Autistic-Animal Analogies and the Ableist-Speciesist Nexus." *Rhetoric, Politics & Culture* 1, no. 2 (2021): 195–225. https://doi.org/10.1353/rhp.2021.0019.

Nolan, Hamilton. "The Animal Legal Defense Fund Is Busting Its Union with a Smile." *In These Times*, January 13, 2021. https://inthesetimes.com/article/animal-legal-defense-fund-busting-union-labor.

NPEU. "Animal Legal Defense Fund Staff Form Union." *Nonprofit Professional Employees Union*, December 14, 2020. https://npeu.org/news/2020/12/14/animal-legal-defense-fund-staff-form-union.

NPEU. "Animal Legal Defense Fund Staff Union Files for NLRB Election after Management Refuses to Recognize." *Nonprofit Professional Employees Union*, December 28, 2021. https://npeu.org/news/2020/12/28/animal-legal-defense-fund-staff-union-files-for-nlrb-election-after-management-refuses-to-recognize.

Porcher, Jocelyne and Jean Estebanez. *Animal Labor: A New Perspective on Human-Animal Relations*. Human-Animal Studies. Bielefeld: transcript Verlag, 2019.

Souza, Kim. "Tyson Foods' Green Forest Plant Implicated in Child Labor Investigation." *Talk Business & Politics*, March 1, 2023. https://talkbusiness.net/2023/03/tyson-foods-green-forest-plant-implicated-in-child-labor-investigation/.

Stancil, Kenny. "GOP Assault on Child Labor Laws Under Fresh Scrutiny After 16-Year-Old Dies at Poultry Plant." *Common Dreams*, July 19, 2023. https://www.commondreams.org/news/mississippi-poultry-plant-teen-dies.

Valentine, Riley Clare. "When Care Is Ordinary: A Care Ethics Critique of Carceral Veganism." Essay. In Z. Zane McNeill (ed.), *Vegan Entanglements: Dismantling Racial and Carceral Capitalism*. New York: Lantern Publishing & Media, 2022.

Section 1 The Necropolitics of Laboring in the Abattoir

Unfulfilled Resistance: The Labor of Not Surviving

CATHERINE OLIVER

In January 1998, two pigs escaped from a lorry at an abattoir in England. *The Tamworth Two*, later named Butch and Sundance, used "wily tricks" to escape their fate and in doing so, captured the empathy of the British public. The resourceful pigs slipped under a fence and swam across a river in their dash for freedom, hiding in a thicket for six days before capture. The pair were rescued from slaughter by a journalist, Barbara Davies, and rehomed at the Rare Breeds Centre in Kent. Fourteen years later, the deaths of first Butch and then Sundance were announced. They could not resist death forever. This story received widespread attention as a story of animals' escape, adventure, and struggle for freedom.

Following Butch's death (at a slaughterhouse after a short illness) in 2012, the journalist who led the call to save them in 1998 said:

> I'm devastated to hear of her death but it's comforting to know that she lived a long and full life. She and Sundance might so easily have ended up in the abattoir, but they shared a spirit of survival which struck a chord, particularly with the British, but also with animal lovers all over the world.

The Tamworth Two "struck a chord" with a British public who kill almost 11 million pigs annually for food (Animal Clock, 2021). The pigs' *spirit of survival* made them exemplary animals through an empathetic resistance. Ultimately, they did end up in the abattoir, albeit 14 years later, but their act of resistance through escape broke them out of the "farmed animal" category and into one of beloved national symbol of hope. But this story is an outlier in the history of capitalist human relations with animals. Indeed, animal resistance has been the target of physical, technological, and scientific manipulations to breed docility in farmed animals.

As the experiences of farmed animals are increasingly framed—uncomfortably—as *labor* in the fight for interspecies justice (see Blattner, Coulter & Kymlicka's, 2020 collection), the question of labor rights for animals is increasingly pertinent (Cochrane, 2016). Within this growing theoretical and practical field of ideas around animal labor and animal labor rights, resistance becomes an important form of animal agency (Beldo, 2007)—one of few available to them in places like the factory farm. Historian Jason Hribal (2007, 103) has described everyday forms of resistance as more than a human action:

> Donkeys have ignored commands. Mules have dragged their hooves. Oxen have refused to work. Horses have broken equipment. Chickens have pecked people's hands. Cows have kicked farmers' teeth out. Pigs have escaped their pens. Dogs have pilfered extra food. Sheep have jumped over fences.

Building on Hribal's work on resistance and class, Charlotte Blattner (2019, 99) adds further examples of animals' refusal to labor:

> At work, animals feign ignorance, reject commands, slow down work processes, refuse to work in heat or without adequate food, take breaks without permission, reject overtime, complain vocally, engage in open pilfering, break equipment, rebuff new tasks, escape...

And, in this book, Will Boisseau brings together Critical Animal Studies and Anarchist Studies to explore the precarious class position of workers in the animal-industrial complex, indicating further nuances of class, labor, and resistance.

For readers who have lived with or been companions of animals, you might be familiar with a dog's refusal to walk, a cat turning their nose up at your choice of food for them, or, in my own case, a guinea pig dashing to hide rather than have their nails clipped. Much like the complex interpretations of animal voices (Meijer, 2019) or attempts to move beyond anthropocentric systems towards "more-than-human" societies (Deckha, 2020), understanding and attending to animal resistance in its myriad forms requires a desire and effort to meet animals on their own terms (Midgley, 1983). Animal resistance has, unsurprisingly, become a fertile space for advocates to hold up as evidence of the ills of the treatment of animals in contemporary (and historical) life. And, as Hribal (2007, 110) has shown, the entanglement of animal and class solidarity can prove an important one in "the creation of social change."

Where human workers' rights have been won through the resistance of workplace organizing, striking, and industrial disputes (O'Brien, 2011), the welfare of animals in law and policy usually treats farmed animals as lively commodities (Collard & Dempsey, 2013), with a duty of care to *reduce* suffering that rarely disrupts speciesist perceptions of animals (Oliver, 2022). Animal rights philosophers have debated for decades whether the best way forward is fundamentalist or pragmatic (see Sztybel, 2007), with an umbrella of approaches established, from political lobbying to animal liberation. The political advocacy of animal rights organizations and an increasing scholarly theorization of animals as *agents* to "subvert work that presents animals as *things* that are mere background in human lives (Srinivasan, 2016, 76), which in turn is essential to changing the *ethical* status of animals. Nonetheless, there are fruitful solidarities and lessons to be learned from taking a connected and intersectional approach to animal issues, as demonstrated by Aph and Syl Ko's Black veganism (2017); Carol J Adams' feminist veganism (1990); Sunaura Taylor's animal and disability liberation (2017); A Breeze Harpers's Black feminist veganism; Margaret Robinson's (2013, 2018) Indigenous veganism; and Zane Mcneill's (2020) queer vegan scholarship. Sitting within a collection on labor, this chapter takes the opportunity to think about animal labor and resistance as both a leftist issue *and* an issue that is not fully being engaged with by the mainstream vegan movement, overlapping with other work in this collection such as Hailey Huget's chapter on abolishing the meat industry.

Specifically, I center three questions: what *is* animal labor, and why does it matter? What has resistance got to do with (enforced) animal labor? And, finally, does this resistance *matter* when it is almost always unfulfilled, especially in relation to animal rights organizing?

Work, Labor, Rights and Resistance for/by/with Non-human Animals

Increasingly, (some) animals are being recognized as workers, whose labor is conscripted in both classic and novel forms in the farm, the laboratory, the zoo, and even the home. This animal work is being used to further both academic and activist arguments, ultimately aiming to find both theoretical and practical more-than-human solidarities. For Porcher and Estebenaz (2019, n.p.) "to study animal work means to look at animals in new ways and to discover in them unsuspected skills and knowledge that open up new ethical and political horizons," specifically looking at work *done by* animals, as opposed to Arluke and Sanders' (1996) definition of work *with* animals. Labor studies scholar Kendra Coulter (2016) sees animal work as a fruitful interface for work done by, with *and for* animals, thinking about both species and individual animals. The relationship between work, labor, and rights has been widely considered by animal studies scholars from a range of disciplines, but before moving to consider the core questions of this chapter, it is necessary to briefly unpack the relationship between work, labor, rights, and resistance, and how this extends or can be applied to non-human life.

Amongst social scientists, there is "no common definition of the key concept 'work' or 'labor'" (Karlsson & Månson, 2017, 107), and the key influences in social theory of work and labor—Marx, Durkheim, and Weber—differ in their definitions and usages of the terms. Marx's approach to work and labor is the most cohesive in distinguishing between the capacity to do work (labor power) and the physical act of working (labor). Linguist Olivier Fraysse has argued that "in the Marxist tradition, the word labor has been associated with alienated and exploited work, a historical category, as opposed to work, an anthropological category, quintessential to the human species." Distinguishing between work and labor can be seen, therefore, as a question of *exchange*, which has "acquired specific meanings through the implication in key historical transitions as the rise of capitalism and the growth of industrial manufacture" (Ingold, 1995, 5). Work and labor are not interchangeable terms but represent different relationships to activity, wages, and capitalism.

Under wage capitalism, labor is sold and, accordingly has certain "rights" attached to it: labor rights. Labor rights are "the set of rights that humans possess by virtue of their status as workers" (Kolnen, 2009, 453) and depends on contested ideas of what constitutes work or labor. For example, domestic work does not have associated labor rights—an activist issue first raised in the 1970s—but it is undeniably labor (Federici, 1975). Labor rights are not extended equally, often excluding the most marginalized in society. These rights have often been won through specific campaigns of resistance—from workers themselves, unions, and political party buy-ins—that seek to redress the balance of power between bosses and workers, albeit minimally. There are different modes of worker resistance, from retraction of labor through strikes to more everyday forms of resistance such as gossip and resignation to, more occasionally, sabotage, or non-cooperation (Tucker, 1993). David Graeber (2019) recently documented novel forms of what might be considered worker resistance resulting from a feeling of pointlessness in their roles, in his book *Bullshit Jobs*. As David Frayne (2015, 5) has shown in the UK, however, "the stripping back of the welfare state ... has significantly reduced the latitude for resistance to work" and *working* has taken on a political salience as "good." Resistance to and in work has shifted from a collective struggle against the inequality of the capitalist labour process to "a matter of personal problems within the worker—a negative attitude, an inability to be a team player or shirking one's duties" (Fleming & Spicer, 2003, 174). As exemplified in Drew Winter's chapter in this book, this collective struggle is also necessary within animal rights labor.

The relationship between work, labor, rights, and resistance is complex and changeable, responding to local and global powers and processes. And this is before these ideas are even extended beyond the human! Of course, animals cannot exchange their labor in the marketplace: labor is conscripted from them, in ever-diminishing circumstances. Intimate and expansive knowledge of their relationships, behaviors, and biology have been put to work in making them more efficient laborers (Boyd, 2001; Blanchette, 2020). For example, the broiler chicken is the result of almost a century of intimate knowledge of chickens, intensifying their labor to grow fast and large (Oliver & Turnbull, 2021). However, social scientists such as those already cited here have long been arguing that animals *do* work and that they *do* labor and, as such, labor rights are also due to them (see, for example, Cochrane, 2016), specifically in the circumstances controlled and directed by human employers. It is also important to note that the *kinds* of work that animals are employed in is also ever-changing and expanding. Outside of the obvious industries of agriculture, entertainment, and clothing, animals are also employed in human healthcare (Gorman, 2017), as digital entertainers (Parkinson, 2019; Mills, 2015), as waste disposal (Zhang, 2020), and in habitat restoration pro-grammes (Lorimer, 2018). With new kinds of labor employing animals, the question of animal labor rights is far from settled.

However, as Guthman (2011) has argued, labor and work aren't exclu-sively human, and the concept of animal rights has existed in some form for centuries, and nor is *resistance* solely a human activity. It might be assumed that animals have no recourse to resist their circumstances, but the very exis-tence of technologies to quash resistance such as breeding for docility, or the machination of agriculture are evidence that non-human resistance exists (Wadiwel, 2018) and that this resistance has implications for the industries extracting and exploiting animal labor. However, with the obvious imbal-ances of power and domination, animal resistance is rarely seen or considered "successful" and most animals do not escape the farm, the laboratory, the zoo, or death itself. This does not invalidate their effort nor their resistance, and indeed this resistance still requires their labor. While many species could be used to illustrate the relationship between labor and resistance, I will spend the rest of this chapter focusing primarily on the chicken as a unique case for thinking about the excesses of labor writ into the chickens' body (Boyd, 2001) under capitalist relations with nature need to produce Cheap lives, both human and non-human (Moore, 2015). I will then look to what the exemplar of the chicken can teach us about animal labor more broadly in the concluding section of this chapter.

Chicken Labor

The chicken's body is both commodity and producer and, with around 26 billion chickens alive on the planet at any given time, their labor is far from insignificant. But what, exactly, is the labor of the chicken? Obviously, the chickens' labor extracted by humans is (at least) twofold: to grow big and fleshy for meat, a form of metabolic labor (Beldo, 2017), or to produce eggs at a rapid rate, a kind of reproductive or byproductive labor (Oliver, 2021). Individual chickens do not, generally, perform *both* kinds of labor, as broiler chickens are killed at between 8 and 12 weeks old and laying does not begin until around 18 weeks, lasting to around 18 months before hens slow down and are "dispatched." The genome of *G. gallus domesticus* actually split in 1900 (Rubin et al., 2020), separating these two birds into distinct morphotypes. The two kinds of labor are distinct but share one core similarity: chickens are to live in enclosed conditions close together, eat vitamin and nutrient enriched layers pellets, digest this food, and turn it into food for humans (Beldo, 2017).

Over the past century, chickens have become the most "popular" meat on earth, with broiler business eclipsing that of the egg industry in the past 25 years (Bell & Weaver, 2002), with consumption of chicken flesh up by 70% since 1990 (The Economist, 2019). In the past century, as the conditions of the factory have worsened, the labor of the chicken has intensified, with catastrophic effects on chickens' bodies. Forced molting, vitamin deficiencies, light restriction, and cramped conditions see birds not just in conditions too cramped to move, but with overweight and disproportionate bodies making them physically unable to do so (Davis, 2009). In July 2020, KFC "admitted" that more than 1 in 3 of the birds they raise for food in the UK suffer from footpad dermatitis, a painful inflammation caused by poor ventilation and hygiene standards, which prevents birds from walking normally (The Guardian, 2020). One in ten suffer with hock burn, caused by ammonia burning through the skin of the leg. The moral outrage at chickens being unable to walk should however be couched in the knowledge that "nearly all the chickens reared for KFC are fast-growing breeds that take just 30 days to reach slaughter weight." It is no wonder that Raj Patel and Jason W Moore have contended that: "the most telling symbol of the modern era isn't the automobile or the smartphone. It's the chicken nugget" (2018).

Chicken Resistance

In the tightly enclosed space of the chicken farm and the century of breeding creating today's chickens, "resistance" is the enemy of efficiency. Behaviors that are controlled or discouraged in commercial hens, such as pecking the ground or dust-bathing, are directly caused by chickens' attempting to find space to be themselves; chickens resist and remain "'wild' in the face of machines that seek to make them docile" (Wadiwel, 2018, 528). As Hribal (2011) has argued, many of the everyday actions of animals against their circumstances can be thought of "resistance," because the work that animals are doing is labor that leads to the humans exploiting this labor to react to it, "forcing"

> owners and supervisors to negotiate the applicability and limits of that exploita-
> tion. Are you going to beat them more? Are you going to surgically alter them
> in an attempt to decrease their resistance? Are you going to invent a device
> that seeks to prevent this behavior? Are you going to treat them better? Are
> you going to give up on trying to exploit one particular creature and switch to
> another? Are you going to quit all together and try a new occupation or busi-
> ness? (Hribal, 2007, 105).

The answer to most of these questions, in the case of the chicken, is yes: confinement, the removal of human interaction, "enriched" cages... attempts to make exploitation efficient for chickens have seen their natural behaviors (here thought of as "resistance") become a challenge to "solve." However, as Hribal (ibid) continues,

> the labor and resistance of animals have influenced other members of human
> society—some of whom saw commonalities in their mutual struggles against
> such forms of exploitation.

This solidarity between humans and animals is not new but thinking of "natural" behaviors as a form of resistance raises interesting questions about the similarities and empathies between exploited human *and* non-human labor under capitalist systems. This relationship between existence and/as resistance is one pioneered by black feminists (see Augusto & Mali, 2018; Haynes et al., 2020) and which, through an intersectional lens, can be used not to compare clearly distinct oppressions, but to understand the shared carceral logics that inspire solidarity in resistance to oppressive systems (Morin, 2018). The structures of society demanding efficiency are not limited to animals, but rather to life itself. As anarchist David Graeber wrote in an essay on "play," in the new full-blown capitalist version of evolution, where the drive for accumulation had no limits, life was no longer an end in itself, but a mere instrument for the propagation of DNA sequences (2014, n.p.).

This succumbing to a capitalist vision of life was considered by Mark Fisher (2009) as "capitalist realism," whereby people could not imagine beyond the current organization of society (and everything else). For Fisher, this produced "affective disorders [as] forms of captured discontent" (p. 80) that needed re-framing to affective *antagonisms* in which alternative organizations could be imagined. With this question of life and control, I want to return to the chicken and their specific forms of resistance to control of their everything, from their genome to their environments, to ask: what kind of resistance can we see in chickens? And what does it mean? As Wadiwel (2018, 536) argues, "the violence experienced by animals in this production process is shaped by this mix of imperatives to both make life endure in such a way as to maximally congeal value and simultaneously shorten life in order to reduce animal labor time (and the production cycle itself)."

Having worked and lived with ex-commercial chickens for the last six years, I have some observational insights into how chickens resist, but I have also been reading "agricultural science" literature and attending their community events to understand why resistance poses such a problem, how they are centering "docility" as the goal, and what this means, materially, for chickens. From these two separate strands of engagement with chickens, there are two kinds of resistance that become important: the everyday and the exceptional, and these are related to the wider activities that chickens are being conscripted into. Everyday resistances can be found in the chickens attempts to find space for themselves and their natural behaviors (Davis, 2009). Sadly, the result of attempts to find space can lead to violence and even killings between birds. Exceptional resistance occurs in the moments of "transition" of chickens' lives, notably when they are being moved from farm to processing plant or, for layers, to be disposed.

> Chickens increasingly no longer confront humans in production processes, but instead almost always encounter machines. The "harvesting" machine takes different forms: some look like wide-mouthed vacuum cleaners, larger than a motor vehicle; while another variation uses "foam paddles to place birds on inclined conveyor belts that carry the birds into crates" (Schilling et al. 2008: 163–164). This device is usually rolled over a darkened compound containing thousands of chickens, who desperately climb over each other to escape. The speed of capture is dizzying. As the chickens succumb to the machine, they are sucked into its internality, whisked away almost seamlessly, and thrust into crates (Wadiwel, 2018, 527–528)

Of course, as we know, of the billions of chickens on Earth, *all* of them participate in and enact resistance—both mundane and exceptional. However, very few of them *fulfil* the aims of their resistance, which is, we can safely assume, to escape their confinement or at least to improve their circumstances. So, what of this *unfulfilled resistance*? Does it not count because it was unsuccessful? And, with the turn away from human labor to machinic interactions, what might solidarity and resistance *with* chickens look like?

Conclusion: Unfulfilled Resistance

Writing about resistance in the contemporary workplace, Fleming and Sewell (2002, 868–869) argue that "the criteria by which we judge 'successful' and 'unsuccessful' workplace resistances needs more reflection because it would seem that *different* forms of resistance might be effective in challenging *different* forms of power." The kinds of resistance that I have written about in this chapter—and indeed most forms of non-human animal resistance against not just humans but their indoctrination in capitalist systems—are quite obviously in circumstances where the odds are stacked against animals. These odds are not just the current environments of animal exploitation, but centuries of breeding, meddling, and manipulating non-human animals for human convenience. But the relationship between power and resistance isn't a simple one, and nor is it stable (Hughes, 2022): it is messy and ambiguous, and there is room for disruption and disturbance as a result of spontaneous resistance. Resistance isn't always about form (Hughes, 2020) but nor is it always—or even often—about results.

This messiness and complexity of these labor relations and resistance are perhaps most tangible in the echoing situations of chickens and poultry house workers. The labor of chickens in intensive agriculture is devastating, but this is not the only kind of exploited labor in the farm or the processing plant. The lives and deaths of chickens under inhumane conditions are inseparable from the lives and deaths of human workers in these spaces. As Blanchette (2020) has found, slaughterhouse workers share "embodied bonds" with the animals that they kill, being physically reshaped by the gruelling labor of work on the disassembly line. The farm and slaughterhouse through their "structural design and disciplinary technologies and practices terrorize animal and human bodies" (Morin, 2018, 41) working to control both human and non-human life and extract labor. The "dirty work" of chicken "processing" is usually done by poorer, racialized, male, and often migrant workers for whom dangerous work is expected and denigrated.

Chicken and human workers are not separate subjects but intimately connected—and nor should their labor be considered as siloes, but as similarly extracted and exploited under capitalist systems. In Marek Muller's chapter in this book, they put forward a case for solidarity with slaughterhouse workers, who are often subjected to unsafe working environments and exploitation. In the American chicken industry, many workers are precarious migrants for whom the processing plant and slaughterhouse are carceral spaces that affect their physical and mental health, as Kelly Shanahan explores in this book. Through the case of the chicken, the labor of being killed and killing intermingle.

In this chapter, I have turned to chickens, the avian species "most exploited and least respected" (Potts, 2012) to explore how resistance still *matters* even when, and perhaps especially, when it isn't fulfilled. Across the world, billions of animals suffer, struggle but, ultimately, still die. In her book, *Chickens' Lib*, Clare Druce writes about a campaign set up by herself and her mother in the 1970s, saying that in making decisions from the very start, they would:

> limit our campaign to the plight of battery hens. Being obtainable and transportable, their extreme deprivation would be the easiest to highlight: hens trapped for like in metal cages, forced to stand on sloping wire, living in semi-darkness, unable to take a normal step *ever*. Surely these images would resonate with the public?

Fifty years ago, remember, the plight of the chicken was both different and the same as it is today in the UK: while the birds now have some (very minimal) welfare and space standards, with battery systems being illegal, those chickens have seen huge transformations in their physiology as efficiency in growing large and fast has reigned over the poultry sector. Thinking about animal resistance often involves including the humans who intervene to enable or highlight animal resistance. But, challenging that problematic slogan of "giving voice to the voiceless" (see Birke, 2014), animals *have* their own voices (Midgley, 1983), and their resistance is one way that they enact not just this voice, but their desires and needs.

Animal resistance does not always look like human resistance, specifically in the labor movement. After all, chickens have not yet unionised or engaged in organized collective action—but nor should we expect them to. These unseen, disrespected forms of resistance considered in this chapter and, conversely, the scale of oppression and domination in the long history of chicken farming are testament to the everyday modes of resistance that chickens can and do engage in. Animal activists turn to narratives and the power of storytelling to connect with and share the stories of animals, as exemplified in the opening vignette of this chapter, but a true movement of solidarity relies on moving *beyond* expectations of animals to be fought back—when there are centuries worth of structural containment from the cellular to infrastructural level that compels them *not* to fight back.

In this chapter, I have argued that these kinds of resistance must be understood as sites of shared labor struggles. Specifically, I looked at three questions: (1) what *is* animal labor, and why does it matter? (2) What has resistance got to do with (enforced) animal labor? and, finally, (3) does this resistance *matter* when it is almost always unfulfilled? To conclude this chapter, I want to return to these questions and reflect on what we can learn from the case of the chicken about interspecies solidarity and understanding how the specific—and changing—conditions of animal labor and resistance are inimical to collective liberation. To do so, I situate this chapter within the wider work in this book on animal labor rights and organizing, pointing towards how advocates and activists can imagine anti-oppression liberation movements.

The idea that animals can work and/or labor has been contested and theorized by a range of academic actors and while no common definition exists for labor or work (in human or non-human terms), the notion that animals *can* and *do* work has inspired a range of theoretical and empirical scholarship. However, the idea that animals might *labor*—and therefore be considered as having access to *rights* related to that labor has proven far more controversial. In any case, there are broader ethical and political concerns over the *kinds* of work that animals are engaged in, which cannot be bound by employment law, contracts, or even consent. Most animal labor is conscripted, involuntary, and non-optional. For example, in the case of the chicken, the metabolic labor of growing or laying is non-optional and involuntary as it is also equated with life itself, but it is also conscripted for profit. These leads to the second question—what has resistance got to do with animal labor? Where there is work, there is resistance—especially where that work is non-optional. In this chapter, I have looked at how chickens resist their labor conditions through maintaining their "wildness" and refusing to be docile in the face of human violence.

Chicken resistance is then taking as an exemplar of how taking seriously animals as exploited laborers can inform the fight for animal labor rights, as part of a broader cosmology of anti-speciesist and vegan-led animal rights. Notably, these labor rights in their radicality include the right to *not work*, that work does not determine our value, as individuals nor as a species (cf. Taylor, 2004). Thinking through the frame of resistance, and again taking the example of the chicken, there is the possibility for radically emancipatory perspectives *against* work to flourish, with connections to be made and solidarities forged between workers' and animals' movements that aim for us all to be liberated from economic labor. Yet, this resistance of chickens—like so much of our own human resistance—seems on the surface to have little impact. They are still worked to their deaths, *for* their deaths. What we can learn *with* the unfulfilled resistance of chickens, then, is vital to a broader cosmology of interspecies (vegan) labor and (anti-) work politics.

Thinking beyond the limits of this chapter, then, raises the question of what it would mean to center animal resistance in animal rights organizing. If animals labor, then they resist, but how can this resistance be incorporated into and perhaps even centered within animal rights organizing? Witnessing and uncovering animal suffering have long been at the heart of animal rights organizing, but there may also be opportunities to center non-human resistance through these same processes. Rather than chickens depicted as corpses or docile bodies, could animal rights activists showcase them as wild, bold, and free beings, who fight for their freedom, even though they inordinately fail? Or, within the contemporary landscape of animal rights organizing, itself plagued by inequality and oppression of human workers, are depictions of resistance too radical? The case of the chicken, then, offers not just reflections on labor or resistance in the non-human realm, but opens new questions of solidarity and organizing that transcend species.

References

Adams, C.J. (1990) *The sexual politics of meat.*

Animal Clock: https://animalclock.org/uk/ accessed 17/06/2022.

Arluke and Sanders' (1996) *Regarding animals.* Temple University Press.

Augusto, C. and Mali, Y. (2018) *Existence necessitates resistance: How Black women's survival in modern day America under conditions of police brutality is a radical act of resistance* [thesis] https://keep.lib.asu.edu/items/133770

Beldo, L. (2017) Metabolic labor: Broiler chickens and the exploitation of vitality. *Environmental Humanities,* 9(1), pp. 108–128.

Bell, D.D. and Weaver, W.D. (2002) *Commercial chicken meat and egg production.* Springer.

Birke, L. (2014) Listening to voices. In Taylor, N. and Twine, R. (eds.), *The rise of critical animal studies.* Routledge.

Blanchette, A. (2020) *Porkopolis.* Verso.

Blattner, C.E. (2020). Animal labour: Toward a prohibition of forced labour and a right to freely choose one's work. *Animal Labour: A New Frontier of Interspecies Justice,* pp. 91–115.

Blättner, C.E., Coulter, K. and Kymlicka, W. (eds.) (2020) *Animal labour: A new frontier of interspecies justice?*. Oxford University Press.

Boyd, W. (2001) Making meat: Science, technology, and American poultry production. *Technology and Culture, 42*(4), pp. 631–664.

Cochrane, A. (2016) Labour rights for animals. *The Political Turn in Animal Ethics*, pp. 15–32.

Collard, R.C. and Dempsey, J. (2013) Life for sale? The politics of lively commodities. *Environment and Planning A, 45*(11), pp. 2682–2699.

Coulter, K. (2016) *Animals, work and the promise of interspecies solidarity*. Palgrave Macmillan.

Davis, K. (2009) *Prisoned chickens, poisoned eggs*. Book Publishing Company Ltd.

Deckha, M. (2020) Unsettling anthropocentric legal systems: Reconciliation, indigenous laws, and animal personhood. *Journal of Intercultural Studies, 41*(1), pp. 77–97.

Druce, C. (2013) *Chickens' lib*. Bluemoose Book.

Federici, S. (1975) *Wages against housework* (pp. 187–194). Bristol: Falling Wall Press.

Fisher, M. (2009) *Capitalist realism: Is there no alternative?* Zero books.

Fleming, P. and Sewell, G. (2002) Looking for the good soldier, Švejk: Alternative modalities of resistance in the contemporary workplace. *Sociology, 36*(4), 857–873.

Fleming, P. and Spicer, A. (2003) Working at a cynical distance: Implications for power, subjectivity and resistance. *Organization, 10*(1), pp. 157–179.

Frayne, D. (2015) *The refusal of work*. Zed Books.

Frayssé, O. (2014) Work and labour as metonymy and metaphor. *triple*C, *12*. https://doi.org/10.31269/triplec.v12i2.546

Gorman, R. (2017) Therapeutic landscapes and non-human animals: The roles and contested positions of animals within care farming assemblages. *Social & Cultural Geography, 18*(3), pp. 315–335.

Graeber, D. (2014) What's the point if we can't have fun? *The Baffler*. https://thebaffler.com/salvos/whats-the-point-if-we-cant-have-fun

Graeber, D. (2018) *Bullshit jobs*. Allen Lane.

Guthman, J. (2011) *Weighing in: Obesity, food justice, and the limits of capitalism* (Vol. 32). University of California Press.

Haynes, C., Taylor, L., Mobley Jr., S.D. and Haywood, J. (2020) Existing and resisting: The pedagogical realities of Black, critical men and women faculty. *The Journal of Higher Education, 91*(5), pp. 698–721.

Hribal, J. (2011) *Fear of the animal planet: The hidden history of animal resistance*. AK Press.

Hribal, J.C. (2007) Animals, agency, and class: Writing the history of animals from below. *Human Ecology Review*, pp. 101–112.

Hughes, S. (2022) (In)coherent subjects? The politics of conceptualising resistance in the UK asylum system. *EPC: Politics and Space, 40*(2), pp. 541–560.

Hughes, S.M. (2020) On resistance in human geography. *Progress in Human Geography, 44*(6), pp. 1141–1160.

Ingold, T. (1995) Work, time and industry. *Time and Society*, 4(1), pp. 5–28.

Karlsson, J.Ch. and Månson, P. (2017) Concepts of work in Marx, Durkheim and Weber. *Nordic Journal of Working Life Studies*, 7(2), pp. 107–119.

Ko, A. and Ko, S. (2017) *Aphro-ism: Essays on pop culture, feminism, and Black veganism from two sisters.* Lantern Publishing & Media.

Kolnen, K. (2009) Labor rights as human rights. *Va. J. Int'l L.*, 50, p. 449.

Lorimer, J. (2018) Leave it to beavers: Animal work in austerity environmentalism. *Theorizing the Contemporary, Fieldsights*, July 26. https://culanth.org/fieldsights/leave-it-to-beavers-animal-work-in-austerity-environmentalism

McNeill, Z. (2020) Queer Appalachia and vegan activism. https://veganfeministnetwork.com/queer-appalachia-and-vegan-activism/

Meijer, E. (2019) When animals speak. In *When animals speak.* New York University Press.

Midgley, M. (1983) *Animals and why they matter.* Athens: University of Georgia Press.

Mills, B. (2015). Towards a theory of documentary representation for animals. *Screen*, 56(1), pp. 102–107.

Moore, J.W. (2015) *Capitalism in the web of life.* Verso.

Moore, J.W. (ed.) (2016). *Anthropocene or capitalocene?: Nature, history, and the crisis of capitalism.* PM Press.

Morin, K. (2018) *Carceral space: Prisoners and animals.* Routledge.

O'Brien, K. (1996). Rightful resistance. *World Politics*, 49(1), pp. 31–55. doi: 10.1353/wp.1996.0022.

Oliver, C. (2021) *OurChickenLife*, http://www.digicologies.com/2021/05/06/catherine-oliver/

Oliver, C. (2022) *Veganism, archives and animals: Geographies of a multispecies world.* Routledge.

Oliver, C. and Turnbull, J. (2021) A conduit for value? More-than-human experiments with chicken metabolisms. *CRASSH.* https://www.crassh.cam.ac.uk/blog/a-conduit-for-value-more-than-human-experiments-with-chicken-metabolisms/

Parkinson, C. (2019). Animal stars: A critical view of creaturely celebrity. *Czech and Slovak Journal of Humanities*, 2019(1), pp. 40–51.

Patel, R. and Moore, J.W. (2018) How the chicken nugget became the true symbol of our era https://www.theguardian.com/news/2018/may/08/how-the-chicken-nugget-became-the-true-symbol-of-our-era

Pendergrass, D. and Vettesse, T. (2022) *Half-Earth socialism.* Verso.

Potts, A. (2012) *Chicken.* Reaktion Books.

Robinson, M. (2013) Veganism and Mi'kmaq legends. *The Canadian Journal of Native Studies*, XXXIII(1), pp. 189–196.

Robinson, M. (2018) The roots of my Indigenous veganism. In Matsuoka, A. and Sorenson, J. (eds.), *Critical animal studies: Towards trans-species social justice.* Rowman and Littlefield International.

Rubin, C.J., Zody, M.C., Eriksson, J. et al. (2010) Whole-genome resequencing reveals loci under selection during chicken domestication. *Nature, 464*(7288), pp. 587–591. Scholssberg, 2020.

Seyferth, P. (2019). Anti-work: A stab in the heart of capitalism. In *Routledge handbook of radical politics* (pp. 371–390). Routledge.

Srinivasan, K. (2016) Towards a political animal geography? *Political Geography, 50*, pp. 76–78.

Sztybel, D. (2007) Animal rights law: Fundamentalism versus Pragmatism. *Journal for Critical Animal Studies*, 5(1), pp. 1–35.

Taylor, S. (2004). The right not to work: Power and disability. *Monthly Review-New York*, 55(10), pp. 30–31.

The Economist (2019) How chicken became the rich world's most popular meat. The Economist.

The Guardian (2020) KFC admits a third of its chickens suffer painful inflammation. https://www.theguardian.com/environment/2020/jul/30/kfc-admits-a-third-of-its-chickens-suffer-painful-inflammation

Tucker, 1993

Wadiwel, D. (2018) Chicken harvesting machine: Animal labor, resistance, and the time of production. *South Atlantic Quarterly, 117*(3), pp. 527–549.

Violence Begets Violence: The Necessity of Solidarity with U.S. Slaughterhouse Workers

S. Marek Muller

It's often said that consumers are disconnected from the meat we eat. Rarely noted is the fact that the slaughterhouse is a site of unfathomable connectivity. The most intimate and bloodstained bond between humans and the animals we consume is forged between nearly voiceless slaughterhouse workers and the animals they're employed to kill.—James McWilliams, Texas Observer, "PTSD in the Slaughterhouse"

Introduction

For many people, the global COVID-19 pandemic changed everything. Out of nowhere, people were separated from their friends and family through quarantine. Stores closed, economies crashed, and many lost their jobs. And, of course, far too many lost their lives to the virus itself. However, for those employed on the front lines of the U.S. American meatpacking industry, perhaps far too little changed. According to Kim Cordova, president of the United Food and Commercial Workers Local 7 in Greeley, Colorado, "What COVID did was just really shed light on what workers dealt with anyway."[1]

Due to quarantined Americans insatiable demand for nonhuman animal flesh, abattoirs stayed open even as local restaurants closed. "Social distancing," wrote Smithfield CEO Kenneth Sullivan, "is a nicety that makes sense only for people with laptops."[2] President Donald Trump signed an executive

---

1 Quoted in Alvin Chang, Michael Sainato, Nina Lakhani, Rashida Kamal, and Aliya Uteunova, "The Pandemic Exposed the Human Cost of the Meatpacking Industry's Power: 'It's Truly Frightening," *The Guardian*, November 21, 2021, https://www.theguardian.com/environment/2021/nov/16/meatpacking-industry-covid-outbreaks-workers.

2 Ibid.

order forcing meatpacking plants to stay open since, as slaughterhouse Tycoon John Tyson posted in multiple newspaper ads, access to animal flesh "is as essential as healthcare."[3]As a result, the 500,000 people working in meatpacking were connected to 6–8% of all early-pandemic COVID cases and 3–4% COVID deaths.[4] A lawsuit filed against Tyson Foods in Waterloo, Iowa even alleged that supervisors and managers participated in a betting pool on how many meatpackers would test positive for coronavirus.[5] Per Cordova, "This needs to go down in the history books as one of the biggest failures to the working man or woman that this country's ever seen."[6]

As other chapters in this collection will attest, abusive labor practices in the nonhuman animal slaughter industry have been documented for years. Most obviously, Chicago's meat-packing workers famously went on strike in 1904 to protest conditions in the Union Stockyards. More recently, the 1980s saw a massive decline in worker pay as practices of vertical integration allowed companies to relocate their meatpacking plants from urban centers to rural locations near feedlots.[7] The organization Human Rights Watch published a 2004 report called "Blood, Sweat, and Fear" purported that "workers in this industry face more than hard work in tough settings. They contend with conditions, vulnerabilities, and abuses which violate human rights."[8] Today, conditions are no better. Working twelve hour shifts for under $15/hour pay, workers have persistently high injury rates, so much so that in 2014, the National Institute for Occupational Safety and Health (OSHA) reported repetitive motion injuries in beef and pork processing workers were seven times that of other industries.[9] In 2016, Oxfam America reported that poultry

---

3 Quoted in Chang et al., "Human Cost of the Meatpacking Industry's Power."

4 Charles A. Taylor, Christopher Boulos, and Douglas Almond, "Livestock Plants and COVID-19 Transmission." *Proceedings of the National Academy of Sciences* 117, no. 50 (2020): 31706–31715.

5 Colin Gordon, "Meatpacking Bosses in Iowa Allegedly Organized a Betting Pool on How Many Workers Would Get Covid," *Jacobin Magazine,* November 20, 2020, https://jacobinmag.com/2020/11/meatpacking-iowa-tyson-lawsuit-work-conditions-covid-19

6 Quoted in Chang et al., "Human Cost of the Meatpacking Industry's Power."

7 See Amy J. Fitzgerald, "A Social History of the Slaughterhouse: From Inception to Contemporary Implications." *Human Ecology Review* (2010): 58–69; Upton Sinclair, *The Jungle: The Uncensored Original Edition.* See Sharp Press, 2003 (original version published in 1906); among others.

8 Human Rights Watch, *Blood, Sweat, and Fear* (New York, NY: Human Rights Watch, 2004), p. 1, https://www.hrw.org/sites/default/files/reports/usa0105.pdf

9 Peggy Lowe, "Working 'The Chain,' Slaughterhouse Workers Face Lifelong Injuries," *National Public Radio,* August 11, 2016. https://www.npr.org/sections/

workers were denied bathroom breaks to the point that many had resorted to wearing diapers on the factory line.[10] And, of course, the COVID-19 pandemic exacerbated these conditions.

But why should animal liberationists fight on behalf of those who *choose* to commit slaughter for a living? After all, employment in a murderous industry, no matter how exploitative of its workers, does not excuse murder. In 2017 alone, approximately 8,916,097,000 chickens, 240,011,000 turkeys, 121,372,000 pigs, 32,189,000 adult cattle, 512,000 calves, 26,628,000 ducks, and 2,178,000 sheep were slaughtered for human consumption through the U.S. American agriculture industry.[11] However, if animal liberationists are truly committed to the dissolution of speciesism—the unjust elevation of one species (usually human) over another (usually nonhuman)— they ought to take a second glance at the working conditions faced by those tasked with the slaughter of nonhuman animal subjects.

In a capitalist labor context, many workers' "choice" of profession is limited, as are their options for making the workplace humane. One need not "like" their job to do it well. On the contrary, "liking" one's work is not the point in unchecked capitalist systems. The point is merely profit—profits that, for abattoir workers, are barely enough to survive. Scholar-activist Nekeisha Alexis explains that "although cruelty must not be excused, it is crucial to link the trauma factory farm employees undergo to the trauma they inflict on the animals. Without an intersectional approach, animal advocates fail to unmask the full extent of the violence."[12] In other words, while animal liberationists can and should center nonhuman animals in their praxis, fighting for one marginalized group *at the expense of the other* is not an effective form of social justice communication.[13] Neither is refusing opportunities for

thesalt/2016/08/11/489468205/working-the-chain-slaughterhouse-workers-face-lifelong-injuries.pdf

10 Elizabeth Chuck, "Poultry Workers, Denied Bathroom Breaks, Wear Diapers: Oxfam Report," *NBC*, May 12, 2016, http://www.nbcnews.com/business/business-news/poultry-workers-denied-bathroom-breaks-wear-diapers-oxfam-report-n572806.

11 U.S. Department of Agriculture, "Livestock Slaughter 2017 Summary April 2018," http://usda.mannlib.cornell.edu/usda/current/LiveSlauSu/LiveSlauSu-04-18-2018.pdf; U.S. Department of Agriculture, "Poultry Slaughter 2017 Summary February 2018," http://usda.mannlib.cornell.edu/usda/current/PoulSlauSu/PoulSlauSu-02-26-2018.pdf.

12 Nekeisha Alayna Alexis, "Beyond Suffering: Resisting Patriarchy and Reproductive Control," in *Anarchism and Animal Liberation: Essays on Complementary Elements of Total Liberation*, ed. Anthony Nocella II, Richard White, and Erika Cudworth (Jefferson, NC: McFarland, 2012), 112.

13 A frequent weakness of the animal liberation movement (and many other social justice movements) is members' often shallow use of the term "intersectionality." The

cross-movement coalition building when the parties involved are both victims to the same speciesist, capitalist systems. After all, as Alexis warns, "without meaningful legal protections, employees are compelled to remain silent about these conditions and the aggression used against nonhuman animals."[14]

Humans are animals—we are, after all, part of Kingdom *Animalia* just like dogs, horses, etc. If humans are animals and slaughterhouse workers are humans, then these employees are literally animals tasked with the routinized murder of other animals. They are all embedded in the "animal-industrial complex," which anthropologist Barbara Noske identifies as a form of "capitalist biopolitics" which "operate[s] via an assumption of human/animal hierarchy, but collectively resource humans and animals alike for capitalization often in the same places and at the same times."[15] Put more simply, the animal-industrial complex functions through the oppressive intersections of unchecked capitalist greed and unquestioned human supremacy. The pursuit of animal liberation calls for a critical interrogation of how best to liberate the human *and* nonhuman animal victims of this industry, how to problematize processes of dehumanization and animalization. This process must also involve a critical interrogation of how animal liberationists themselves "animalize" other humans (such as slaughterhouse workers) specifically to deny them empathy, concern, and moral consideration.

Who Is a Human and Who Is an Animal?

One iteration of the animal-industrial complex in action is in the dehumanization (that is to say, the animalization) of those vulnerable persons tasked with murdering nonhuman animals for profit.[16] A common term for the de-elevation of human status through discriminatory language and action is "dehumanization," defined as a form of moral and social exclusion in which

term originates from critical legal studies, specifically in Kimberle Crenshaw's analysis of black women under the law. While all beings have multiple and intersecting identities, the term should not be divorced from its origins and intended application toward racial justice. Deploying the term in animal liberation circles must entail an equal commitment to the dissolution of speciesism and systemic racism, even where investments in Whiteness might make animal activism easier.

14 Ibid.

15 Barbara Noske, *Humans and Other Animals: Beyond the Boundaries of Anthropology* (London: Pluto Press, 1989).

16 See Natalie Khazaal and Núria Almiron, *Like an Animal: Critical Animal Studies Approaches to Borders, Displacement, and Othering* (New York: Brill, 2021) for a thorough, anti-speciesist explanation of how animalization functions through discourse practices of Othering, particularly as it relates to borders, place and placelessness.

certain humans are moved "outside the boundary in which moral values, rules, and considerations of fairness apply."[17] However, the process of dehumanization is inherently bound to the conceptualization of the nonhuman animal. Psychologists Nick Haslam and Steve Loughnan conclude "There is now substantial evidence that the lowest of the low are most vulnerable to dehumanization, especially when humanness is understood as human uniqueness, a vertical dimension of comparison in which being human amounts to being above animals."[18] Ergo, a more effective term for dehumanizing language and action is "animalization." By virtue of the human/nonhuman animal binary, wherein the homo sapien is cast as morally and legally superior to other savage species, human-on-human discrimination is not only made possible, but perpetuated by speciesist rationalizations.

There is nothing inherently wrong about being "an animal," but in a speciesist society, animalization is an intentionally harmful process. For instance, the animal-industrial complex thrives on racial hierarchy, and such hierarchies depend on dehumanization/animalization. Authors like Aph Ko, Amie Breeze Harper, and Christopher Sebastian have long described how speciesism and racism are similar structures that oppress subjects identified as bestial, closer to nature, or sufficiently 'Other.'[19] To wit, New York Times journalist Charlie LeDuff's famous investigation into abattoirs reported that workplace racial segregation was the norm:

> The few whites on the payroll tend to be mechanics or supervisors. As for the Indians, a handful are supervisors; others tend to get clean menial jobs like warehouse work. With few exceptions, that leaves the blacks and Mexicans with the dirty jobs at the factory. ... The locker rooms are self-segregated and so is the cafeteria. The enmity spills out into the towns. The races generally keep to themselves. ... Language is also a divider. ... This means different groups don't re-ally understand one another and tend to be suspicious of what they do know.[20]

---

17 Susan Opotow, "Moral Exclusion and Injustice: An Introduction." *Journal of Social Issues* 46, no. 1 (1990): 1.
18 Nick Haslam and Steve Loughnan. "Dehumanization and Infrahumanization." *Annual Review of Psychology* 65 (2014): 410.
19 See: Aph Ko and Syl Ko, *Aphro-ism: Essays on Pop Culture, Feminism, and Black Veganism from Two Sisters* (Lantern Publishing, 2017); A. Breeze Harper, *Sistah Vegan: Black Female Vegans Speak on Food, Identity, Health, and Society* (Lantern Publishing, 2009); among others.
20 Charlie LeDuff, "At a Slaughterhouse, Some Things Never Die," *New York Times*, June 16, 2000, https://partners.nytimes.com/library/national/race/061600leduff-meat.html

Perhaps unsurprisingly, the low pay and dangerous work environment of abattoir work means that the most vulnerable and most racialized populations are those most likely to be employed on the line. Slaughterhouse laborers are often recent immigrants and refugees. Meatpacking currently has the fifth-highest concentration of refugee workers. The *Los Angeles Times* reported that as of May 2020, there were 156,000 immigrants employed in meatpacking—approximately 40% of the industry. Numbers are even higher in areas like South Dakota, where they made up 58% of workers. However, these numbers are likely much higher due to the difficulty of counting undocumented populations. Estimates place undocumented worker populations as high as 14% in some plants.[21] These numbers are hardly a product of recent times. In fact chicken plants recruited immigrants in the 1990s as a union-busting tactic against majority African American workers. Although immigrants with work authorization were initially used to push out unionizers, over time they were replaced by undocumented populations. When workers pushed for fairer conditions, companies began immigration raids—in fact, a 2006 raid of Swift & Co. remains the largest single worksite raid in U.S. history. With conditions so low-paying and so intense, turnover is often 100%. However, by the 2000s, explain journalists Stephen Groves and Sophia Tareen, "the labor pool was self-sustaining with word-of-mouth."[22] In other words, so long as workers are desperate to eat, meatpacking positions will inevitably be filled.

Given the raced and classed composition of typical slaughterhouse floor workers, it should not be controversial to argue that the abattoir is a site of animalization. That is to say, workers are dehumanized to the point where they are "treated like animals" in close proximity to the very beings whose "animal" status was used to deny them life and liberty. Abattoir workers are not marched to their literal deaths like their nonhuman animal cohabitants inside the slaughterhouse walls. However, all inhabitants' inhumane conditions and liminal citizenship statuses result in what historical sociologist Orlando Patterson calls "social death," which is essentially a status of not-quite-human and definitely-not-citizen.[23] As nonhuman animals are chattel (or property), they by definition must be socially dead. At the same time,

---

21 Stephen Groves and Sophia Tareen, "U.S. Meatpacking Industry Relies on Immigrant Workers. But a Labor Shortage Looms," *Los Angeles Times,* May 26, 2020, https://www.latimes.com/food/story/2020-05-26/meatpacking-industry-immigrant-undocumented-workers

22 Ibid.

23 Orlando Patterson, *Slavery and Social Death* (Cambridge, MA: Harvard University Press, 1982), 15.

however, those floor workers assigned to slaughter them are shoved to the margins of civic life where they "engage in acts of violence deemed unsuitable for genteel middle class life."[24] Out of sight and out of mind, floor workers become as invisible and powerless as the nonhuman animals they are assigned to kill.

Who Labors and for Whom?

Their voices silences, it is easier for animal liberationists to falsely paint workers as "beasts" who enjoy animal abuse instead of interrogating the complex savagery of the meatpacking industry itself. When vulnerable populations make up the majority of a labor force, capitalist norms inevitably exploit those workers' labor for maximum output while minimizing workers' chances for collaborative action against this exploitation. After all, the slaughterhouse is a labor site that relies upon a flesh-craving public's willful ignorance of the human and nonhuman animals mistreated behind its walls. Timothy Pachirat describes how working the line is "a labor considered morally and physically repellant by the vast majority of society"—despite the majority of society itself demanding that labor so that their own routines of meat consumption can continue unquestioned.[25] In other words, the animal-industrial complex makes use of the walled-off, purposefully ignored slaughterhouse populations to strip these subjects of their agencies, to "castrate acts of resistance, and to ultimately reify the culturally constructed subhumanity of slaughterhouse inhabitants to further the capitalist cause."[26]

Traditionally, slaughterhouse wages were above the average manufacturing wage. After all, it was the multi-ethnic meatpacking unions of the early 20th century that served as shining examples for collecting labor organizing during the height of the U.S. Labor Movement. Historian Roger Horowitz explains:

> They tapped ethnic, familial, and neighborhood networks of packinghouse workers, secured support from white and black religious leaders, and brought respected group leaders into the center of the organizing drive. And they used National Labor Relations Board certification elections to give legitimacy to their efforts.[27]

24 S. Marek Muller, "Zombification, Social Death, and the Slaughterhouse: US Industrial Practices of Livestock Slaughter," *American Studies* 57, no. 3 (2018): 88.
25 Timothy Pachirat, *Every Twelve Seconds: Industrialized Slaughter and the Politics of Sight* (New Haven, CT: Yale University Press, 2011), 11.
26 Muller, "Zombification, Social Death, and the Slaughterhouse," 88.
27 Quoted in Gordon, "Meatpacking Bosses in Iowa."

Organizations like the United Packinghouse Workers of America and the Independent Union of All Workers won substantial worker rights throughout the Midwest from the 1930s through the 1950s. Wages in some plants topped $30 (in 2022 dollars) along the line.[28]

In recent decades, however, vertical integration has resulted in conglomerates like Tyson and Cargill taking control of the meatpacking industry and quashing attempts at labor organizing. The development of the Interstate Highway system and refrigerated transportation further hampered union efforts by allowing meatpacking conglomerates to move away from unionized cities toward other states and small towns.[29] According to Colin Gordon:

> The new firms, led by Holman and Anderson's Iowa Beef Processors (IBP), pushed production into the cornfields of Iowa, Nebraska, and Missouri. Their exodus undercut the political and community alliances that had sustained the UPWA and eroded the union's ability to organize across plants or secure master agreements.[30]

Today, employees are lucky to earn $26,000 per year (on the high end) with little to no benefits. Processes such as the aforementioned racial segregation along the line is a process of stifling group solidarity more than encouraged by industry supervisors. Furthermore, undocumented workers live in fear deportation for speaking out. Beginning in the late 20th century and continuing through today, Gordon explains:

> Firms recruited aggressively abroad, seeking not only those willing to work for low wages but new immigrants (documented and undocumented) who were either unfamiliar with labor law and labor standards or lacked the legal status to challenge employers who violated them. Meatpacking companies became synonymous with extreme exploitation, high worker turnover, and callous disregard for the law.[31]

Thus, by 2002, line worker profits were 24% lower than the average manufacturing wage.[32]

---

28 See: Luke X. Martin, "How Multi-Ethnic Stockyard Workers Propelled Kansas City into the Modern Age," *National Public Radio,* April 28, 2019, https://www.kcur. org/show/up-to-date/2019-04-28/how-multi-ethnic-stockyard-workers-propelled-kansas-city-into-the-modern-age.
29 Gordon, "Meatpacking Bosses in Iowa."
30 Ibid.
31 Ibid.
32 Jennifer Dillard, "A Slaughterhouse Nightmare: Psychological Harm Suffered by Slaughterhouse Employees and the Possibility of Redress through Legal Reform," *Georgetown Journal on Poverty Law and Policy* 15 (2008): 392.

In this "new normal of deunionized meatpacking," practices such as wage left run rampant. For example, one turkey processing plant in Iowa utilized labor brokers to staff the line with developmentally disabled men, collect their wages *and* social security payments, and pay the workers only 41 cents per hour. This practice continued for 30 years until the company was fined for over nine thousand labor violations in 2011. Since 2000, Tyson has paid out more than $75 million to settle claims against its practice of discounting "donning and docking" time from line workers' paychecks.[33] This experience is best summarized by one of the workers in LeDuff's investigation: "They [not only] kill pigs in the plant, they kill people."[34]

Divisions between workers (and subsequently union members) have even hobbled active strikes. Stephen Thierman argues:

> The people in this environment have a hard time seeing each other and this inability leads to distrust, segregation, and animosity. A very tangible effect of these reductions seems to have been the stifling of attempts at collective action with respect to unionization.[35]

Perhaps the most famous recent labor dispute between meatpacking executives, union leadership, and vulnerable line workers was the 1985 Hormel Strike in Minnesota. The 1,500 strikers belonged to United Food and Commercial Workers' Local P-9 and walked out due to wage freezes during a recession, 23% wage cuts, and dangerous working conditions. Protests including roving picket lines and blockades. Management offered some employees retirement benefits to stop striking and hired non-union workers composed mostly of Mexican migrants to cross the picket line. Although the initial protest was peaceful, the Minnesota National Guard was called in to protect the non-union workers. As frustrations boiled over—spurred in part by the P-9's parent union showing support for Hormel management instead of the strikers—riots broke out. Eventually, local police used tear gas and arrested protestors. The UFCW ultimately suspended P-9 leadership, effectively ending the strike. Only 20% of strikers were re-employed after a new contract was ratified with Hormel.[36]

---

33 Gordon, "Meatpacking Bosses in Iowa."

34 Leduff, "At a Slaughterhouse, Some Things Never Die."

35 Stephen Thierman, "Apparatuses of Animality: Foucault Goes to a Slaughterhouse," *Foucault Studies* 9 (2010): 106.

36 Susan Marks, "The 1985 Hormel Strike Was One of Minnesota's Most Contentious Labor Disputes," *Minnesota Post*, August 12, 2019, https://www.minnpost.com/mnopedia/2019/08/the-1985-hormel-strike-was-one-of-minnesotas-most-contentious-labor-disputes/.

There is a much longer labor history of meatpacking that spans the whole of the 20ᵗʰ and 21ˢᵗ centuries and is full of union wins and losses. Regardless, working the line is now one of the most dangerous jobs in the country and is largely staffed by the country's most vulnerable.

Who Is Cruel and Why?

When animal liberationists fail to recognize the rights of slaughterhouse workers, they become complicit in animalization. By painting workers with broad brushes as sadists, thugs, or other "beastly" constructions, those wanting to protect animals end up creating another symbolic "predator" working the slaughterhouse line. In the same way that a coyote is more than some sort of predatory sadist when he kills a family's cat, a slaughterhouse employee is more complex than her place of employment. They kill to live, but they do not live to kill. And, given the labor violations these employees endure, one would assume that many would choose an alternate profession if presented with reasonable alternatives.

Animal rights and welfare organizations often release undercover footage showing the abhorrent treatment of nonhuman animals en route to slaughter. The old adage goes, after all, that if slaughterhouses had glass walls, everyone would go vegan. One video released by the Humane Society showed floor workers at Bushway Packing Inc. shocking and beating baby calves that still had their umbilical cords attached. The video was unquestionably horrific. However, it is simplistic to grimace and ask: "What kind of person would do such a thing?" After all, industry executives would have the public believe that such actions are the results of a few "bad apples." The tougher and more fruitful question, however, is "What kind of working conditions make possible and probable these violent situations?"

The floor workers who sustain the meatpacking industry are *not* inherently cruel individuals. Rather, *the nature abattoir work itself produces violent behaviors on and beyond the slaughterhouse floor.* Jennifer Dillard observes that while the average American "will never see the inside of a slaughterhouse and may be able to eat a hamburger without confronting the pain and terror of a cow's final moments" slaughterhouse workers "face that troubling predicament every day, creating an employment situation ripe for psychological problems."[37] These conditions include: intense noise attributed to hearing loss; extreme temperatures increasing risk of overheating or hypothermia; physical labor attributed to musculoskeletal disorders; exposure to harsh

37 Dillard, "A Slaughterhouse Nightmare," 395.

chemicals and bacteria connected to the contraction of zoonotic disease; ever-increasing speeds of the line which exacerbate risks of exhaustion; and, of course, the killing of hundreds of nonhuman animals per day.[38]

The nature of killing-as-profession inevitably results in exponentially more violent acts along the slaughterhouse line. These acts, however, are not due to some inherent violent-ness in the individual, but rather the traumatic nature of the work itself. Rachel MacNair suggests that people placed in traumatic workplaces—specifically workplaces in which performing violence is the job—often develop a form of posttraumatic stress disorder called P.I.T.S— "perpetration-induced traumatic stress."[39] Unlike traditional traumatic stress disorders in which result from a person being the victim of a traumatic situation, sufferers of P.I.T.S. are instead "causal participants" in such situations. They are, as Michael Lebwohl explains, "the direct reason for another being's trauma. Living with the knowledge of their actions causes symptoms similar to those of individuals who are recipients of trauma: substance abuse, anxiety issues, depression, and dissociation from reality."[40]

Worker narrations shed more light on the nature of P.I.T.S. and how, as James McWilliams says, "the psychological weight of their work erodes their wellbeing."[41] Laborers recount persistent and disturbing flashbacks and nightmares."[42] One recalled "I dream about the cattle, when you stun it, it just fall down, after falling down, when you open the door it will ask you: 'Why are you killing me?'"[43] Another remembers "One day I dream that the cow gets out at the stunning box. It was alive…The cow is coming and you fall down! You fall down!"[44] Karen Victor and Antoni Barnard's study of abattoir floor workers' lived experiences showed workers resorting to maladaptive coping

38 Tani Khara, "Animals Suffer for Meat Production—And Slaughterhouse Workers Do Too," *The Conversation*, February 4, 2020. https://theconversation.com/anim als-suffer-for-meat-production-and-abattoir-workers-do-too-127506

39 Rachel MacNair, *Perpetration-Induced Traumatic Stress: The Psychological Consequences of Killing* (Westport, CT: Greenwood, 2002).

40 Michael Lebwohl, "A Call to Action: Psychological Harm in Slaughterhouse Workers," *Yale Global Health Review*, January 25, 2016, https://yaleglobalhealt hreview.com/2016/01/25/a-call-to-action-psychological-harm-in-slaughterhouse-workers/.

41 James McWilliams, "PTSD in the Slaughterhouse," *Texas Tribune*, "February 7, 2012," https://www.texasobserver.org/ptsd-in-the-slaughterhouse/.

42 Karen Victor and Antoni Barnard. "Slaughtering for a Living: A Hermeneutic Phenomenological Perspective on the Well-being of Slaughterhouse Employees." *International Journal of Qualitative Studies on Health and Well-Being* 11, no. 1 (2016): 30266.

43 Ibid.

44 Ibid.

mechanisms to live with the violence they inflicted: "Fear and anger coupled with guilt and shame (from the adjustment phase) seem to evolve into a response of emotional detachment."[45] So severe was the emotional dissociation that one worker recalled an incident the prior night in which "someone was cut in the stunning area, by one of his friends. He didn't even say sorry. He said it was an accident, turned around and continued cutting open the cattle."[46]

Violence begets violence. Ergo, the violence required of employees *inside* the abattoir inevitably impacts workers' lives *outside* the abattoir as well. Communities with larger proportions of slaughterhouse employees tend to have greater violent crime rates, specifically domestic violence, rape, and murder.[47] Criminologist Amy Fitzgerald proposed that the inhumane nature of the profession "desensitized" abattoir workers to violence.[48] While attributing these statistics entirely to one's profession would be disingenuous (after all, violent crime is also linked to issues of childhood trauma, mental illness, and sustained poverty), courts of law have at times *used the slaughterhouse to argue a defendant's guilt.* According to Dillard, "the defendant's occupation at the slaughterhouse was seen as an occupation that enhanced a person's tendency to commit—or at least to be comfortable with—violent acts."[49]

In other words, it is perfectly *legal* for corporations to employ vulnerable workers and require them commit mass murder against nonhuman animals while experiencing physical and psychic harm. And, at the same time, the inherent psychological consequences of that profession are used against line workers to blame them for any *illegal* activity. White-collar executives, meanwhile, enjoy the profits of the violence they themselves demanded of their workers.

Concluding Remarks

So then, why should those activists specifically concerned with the lost lives of nonhuman animals fight for the labor rights of the very people whose job it is to end those animals' lives? As with most animal liberation issues,

---

45 Ibid.
46 Ibid.
47 Amy J. Fitzgerald, Linda Kalof, and Thomas Dietz, "Slaughterhouses and Increased Crime Rates: An Empirical Analysis of the Spillover from "The Jungle" into the Surrounding Community," *Organization and Environment* 22, no. 2 (2009): 158–184.
48 Ibid.
49 Dillard, "A Slaughterhouse Nightmare," 391.

the answer comes back to speciesism. The human/nonhuman animal binary undergirds most, if not all, sociocultural institutions.[50] Whereas bioethicist Peter Singer's *Animal Liberation* focused on speciesism's application toward nonhuman animals, researchers and activists interested in race, class, gender, and disability justice consistently show how the category of "human" is—morally and legally speaking—hardly a homogenous bloc. On the contrary, the "ideal human subject" is bound to the identity categories of those *homo sapiens* with social and cultural capital. Those outside of this capital-N Norm are treated with various levels of "sub" humanness, a categorization which provides moral justification for immoral treatment.[51] Labor practices are embedded in this speciesist practice.

In other words, although two humans might be members of the same species, their opportunities for participation and/or advancement in human society could be very different by virtue of their (in)sufficiently human traits. The slaughterhouse is just that: a site of slaughter. It is a violent institution kept hidden from the average U.S. American's view that perpetuates speciesist norms and encourages the consumption of animal flesh for capitalist profit. For good reason, animal liberationists detest these institutions and fight for their abolition. That being said, nonhuman animals are not the only living animal subjects who suffer in the abattoir. The very workers assigned to kill these nonhuman animals are themselves dehumanized/animalized on a daily basis. Their labor conditions are appalling and their post-work psyches are perhaps even worse. These marginalized workers' perspectives are kept from public view both due to the animal-industrial complex's determination to keep slaughterhouse insides hidden from view and due to the liminal, vulnerable status of so many employees. And, due to their liminal status, it is all too easy for animal liberationists to beastialize these workers and portray them as predators in need of a cull.

In short, *all* animals trapped behind slaughterhouse walls deserve consideration—even those human animals tasked with the terrible, murderous, trauma-inducing job that the average omnivore prefers to ignore.

---

50 Kelly Struthers Montford, "Dehumanized Denizens, Displayed Animals: Prison Tourism and the Discourse of the Zoo." *PhiloSOPHIA* 6, no. 1 (2016): 73–91.
51 See: Maneesha Deckha, "The salience of Species Difference for Feminist Theory." *Hastings Women's Law Journal* 17 (2006): 1–38; Sylvia Wynter, "Unsettling the Coloniality of Being/Power/Truth/Freedom: Towards the Human, After Man, Its Overrepresentation—An Argument." *CR: The New Centennial Review* 3, no. 3 (2003): 257–337; among others.

References

Alayna Alexis, Nekeisha. "Beyond Suffering: Resisting Patriarchy and Reproductive Control," in *Anarchism and Animal Liberation: Essays on Complementary Elements of Total Liberation*, ed. Anthony Nocella II, Richard White, and Erika Cudworth (Jefferson, NC: McFarland, 2012), 112.

Chang, Alvin, Michael Sainato, Nina Lakhani, Rashida Kamal, and Aliya Uteunova. "The Pandemic Exposed the Human Cost of the Meatpacking Industry's Power: 'It's Truly Frightening," *The Guardian*, November 21, 2021, https://www.theguardian.com/environment/2021/nov/16/meatpacking-industry-covid-outbreaks-workers.

Chuck, Elizabeth. "Poultry Workers, Denied Bathroom Breaks, Wear Diapers: Oxfam Report," *NBC*, May 12, 2016, http://www.nbcnews.com/business/business-news/poultry-workers-denied-bathroom-breaks-wear-diapers-oxfam-report-n572806.

Deckha, Maneesha. "The Salience of Species Difference for Feminist Theory." *Hastings Women's Law Journal* 17 (2006): 1–38.

Dillard, Jennifer. "A Slaughterhouse Nightmare: Psychological Harm Suffered by Slaughterhouse Employees and the Possibility of Redress through Legal Reform," *Georgetown Journal on Poverty Law and Policy* 15 (2008): 392.

Fitzgerald, Amy J. "A Social History of the Slaughterhouse: From Inception to Contemporary Implications." *Human Ecology Review* (2010): 58–69.

Fitzgerald, Amy J., Linda Kalof, and Thomas Dietz. "Slaughterhouses and Increased Crime Rates: An Empirical Analysis of the Spillover from "The Jungle" into the Surrounding Community," *Organization and Environment* 22, no. 2 (2009): 158–184.

Gordon, Colin. "Meatpacking Bosses in Iowa Allegedly Organized a Betting Pool on How Many Workers Would Get Covid," *Jacobin Magazine*, November 20, 2020, https://jacobinmag.com/2020/11/meatpacking-iowa-tyson-lawsuit-work-conditions-covid-19

Groves, Stephen and Sophia Tareen. "U.S. Meatpacking Industry Relies on Immigrant Workers. But a Labor Shortage Looms," *Los Angeles Times*, May 26, 2020, https://www.latimes.com/food/story/2020-05-26/meatpacking-industry-immigrant-undocumented-workers

Harper, A. Breeze. *Sistah Vegan: Black Female Vegans Speak on Food, Identity, Health, and Society* (Lantern Publishing, 2009).

Haslam, Nick and Steve Loughnan. "Dehumanization and Infrahumanization." *Annual Review of Psychology* 65 (2014): 410.

Human Rights Watch. *Blood, Sweat, and Fear* (New York, NY: Human Rights Watch, 2004), p. 1, https://www.hrw.org/sites/default/files/reports/usa0105.pdf

Khara, Tani. "Animals Suffer for Meat Production—And Slaughterhouse Workers Do Too," *The Conversation*, February 4, 2020. https://theconversation.com/animals-suffer-for-meat-production-and-abattoir-workers-do-too-127506

Khazaal, Natalie and Núria Almiron. *Like an Animal: Critical Animal Studies Approaches to Borders, Displacement, and Othering* (New York: Brill, 2021).

Ko, Aph and Syl Ko. *Aphro-ism: Essays on Pop Culture, Feminism, and Black Veganism from Two Sisters* (Lantern Publishing, 2017).

Lebwohl, Michael. "A Call to Action: Psychological Harm in Slaughterhouse Workers," *Yale Global Health Review*, January 25, 2016, https://yaleglobalhealthreview.com/2016/01/25/a-call-to-action-psychological-harm-in-slaughterhouse-workers/.

LeDuff, Charlie. "At a Slaughterhouse, Some Things Never Die," *New York Times*, June 16, 2000, https://partners.nytimes.com/library/national/race/061600leduff-meat.html

Lowe, Peggy. "Working 'The Chain,' Slaughterhouse Workers Face Lifelong Injuries," *National Public Radio*, August 11, 2016. https://www.npr.org/sections/thesalt/2016/08/11/489468205/working-the-chain-slaughterhouse-workers-face-lifelong-injuries.pdf

MacNair, Rachel. *Perpetration-Induced Traumatic Stress: The Psychological Consequences of Killing* (Westport, CT: Greenwood, 2002).

Marks, Susan. "The 1985 Hormel Strike Was One of Minnesota's Most Contentious Labor Disputes," *Minnesota Post*, August 12, 2019, https://www.minnpost.com/mnopedia/2019/08/the-1985-hormel-strike-was-one-of-minnesotas-most-contentious-labor-disputes/.

Martin, Luke X. "How Multi-Ethnic Stockyard Workers Propelled Kansas City into the Modern Age," *National Public Radio*, April 28, 2019, https://www.kcur.org/show/up-to-date/2019-04-28/how-multi-ethnic-stockyard-workers-propelled-kansas-city-into-the-modern-age.

McWilliams, James. "PTSD in the Slaughterhouse," *Texas Tribune*, "February 7, 2012," https://www.texasobserver.org/ptsd-in-the-slaughterhouse/.

Muller, S. Marek. "Zombification, Social Death, and the Slaughterhouse: US Industrial Practices of Livestock Slaughter," *American Studies* 57, no. 3 (2018): 88.

Opotow, Susan. "Moral Exclusion and Injustice: An Introduction." *Journal of Social Issues* 46, no. 1 (1990): 1.

Pachirat, Timothy. *Every Twelve Seconds: Industrialized Slaughter and the Politics of Sight* (New Haven, CT: Yale University Press, 2011), 11.

Patterson, Orlando. *Slavery and Social Death* (Cambridge, MA: Harvard University Press, 1982), 15.

Taylor, Charles A. Christopher Boulos, and Douglas Almond, "Livestock Plants and COVID-19 Transmission." *Proceedings of the National Academy of Sciences* 117, no. 50 (2020): 31706–31715.

Thierman, Stephen. "Apparatuses of Animality: Foucault Goes to a Slaughterhouse," *Foucault Studies* 9 (2010): 106.

U.S. Department of Agriculture. "Livestock Slaughter 2017 Summary April 2018," http://usda.mannlib.cornell.edu/usda/current/LiveSlauSu/LiveSlauSu-04-18-2018.pdf; U.S. Department of Agriculture, "Poultry Slaughter 2017 Summary

February 2018," http://usda.mannlib.cornell.edu/usda/current/PoulSlauSu/Pou lSlauSu-02-26-2018.pdf.

Victor, Karen and Antoni Barnard. "Slaughtering for a Living: A Hermeneutic Phenomenological Perspective on the Well-being of Slaughterhouse Employees." *International Journal of Qualitative Studies on Health and Well-Being* 11, no. 1 (2016): 30266.

Wynter, Sylvia. "Unsettling the Coloniality of Being/Power/Truth/Freedom: Towards the Human, After Man, Its Overrepresentation—An Argument." *CR: The New Centennial Review* 3, no. 3 (2003): 257–337.

Section 2 The Animal Advocacy Nonprofit Sector and the Reification of Carceral and Racial Capitalism

Undercover Investigations and Carceral Veganism: The Limitations of "Removing the Veil"

ELLYSE WINTER

Introduction

The production of meat, eggs, and dairy products within the United States and Canada comes at significant cost to the environment and to the well-being of both humans and animals.[1] These implications are inextricably bound to the overlapping structures of White privilege and capitalism that normalize and depend upon exploitation, maximizing productivity and profits, and the privatization of resources and spaces.[2] Such logic manifests within industrial agriculture wherein animals are often produced in barren and restricted environments and subject to a range of physical and psychological stressors[3] where slaughterhouse workers—a workforce comprised primarily of racialized people, immigrants, and refugees—face deplorable working conditions and an injury rate five times higher than the national average,[4] and where the contribution to some of the most serious environmental problems, including greenhouse gas emissions, water pollution and depletion, land degradation, and biodiversity loss far exceeds that of other industries.[5] Moreover, it is the logic of White privilege and capitalism that masks these implications and

1 Gunderson, 2011; Gunderson & Stuart, 2014; MacDonald & McBridge, 2009; Rossi & Garner, 2014; Walker et al., 2005
2 Gunderson, 2011; Guthman, 2008a, 2008b; Lowe, 2015; Melamed, 2015; Nguyen, 2008; Noske, 1997; Robinson, 2000; Steinfeld et al., 2006
3 Mason & Finelli, 2013; Rossi & Garner, 2014
4 Nibert, 2013; Oxfam America, 2016
5 Oppenlander, 2013; Steinfeld et al., 2006

keeps them largely hidden from consumers.[6] Within the context of this chapter, I will refer to the current model of producing animal (by-) products as the animal-industrial complex. Deriving from earlier concepts of the prison-industrial complex and the military-industrial complex, the animal-industrial complex refers to the largely opaque and overlapping interests of the agricultural sector, the government, agribusiness corporations, and the economy that together result in the commodification and objectification of animals, humans, and the Earth.[7]

In response to the effects of the animal-industrial complex, several individuals and groups have developed spaces of advocacy through non-profit organizations, social media accounts, protests, documentaries, etc. I argue that these spaces of resistance constitute a form of pedagogy in their attempt to serve as an educative bridge between the production and consumption of animal (by-)products and thus "remove the veil" that obscures the resultant socio-ecological implications. However, despite being progressive in some ways, many of these spaces are underpinned by the same White privilege and capitalist logic that sustain the animal-industrial complex and are thus rife with troubling rhetoric, strategies, language, and assumptions. As such, an examination of these spaces must consider the processes of power and oppression that shape the production of resistance efforts and ultimately limit the arguable, fundable, organizable, and capacity for meaningful action.[8] Of particular interest in the context of this chapter, are the ways in which a reliance on the norms, values, and practices associated with White privilege and a capitalist system contributes to the reproduction of the status quo even within efforts to undermine it.[9]

Relying on the theoretical dimensions of critical animal studies (CAS) and the methodological field of critical discourse analysis (CDA), the purpose of this chapter is to examine the ways in which the logic that produced and maintains the current system of animal agriculture in Canada and the United States is re-inscribed in some the emergent spaces of resistance. More specifically, this project will examine the ways in which White privilege and capitalist logic is reproduced via undercover investigations. Part of the work done by some of the larger animal interest groups such as People for the Ethical Treatment of Animals (PETA) and Mercy for Animals (MFA) involves undercover investigations within farms and slaughterhouses across the United States and Canada. These investigations generally involve an animal rights

---

6   Gunderson, 2011; Guthman, 2008a, 2008b; Noske, 1997; Steinfeld et al., 2006
7   Fitzgerald & Pellow, 2014; Noske, 1997; Twine, 2012
8   Coleman & Bassi, 2011; Guthman, 2008a/2008b
9   Coleman & Bassi, 2011

activist posing as an employee and wearing surveillance equipment to capture the lived reality of the animal-industrial complex. Overall, I will argue that despite being valuable in "removing the veil" that obscures the socio-ecological implications of the animal-industrial complex, undercover investigations reproduce White privilege and capitalism by relying on a banking model of education, reproducing an individualized understanding of violence, re-commodifying animals, and utilizing a surveillance and detention framework that often targets marginalized farm and slaughterhouse workers. Taken together, this chapter advances the notion that debates about animal labour cannot be divorced from debates about human labour.[10]

Defining Key Terms

As mentioned, this chapter is concerned with the ways in which White privilege and capitalism both amplify the implications of the animal-industrial complex and frame the advocacy efforts that aim to resist it. With this in mind, I will now briefly outline how White privilege and capitalism are defined within the context of this chapter. White privilege refers to the belief system that rationalizes and reproduces race as a valuable social, political, and economic resource for White people. This has occurred because of unjust policies and practices that endure into the present and grant White people easier access to power and resources within the institutions of society.[11] Moreover, capitalism is characterized by the necessity to grow and the drive to accumulate the greatest profit in the shortest amount of time by maximizing output and minimizing input. Capitalism relies on both a spatial and conceptual distance between the production and consumption of goods to obscure the socio-ecological implications involved in production. However, capitalism is not just an economic system—it is reliant on a political and social system for support where individuals are socialized into accepting greed, individualism, competition, exploitation, and consumerism as natural and necessary for a thriving society.[12] Although I have defined White privilege and capitalism separately, I also want to emphasize that they are in fact overlapping and aid each other in complex ways. The concept of racial capitalism is useful in understanding how capitalism relies on an accumulation of capital that has depended on slavery, violence, and genocide and continues to exploit through

---

10 Blattner, Coulter, & Kymlicka, 2019
11 Bell, Funk, et al., 2016
12 Adams et al., 2016; Albritton, 2012; Fairclough, 2010; Magdoff & Foster, 2010; Stanford, 2008; Weis, 2012

systems of immense inequality.[13] Taken together, White privilege and capitalism create an exploitative and divisive system wherein particular human
populations, animals, and the environment are largely viewed as expendable
resources.[14]

Methodology and Theoretical Framework

This chapter draws on data that were collected as part of my doctoral dissertation, "The Animal-Industrial Complex and the Politics of Resistance" which
examined the ways in which White privilege and capitalist logic are reproduced
and contested in online spaces of vegan advocacy. The project used a qualitative
critical discourse analysis (CDA) to examine social media accounts dedicated to
vegan advocacy. Discourses are mutually supportive frameworks of meaning and
are made up of a particular set of knowledges, assumptions, and judgments.[15] As
a method for collecting and analyzing data, CDA examines the social context
that produced a particular text and the processes through which individuals
and groups create meaning as they interact with texts.[16] More specifically, CDA
posits these texts as a central part of social relations and involves a consideration
of the reciprocity between these forms of meaning making and aspects of social
relations such as social identities, values, and means of production.[17] In this way,
CDA considers the ways in which power relations are reproduced, reinforced, or
challenged within texts and narratives.[18] As such, data were collected from 10
online Facebook pages dedicated to vegan advocacy and included entries posted
by the page administrator(s) within a 6-month period, as well as the top 5 user
comments left on each of these entries. Across all 10 vegan advocacy groups, the
total number of posts analyzed was 3,071 and the total number of user comments analyzed was 8,313. For this chapter, I will focus primarily on the posts
and comments related to undercover investigations.

This chapter is also grounded in the central tenets of critical animal
studies (CAS). Perhaps the most important feature of CAS that makes it an
appropriate theoretical framework for this chosen project is the emphasis on
understanding the connection between multiple forms of oppression and
conceptualizing hierarchical ideologies as parts of a larger system.[19] Relying

---

13 Lowe, 2015; Melamed, 2015; Nguyen, 2021; Robinson, 2000
14 Nibert, 2013
15 Power, 2003
16 Fairclough, 2010; Wodak, 2001
17 Fairclough, 2001
18 Wodak & Meyer, 2009
19 Nibert, 2014

on the theoretical contributions of Patricia Hill Collins, Fellows and Razack (1998) conceptualize interlocking oppressions as follows:

> Systems of oppression rely on one another in complex ways. This "interlocking" effect means that systems of oppression come into existence in and through one another so that class exploitation could not be accomplished without gender and racial hierarchies; imperialism could not function without class exploitation, sexism, heterosexism, and so on. Because the systems rely on one another in complex ways, it is ultimately futile to attempt to disrupt one system without simultaneously disrupting others. (pp. 335–336)

With this context in mind, CAS explores the systemic destructive effects of White privilege and capitalism on humans, animals, and the Earth and rejects single-issue politics that focus strictly on animal interests in favor of solidarity and total liberation.[20] As such, I argue that undercover investigations are antithetic to a total liberation framework in that they largely disregard the harm exerted against human laborers and thus leave intact all harm. Further, both CDA and CAS represent socially committed paradigms that focus not only on engaging in critique, but also on emphasizing alternative ways of being.[21] Overall, CDA and CAS are useful in uncovering and contextualizing the multiple meanings and assumptions underlying online spaces that advocate for a vegan ethic.

The Uneven Burden of the Animal-Industrial Complex

Employees of the animal–industrial complex, particularly within slaughterhouses, face one of the highest risk jobs in the United States.[22] In 2005, the Human Rights Watch identified slaughterhouses as the most dangerous factory job, with an injury rate five times higher than the national average.[23] Employees also endure long hours in difficult conditions and are at an increased risk of developing respiratory disease, hearing loss, musculoskeletal problems, and contracting zoonotic diseases or anti-microbial resistant bacteria.[24] Further, employees have little to no job security or voice in opposing unsafe working conditions and earn disparately low wages.[25] Additionally, research is beginning to address the psychological effects of working in a

---

20 Best, 2009; Institute for Critical Animal Studies, n.d.; Nibert, 2014
21 Fairclough, 2010; Rogers, 2011
22 Glasser, 2011; Ilea, 2009; Oxfam America, 2016; Wrenn, 2015a
23 Glasser, 2011; Ilea, 2009; Nibert, 2014; Oxfam America, 2016
24 Dillard, 2008; Oxfam America, 2016; Rossi & Garner, 2014; Walker et al., 2005
25 Oxfam America, 2016

slaughterhouse and the trauma associated with being responsible for killing countless animals, observing animals being cut and dismembered while still conscious, and interacting with animals in various states of fear and pain.[26] Given the increasingly rapid pace of slaughter that persists to maximize productivity, employees are expected to consistently kill animals using violent methods, causing lasting psychological implications.[27] To this effect, one slaughterhouse worker comments:

> The worst thing, worse than the physical danger, is the emotional toll ... pigs down on the kill floor have come up and nuzzled me like a puppy. Two minutes later I had to kill them—beat them to death with a pipe. I can't care.[28]

It is crucial to acknowledge that these negative implications are unevenly distributed amongst society, as those who already experience vulnerability and marginality within society generally bear the largest burden.[29] As such, a discussion of the animal–industrial complex and the resultant implications must recognize the food system as a racialized and classed project and consider linkages to settler-colonialism and environmental racism.[30] Due to an exceptionally high turnover rate, the animal–industrial complex needs to find new employees, and has thus cultivated a highly vulnerable workforce, comprised largely of BBIPOC communities, working-class individuals, immigrants, and refugees.[31] As such, it is this vulnerable workforce subject to the aforementioned abysmal labour conditions, increased risk of experiencing injury and developing health issues, and psychological implications associated with being surrounded by and implicated in constant fear and death.[32] Overall, those who may already experience social, cultural, economic, and political marginalization are disproportionately impacted by the socio-ecological implications of the animal-industrial complex. In this way, these implications for humans and communities are tied to White privilege and the capitalist drive to maintain the power of elites and to value wealth accumulation above all else. As Rowe (2011) states, "industrial animal production devalues all life, privileging output and efficiency over respect and

26 Dillard, 2008; Rowe, 2011; Weis, 2013
27 Dillard, 2008; Nibert, 2014; Oxfam, 2016; Rowe, 2011
28 Dillard, 2008, p. 391
29 Alkon & Agyeman, 2011
30 Alkon & Agyeman, 2011
31 Nibert, 2014; Oxfam America, 2016; Wrenn, 2015
32 Dillard, 2008; Glasser, 2011; Ilea, 2009; Nibert, 2014; Oxfam America, 2016; Rossi & Garner, 2014; Rowe, 2011; Walker et al., 2005; Weis, 2013; Wrenn, 2015

compassion … [as] animals and humans are nothing but mechanical parts in the engine of corporate productivity and profit" (p. 9).

The Implications of Undercover Investigations

The industrial food system is premised on both a spatial and conceptual distance between the producers and consumers of food.[33] A consequence of this distance is that the socio-ecological implications of the animal–industrial complex are largely hidden from popular consciousness and obscured by market imperatives.[34] Karl Marx referred to this phenomenon as commodity fetishism, whereby the relations and costs involved in the production of commodities are minimized and difficult to comprehend.[35] Commodity fetishism is prevalent in a capitalist system, whereby a consumer's experiences with the production of commodities are limited to the characteristics of the final product itself, such as price, convenience, quantity, and packaging.[36] In this way, consumers engage with a food object that is largely divorced from the socio-ecological implications behind it, are largely discouraged from seeking additional context, and may thus have difficulty recognizing and addressing the resultant implications.[37] Consequently, given that the adverse effects of the animal–industrial complex are purposely hidden or minimized within public consciousness, Davis (2004) suggests, "a problem that remains to be solved … is how to win attention to sufferers or suffering that most people do not want to hear about, or have trouble imagining, or would just soon forget" (p. 3).

As such, undercover investigations, such as those carried out by organizations such as People for the Ethical Treatment of Animals (PETA) and Mercy for Animals (MFA) are potentially valuable in decreasing the distance between production and consumption by detailing the lived reality of the animal-industrial complex. One such example of a post shared by PETA on Facebook features an image of Paul McCartney saying, "I've often said, if slaughterhouses had glass walls, everyone would be vegetarian" and the caption reads "If slaughterhouses had glass walls…#ReasonsToGoVegan." A second example shared by PETA on Facebook features a graphic video of

---

33 Anthony, 2012; Gross, 2011; Hudson & Hudson, 2003; Knezevic, 2012; Weis, 2012/2013
34 Greenebaum, 2017; Gross, 2012; Hudson & Hudson, 2003; Knezevic, 2012; Weis, 2012, 2013
35 As cited in Weis, 2012
36 Hudson & Hudson, 2003; Sage, 2011
37 Hudson & Hudson, 2003; Rowe, 2011; Sage, 2011

pigs being harmed and the caption reads "Is your 'Easter ham' put in a gas chamber? Sound on." A third example shared by MFA on Facebook features a link to an article, "Largest Undercover Dairy Investigation of All Time Exposes Horrific Abuse of Calves" and the caption reads "Fair Oaks is one of the largest dairies in the United States." A fourth example shared by MFA on Facebook features a link to an article, "Angry Customers File Lawsuits After Huge Undercover Dairy Investigation" and the caption reads "In these complaints, Fairlife customers express their rage at being misled, including a claim that the company participated in 'massive consumer fraud.'" A fifth example shared by PETA on Facebook features an image juxtaposing "expectation" vs. "reality" imagery of the lives in chickens and the caption reads "ATTENTION! If you bought Nellie's Free Range Eggs and believe that you were misled by their advertising, we want to hear from you. PETA Foundation attorneys are now representing shoppers who felt misled into buying from Nellie's." Finally, a sixth example shared by PETA on Facebook features a graphic video of an injured cow and the caption read "Four days after this footage was taken, she was found dead. Your cheese is not worth this-NOTHING is worth this." Taken together, these examples depict the discoveries of several undercover investigations conducted by PETA and MFA. Such efforts disrupt the capitalist logic of commodity fetishism and the additional layer of obfuscation added by agribusiness propaganda by "removing the veil" that obscures the implications of the animal-industrial complex for animals.

However, such efforts can simultaneously reinforce capitalist logic and cumulative White advantage by emphasizing individualism and leaving intact larger structural forces. First, a focus on "removing the veil" is largely based on an ignorant mass of people being simply unaware of the socio-ecological implications of the animal–industrial complex, and who, once made aware, are expected to alter their consumption choices in favor of what has been deemed more ethical and sustainable; it presumes that, through principles of supply and demand, a more ethical and sustainable food system would flourish.[38] However, it is problematic to assert that those who purchase and consume foods produced via the animal–industrial complex are fundamentally less knowledgeable or ethically inclined.[39] A focus on personal culpability ignores the collective power and institutional support of the animal–industrial complex and the structural conditions—including White privilege and capitalism—that contribute to a reliance upon it and limit access to alternative

38 Alkon & Agyeman, 2011; Almassi, 2011; Guthman, 2008a, 2011; Weis, 2013
39 Guthman, 2011; Wrenn et al., 2015

foodways.[40] This emphasis on individualist sentiments within resistance discourse aligns with what Freire (1996) called the "banking model of education," whereby individuals are considered empty containers lacking any knowledge of the animal–industrial complex and vegan advocacy groups must impose knowledge on an unintelligible mass. This logic undergirds statements such as "if slaughterhouses had glass walls, everyone would be vegetarian." Such sentiments suggest that the only thing standing between individuals and veg(etari)anism is a lack of knowledge and ignores the larger systemic forces at work. As such, the notion of "removing the veil" to simply create awareness in hope that change will occur at an individual level largely ignores the immense power imbalances that persist within the food system and within society more generally, due at least in part to systems of capitalism and White privilege.

Second, public reception to undercover investigations reinforces a problematic boundary between violence that is deemed acceptable and that which is deemed unacceptable. While some of these investigations have led to cruelty charges filed against individual workers, others have been analyzed by a third party and have been found to include no evidence of abuse but rather to reveal "industry standard methods" of "humane" treatment and slaughter.[41] In this way, efforts to "remove the veil" are limited in their efficacy within a larger social context wherein most of the violence experienced by animals is in fact legal. More specifically, receptiveness to these investigations is bound to the individualistic conceptualization of violence that undergirds Canada's legal system.[42] For example, the Canadian legal system generally recognizes that animals have an interest in experiencing as little suffering as possible but allows for animals to be made to suffer for human benefit.[43] These laws protect fundamentally conflicting interests—those of animals not to suffer and those of people to cause such suffering.[44] Within Canadian legislation regarding animals, there are frequent references to the need for "humane" treatment of animals and the avoidance of "willful," "unnecessary," "undue," or "avoidable" pain and suffering. Bisgould (2011) problematizes the fact that these terms are not adequately defined and reinforce the notion that some degree of violence is acceptable in the name of industry and human interests. This notion of "unnecessary" suffering can thus be understood as those individual acts of violence against animals that are meant to deliberately cause pain

40 Wrenn, 2015; Wrenn et al., 2015
41 Kristof, 2015
42 Bisgould, 2011
43 Bisgould, 2011
44 Bisgould, 2011

without lawful purpose.[45] It is important to note that the words "undue," "willful," et cetera are also used in laws that speak to human suffering and hardship, in recognition that the law cannot be held accountable for eliminating all harm. However, within the scope of this project, I am interested specifically in laws related to the animal–industrial complex, the boundaries that exist between legal and illegal forms of harm, and the larger systemic forces that shape this line-drawing. As an example, the Fair Oaks case highlighted in the examples of Facebook content discussed above demonstrates that the legal system has deemed the slapping, punching, stabbing, and burning of calves and subjecting them to malnutrition and extreme temperatures as "willful" violence and suffering. While I do not disagree that these particular acts of violence did cause "willful" or "unnecessary" suffering, I would suggest that the routinized acts of violence including intensive confinement, the physiological and anatomical manipulation of farmed animals' bodies, continuous artificial ejaculation and insemination, premature separation of newborn animals from their mothers, the denial of species-life behaviors, and transportation and slaughter practices also cause "willful" and "unnecessary" suffering, given that alternative foods and agricultural practices are possible.[46] More specifically, Bisgould et al. (2001) argue that:

> Many, if not all of the practices by which animals are turned into food could be considered to be violations of [the Canadian Criminal Code] in that they cause pain, suffering or injury to animals for an ultimate purpose which is not 'necessary' in any true sense of the word. Relying on animals for food may be done for reasons of custom, habit, or preference, but it cannot be considered 'necessary' in most parts of Canada. (p. 12)

Consequently, the words "willful," "unnecessary," "undue," or "avoidable" within Canadian legislation regarding animal agriculture would be more accurately replaced with "unproductive" or "unprofitable" in reference to the pain and suffering inflicted on animals in the industrial complex. Rather than questioning the ethics of the entire system, by reducing the distance between the production and consumption of animal products and by-products, some of these undercover investigations lead to a compartmentalized, misplaced, and quickly relieved discomfort. Kirts (2020) discusses a relatively recent example in the following passage:

> In 2012, a poultry worker at a Butterball turkey farm in North Carolina became the first person in U.S. history to be convicted of a felony for cruelty to factory farmed birds. The arrest followed an undercover investigation by a prominent

45 Sorenson, 2003
46 Bisgould et al., 2001; Sorenson, 2003

vegan animal advocacy group that led to the employee's sentencing, probation, fines, and subjection to warrantless searches by law enforcement. Butterball management and executives weren't charged or fined for creating the conditions that led to the abuse of turkeys on the farm while the farm worker's arraignment was hailed as a milestone in the vegan movement.

While this example is from the United States, the basic premise has widespread implications. Overall, by relying upon the criminal justice system to protect animals, undercover investigations perpetuate an individualistic conceptualization of violence and leave intact the structural violence inherent to the animal-industrial complex.

Third, in aiming to "remove the veil" that obscures the implications of the animal-industrial complex, I also examined the use of graphic versus non-graphic imagery to illustrate these consequences. In using the term graphic, I am referring to the idiomatic meaning—content that is jarring, explicit, or no-holds-barred. That being said, it could be argued that all these posts illustrate graphic content, particularly when working with a sociology of violence that considers the forms of violence that are socio-politically legitimized and manifest in both physical and psychological forms.[47] As such, it is important to note that this classification of graphic or non-graphic was a subjective interpretation and was based, in large part, on the censorship policy built into Facebook Community Standards. To give users more choice over the content they are exposed to, Facebook adds a warning screen to initially blur particularly graphic or violent content so that it is not available to those under the age of 18 and so that people are able to choose whether to click to remove the blur and reveal the photo or video. Interestingly enough, this functions as an example of a literal veil or a deliberate obscuring of the implications of the animal–industrial complex, leaving consumers with the choice of whether they want to remove that veil. Perhaps unsurprisingly, of the 101 posts coded as graphic, PETA produced 89 of them. As an organization, PETA has come to be known for its controversial campaign strategies, emphasizing one of their central values as "animal rights uncompromised." More specifically, PETA emphasizes they "aren't afraid to make the difficult comparisons, say the unpopular thing, or point out the uncomfortable truth, if it means that animals will benefit." In the frequently asked questions section of its website, PETA defends its choice to use graphic imagery by saying such photographs and videos "are intended to make people angry enough to act ... [as] anger plays an important role in motivating people." While anger is in fact a powerful emotion, research indicates that feelings of anger often cause individuals

47 Cudworth, 2015

to "view negative events as predictably caused by, and under the control of, other individuals."[48] Further, anger has been associated with a "desire to change the situation and 'move against' another person or obstacle by fighting, harming, or conquering it."[49] Taken together, the research on anger as linked to perception and decision-making causes me to question whether a desire to elicit anger via vegan advocacy will result in viewers either blaming individual farm or slaughterhouse workers and/or seeking out "humane" alternatives or advocating for welfare-based reform rather than veganism. The existing research on the efficacy of graphic versus non-graphic content is scarce, but one study conducted by Faunalytics (2012) on behalf of VegFund sampled 500 individuals to assess how individuals responded to varying levels of violence portrayed in vegan advocacy. Interestingly, participants indicated that the video portraying the highest level of graphic content was the most likely to impact their decision to reduce or eliminate animal products and by-products, but it also had the lowest rate of user engagement and retention.[50] Consequently, the warning screen that initially blurs out violent and graphic imagery on Facebook and allows individual users to choose whether or not to view it may lead to minimal user engagement and thus the veil that obscures the socio-ecological implications of the animal–industrial complex may never be removed. The hesitation to watch graphic videos and the tendency to turn them off partway through therefore undermine their efficacy and speak to the natural inclination to turn away during moments of discomfort or avoid them all together. Further, the use of graphic imagery provides a heightened visual representation of animals as commodities. In other words, Facebook users visiting these vegan advocacy pages are still inundated with images of animals in situations that demonstrate their property status and as victims of violence and exploitation. Although the intent is to use this representation to elevate moral consideration towards animals, the representation is still rooted in White privilege and a capitalist logic that enables the total commodification of animals as property. Moreover, these representations largely depict animals as lacking agency and as passively accepting their fate, unable to act in meaningful ways or to make choices about their lives. Continuing to present images of animals as commodities contributes to the existing hegemonic discourse, rather than presenting counter-narratives about the possibilities for their lives outside of the industrial complex or as agents who can "shape elements of their lives, share their views, and make certain choices."[51]

48 Lerner et al., 2015, p. 13
49 Lerner et al., 2015, p. 18
50 Faunalytics, 2012
51 Coulter, 2018, p. 67

Underlying all three of the aforementioned implications of undercover investigations is that they also serve to further marginalize the vulnerable workforce that has been cultivated within the animal-industrial complex. Undercover investigations rely on a surveillance and detection framework, whereby "a felony conviction is a marker of a successful campaign."[52] In doing so, undercover investigations present a narrow and singular view of harm—one that positions animals as victims, workers as villains, and animal rights organizations or the carceral system as heroes—and thus obscures the exploitation of BBIPOC, immigrant, and working-class communities that are disproportionately involved in the production of animal (by-)products.[53] This narrative is made explicit via the Mercy for Animals website that refers to undercover investigators as "hidden heroes" and highlights that "not all superheroes wear capes." This narrative is further reproduced via several user comments that emerged in response to the undercover footage shared via the Facebook pages that were analyzed. Including an analysis of user comments aligned with a central principle of CDA, which considers the processes through which individuals and groups contribute to a shared sense of meaning as they interact with particular texts.[54] Below I will discuss several illustrative examples of the reproduction of this fixed victim-villain-hero narrative by way of accusing workers of being sociopaths and lacking compassion, and by wishing harm and imprisonment upon them. Each of the user comments discussed below are in response to various undercover footage videos and images. User comments included the following statements: "I don't know how a person could sleep at night if that was their job", "How do these people work for these cruel industries perpetuating abuse and death on these innocent precious chicks? You have to be a sociopath!!", "What kind of a person could do this and then go home and be a loving family person...I'd run fast when the question so what do you do for a living and they answer work in a slaughterhouse" and "Imagine how psychotic one must be to have this job." Such comments and the larger narrative within which they are situated demonstrate a failure to understand the ways in which capitalism and White privilege have contributed to the establishment of a highly vulnerable workforce, many of whom are not choosing this type of work but taking it out of necessity. Such comments also fail to recognize the physical and psychological harm enacted upon the workers themselves, as described earlier in this chapter. Additionally, rather than questioning the ways in which violence

---

52 Kirts, 2020, p. 198
53 Harper, 2013; Ornealas, 2011
54 Fairclough, 2010; Wodak, 2001

against animals has become socio-politically legitimized within the industrial complex and broader society, such comments transfer complicity away from both the industry and consumer towards the individual performing the labour. This serves to further alienate the worker, punish the worker for their labour, and reward those who own the means of production—thus reproducing capitalist ideology. In this way, vulnerable human populations are exploited and the larger systemic violence against workers, through violent and dehumanizing working conditions, goes unnoticed.[55]

Next Steps

The empirical work of studying the discourses used in vegan activism generally, and undercover investigations specifically, is not meant to be a purely theoretical exercise. Rather, the purpose is to advocate more effectively and in keeping with an alliance politics. It is important to note that there are many activists working to dismantle oppressive structures within vegan advocacy (i.e., Food Empowerment Project, Striving with Systems, Vegan Hip Hop Movement, and Vegan Voices of Colour), as well as scholars doing the same.[56] I am greatly indebted to these activists and scholars for shaping the direction of my research. In this final section of the chapter, I will highlight what can be learned from the study that will enhance the scholarship and activism in the areas of veganism and intersectional social justice. Given that both critical animal studies and critical discourse analysis are theory-to-action frameworks, and thus understand scholarship, teaching, and activism as intricately connected, I have chosen to collapse my discussion of the implications for both theory and practice.

This study has positioned vegan advocacy as a form of public pedagogy. As is true in traditional educational spaces, teaching is about much more than delivering a message; it is also about the ways in which that message is delivered. Although the underlying message of vegan advocacy may be valid, in many cases these activist groups are applying debunked pedagogical strategies to the delivery. What kinds of education, then, will be respectful and effective in bringing about changes in behavior? While I do want to deflect responsibility from individual consumers, I also believe in the value of education, which depends on a level of transformation within individual minds. There is a need for individual education, or conscientization,[57] which involves

---

55 Wrenn, 2015
56 i.e., Deckha, 2012/2010/2008a/2008b/2006; Harper, 2013/2011a/2011b, 2010a/2010b/2010c
57 Freire, 1996

reflecting on taken-for-granted understandings of the social world and acting against injustice. In *Teaching Community: A Pedagogy of Hope*, bell hooks (2003) argues:

> The purpose of education is not to dominate, or prepare [students] to be dominators, but rather to create the conditions for freedom. Caring educators open the mind, allowing students to embrace a world of knowing that is always subject to change and challenge. (p. 91)

This process of fostering a critical consciousness stands in contrast to a banking model of education,[58] according to which educators must deposit knowledge into otherwise empty minds. Vegan advocacy often relies on a banking model by approaching educative moments assuming their target audience is ignorant, and that providing information will correct their behavior. Moreover, these moments are often approached with hostility and dogmatism and fail to provide space for meaningful dialogue. I emphasize the importance of fostering curiosity or environments where individuals feel safe to try out different ideas and dialogue with one another. If, as activists and teachers, we enter conversations believing that our perception of the social world is the only right one, and if we are unwilling to budge in our views, we will often fail to facilitate meaningful action in the face of oppressive structures. Ultimately, people want to have their identities, knowledge, and experiences heard and validated. Rather than telling people what they should believe, the process of fostering a critical consciousness by using an active and dialogical approach provides space for imperfect dialogue and vulnerability so that individuals can begin to think critically and ask questions of themselves and of others.

Overall, I advocate for the value of nuance within conversation and activism and the notion that "perfect is the enemy of the good." When vegan advocacy pursues absolutism or perfection, activists end up engaging in processes of moral gatekeeping, or a sense of competition over who is "doing veganism the best." Again, if we conceptualize veganism as a means for practicing harm reduction, it is crucial to recognize the social, cultural, and economic positions that shape an individual's ability to pursue perfection and our perception and experiences of harm and, thus value nuance in this dialogue and practice. Overall, to improve pedagogical efficacy, vegan advocacy should focus on fostering a critical consciousness and recognize the underlying generative frameworks that have produced a system that is harmful to animals,

58 Freire, 1996

humans, and the Earth. As such, vegan advocacy must draw attention to the harm of more beings than just animals within its activism.

References

Adams, M., Hopkins, L. E., & Shlasko, D. (2016). Classism. In M. Adams & L. A. Bell (Eds.), *Teaching for diversity and social justice* (3rd ed., pp. 213–254). Routledge.

Albritton, R. (2012). Two great food revolutions: The domestication of nature and the transgression of nature's limits. In M. Koc, J. Sumner, & A. Winson (Eds.), *Critical perspectives in food studies* (pp. 89–103). Oxford University Press.

Alkon, A. H., & Agyeman, J. (2011). Introduction: The food movement as polyculture. In A. H. Alkon & J. Agyeman (Eds.), *Cultivating food justice: Race, class, and sustainability* (pp. 1–20). MIT Press. https://doi.org/10.7551/mitpress/8922.003.0003.

Almassi, B. (2011). The consequences of individual consumption: A defense for threshold arguments for vegetarianism and consumer ethics. *Journal of Applied Philosophy*, 28(4), 396–411. https://doi.org/10.1111/j.1468-5930.2011.00544.x.

Anthony, R. (2012). Building a sustainable future for animal agriculture: An environmental virtue ethic-of-care approach within the philosophy of technology. *Journal of Agricultural and Environmental Ethics*, 25(1), 123–144. https://doi.org/10.1007/s10806-010-9285-z.

Bell, L. A., Funk, M. S., Joshi, K. Y., & Valdiva, M. (2016). Racism and White privilege. In M. Adams & L. A. Bell (Eds.), *Teaching for diversity and social justice* (3rd ed., pp. 133–182). Routledge.

Best, S. (2009). The rise of critical animal studies: Putting theory into action and animal liberation into higher education. *Journal for Critical Animal Studies*, 7(1), 9–52. http://www.criticalanimalstudies.org/wp-content/uploads/2012/09/JCAS-VII-Issue-1-2009.pdf

Bisgould, L. (2011). *Animals and the law*. Irwin Law.

Bisgould, L., King, W., & Stopford, J. (2001). *Anything goes: An overview of Canada's legal approach to animals on factory farms* (pp. 1–65). Animal Alliance of Canada. http://www.animalalliance.ca/wp-content/uploads/2011/07/report-Anything-Goes.pdf

Blattner, C. E., Coulter, K., & Kymlicka, W. (Eds.). (2019). *Animal labour: A new frontier of interspecies justice?* Oxford University Press.

Coleman, L. M., & Bassi, S. A. (2011). Deconstructing militant manhood: Masculinities in the disciplining of (anti-)globalization politics. *International Feminist Journal of Politics*, 13(2), 204–224. https://doi.org/10.1080/14616742.2011.560039

Cudworth, E. (2015). Killing animals: Sociology, species relations and institutionalized violence. *The Sociological Review*, 63(1), 1–18. https://doi.org/10.1111%2F1467-954X.12222

Davis, K. (2004). A tale of two Holocausts. *Animal Liberation Philosophy and Policy Journal, 11*(2), 1–20. http://www.criticalanimalstudies.org/wp-content/uploads/2012/09/JCAS-Vol-2-Issue-2.pdf

Dillard, J. (2008). A slaughterhouse nightmare: Psychological harm suffered by slaughterhouse employees and the possibility of redress through legal reform. *Georgetown Journal on Poverty Law & Policy, 15*(2), 391–408.

Fairclough, N. (2010). *Critical discourse analysis: The critical study of language* (2nd ed.). Routledge.

Faunalytics. (2012, October 9). *What is the most effective veg outreach video?* https://faunalytics.org/what-is-the-most-effective-veg-outreach-video/

Fellows, M. L., & Razack, S. (1998). The race to innocence: Confronting hierarchical relations among women. *The Journal of Gender, Race and Justice, 1*(2), 335–352. https://scholarship.law.umn.edu/faculty_articles/274

Fitzgerald, A. J., & Pellow, D. (2014). Ecological defense for animal liberation: A holistic understanding of the world. In A. J. Nocella, J. Sorenson, K. Socha, & A. Matsuoka (Eds.), *Defining critical animal studies: An intersectional social justice approach for liberation* (pp. 28–50). Peter Lang.

Freire, P. (1996). *Pedagogy of the oppressed.* Continuum.

Glasser, C. L. (2011). Tied oppressions: An analysis of how sexist imagery reinforces speciesist sentiment. *The Brock Review, 12*(1), 51–68. https://doi.org/10.26522/br.v12i1.333

Greenebaum, J. B. (2017). Questioning the concept of vegan privilege: A commentary. *Humanity & Society, 41*(3), 355–372. https://doi.org/10.1177%2F0160597616640308

Gross, J. (2011). Constructing a community food economy. *Food and Foodways, 19*(3), 181–200. https://doi.org/10.1080/07409710.2011.599775

Gunderson, R. (2011). From cattle to capital: Exchange value, animal commodification, and barbarism. *Critical Sociology, 39*(2), 259–275. https://doi.org/10.1177%2F0896920511421031

Gunderson, R., & Stuart, D. (2014). Industrial animal agribusiness and environmental sociological theory. *International Journal of Sociology, 44*(1), 54–74. https://doi.org/10.2753/IJS0020-7659440104

Guthman, J. (2008a). Neoliberalism and the making of food politics in California. *Geoforum, 39*(3), 1171–1183. https://doi.org/10.1016/j.geoforum.2006.09.002

Guthman, J. (2008b). Thinking inside the neoliberal box: The micro-politics of agrofood philanthropy. *Geoforum, 39*(3), 1241–1253. https://doi.org/10.1016/j.geoforum.2006.09.001

Guthman, J. (2011). "If they only knew": The unbearable Whiteness of alternative food. In A. H. Alkon & J. Agyeman (Eds.), *Cultivating food justice: Race, class, and sustainability* (pp. 309–330). MIT Press.

Harper, A. B. (2013). *Vegan consciousness and the commodity chain: On the neoliberal, afrocenric, and decolonial politics of "cruelty free"* [Doctoral dissertation, University of California Davis]. http://www.sistahvegan.com/wp-content/uploads/2013/03/harperpdftelfordupdates.pdf

hooks, B. (2003). *Teaching community: A pedagogy of hope*. Routledge.

Ilea, R. C. (2009). Intensive livestock farming: Global trends, increased environmental concerns and ethical solutions. *Journal of Agricultural and Environmental Ethics*, *22*(1), 153–167. https://doi.org/10.1007/s10806-008-9136-3

Institute for Critical Animal Studies. (n.d.). *About*. http://www.criticalanimalstudies.org/about/

Kim, C. J. (2011). Moral extensionism or racist exploitation: The use of Holocaust and slavery analogies in the animal liberation movement. *New Political Science*, *33*(3), 311–333. https://doi.org/10.1080/07393148.2011.592021

Kirts, L. (2020). Toward an anti-carceral queer veganism. In J. F. Brueck & Z. McNeill (Eds.). *Queer and trans voices: Achieving liberation through consistent anti-oppression*. Sanctuary Publishers.

Knezevic, I. (2012). Labels and governance: Promises, failures, and deceptions of food labeling. In M. Koc, J. Sumner, & A. Winson (Eds.), *Critical perspectives in food studies* (pp. 247–259). Oxford University Press.

Lerner, J. S., Li, Y., Valdesolo, P., & Kassam, K. S. (2015). Emotion and decision making. *Annual Review of Psychology*, *66*(1), 799–823. https://doi.org/10.1146/annurev-psych-010213-115043

Lowe, L. (2015). *The intimacies of four continents*. Duke University Press.

MacDonald, J. M., & McBridge, W. D. (2009). *The transformation of U.S. Livestock agriculture: Scale, efficiency, and risks*. United States Department of Agriculture. https://www.ers.usda.gov/webdocs/publications/44292/13802_eib43fm_1_.pdf?v=41055

Magdoff, F., & Foster, J. B. (2010). What every environmentalist needs to know about capitalism. *Monthly Review*, *61*(10), 1–30.

Mason, J., & Finelli, M. (2013). Brave new farm. In P. Singer (Ed.), *In defense of animals: The second wave* (pp. 104–122). Blackwell.

Melamed, J. (2015). Racial capitalism. *Critical Ethnic Studies*, *1*(1), 76–85.

Nguyen, C. (2020). The relationship between White supremacy and capitalism: A Socioeconomic study on embeddedness in the market and society. *SUURJ: Seattle University Undergraduate Research Journal*, *4*(6), 7–16

Nibert, D. A. (2013). *Animal oppression and human violence: Domesecration, capitalism, and global conflict*. Columbia University Press.

Noske, B. (1997). *Beyond boundaries: Humans and animals*. Black Rose Books.

Oppenlander, R. A. (2013). *Food choice and sustainability: Why buying local, eating less meat, and taking baby steps won't work*. Langdon Street.

Ornelas, L. (2011). An appetite for justice. In L. Kemmerer (Ed.), *Sister species: Women, animals, and social justice* (pp. 152–160). University of Illinois Press.

Oxfam America. (2016). *Lives on the line: The human cost of cheap chicken*. https://www.oxfamamerica.org/static/media/files/Lives_on_the_Line_Full_Report_Final.pdf

Power, M. (2003). Development thinking and the mystical "kingdom of abundance." In *Rethinking development geographies* (pp. 71–94). Routledge.

Robinson, C. (2000). *Black Marxism: The making of the Black radical tradition.* University of North Carolina.

Rogers, R. (2011). Critical approaches to discourse analysis in educational research. In R. Rogers (Ed.), *Critical discourse analysis in education* (2nd ed., pp. 1–20). Routledge.

Rossi, J., & Garner, S. (2014). Industrial farm animal production: A comprehensive moral critique. *Journal of Agricultural and Environmental Ethics, 27*(1), 479–522. https://doi.org/10.1007/s10806-014-9497-8

Rowe, B. D. (2011). Understanding animals-becoming-meat: Embracing a disturbing education. *Critical Education, 2*(7), 1–25. https://doi.org/10.14288/ce.v2i7.182311

Sage, C. (2011). *Environment and food.* Routledge.

Sorenson, J. (2003). "Some strange things happening in our country": Opposing proposed changes in anti-cruelty laws in Canada. *Social & Legal Studies, 12*(3), 377–402. https://doi.org/10.1177%2F09646639030123005

Stanford, J. (2008). *Economics for everyone: A short guide to the economics of capitalism.* Fernwood Publishing.

Steinfeld, H., Gerber, P., Wassenaar, Castel, V., Rosales, M., & de Haan, C. (2006). Executive summary. *Livestock's long shadow: Environmental issues and options* (pp. xx–xxiv). FAO. https://www.fao.org/3/a0701e/a0701e00.htm

Twine, R. (2012). Revealing the "animal–industrial complex": A concept and method for critical animal studies? *Journal for Critical Animal Studies, 10*(1), 12–39. https://tinyurl.com/bp5c3r94

Walker, P., Rhubart-Berg, P., McKenzie, S., Kelling, K., & Lawrence, R. S. (2005). Public health implications of meat production and consumption. *Public Health Nutrition, 8*(4), 348–356. https://doi.org/10.1079/phn2005727

Weis, T. (2012). A political ecology approach to industrial food production. In M. Koc, J. Sumner, & A. Winson (Eds.), *Critical perspectives in food studies* (pp. 104–121). Oxford University Press.

Weis, T. (2013). *The ecological hoofprint: The global burden of industrial livestock.* Zed Books.

Wodak, R. (2001). What CDA is about: A summary of its history, important concepts, and its developments. In R. Wodak & M. Meyer (Eds.), *Methods of critical discourse analysis* (pp. 1–13). SAGE.

Wodak, R., & Meyer, M. (Eds.). (2009). *Methods of critical discourse analysis* (2nd ed.). SAGE.

Wrenn, C. L. (2015). *A rational approach to animal rights: Extensions in abolitionist theory.* Palgrave Macmillan.

Wrenn, C. L., Clark, J., Judge, M., Gilchrist, K. A., Woodlock, D., Dotson, K., Spanos, R., & Wrenn, J. (2015). The medicalization of nonhuman animal rights: Frame contestation and the exploitation of disability. *Disability & Society, 30*(9), 1307–1327. https://doi.org/10.1080/09687599.2015.1099518

Death or Deportation: A Nebraska-Based Study of the Exploitation of Immigrant Workers in Meatpacking Facilities and the Immigration Consequences of the Animal Protection Movement

KELLY SHANAHAN

[TW: this chapter mentions sexual assault and other forms of physical violence]

Imagine. 19 years old, huddling in the corner of your home, you watch as local gang members rape, beat, and murder your younger sister, Alessandra, and your mother, Aniela. Stifling down the screams threatening to erupt from your throat, you sneak out the back door to safety. Well not safety, but at least out of immediate danger. You only have the money in your pocket, your slightly torn t-shirt, your blue jeans, and your worn-down Nikes as you begin the over two-thousand-kilometer journey to a hopeful new life in America, the land of free and the promised American dream.

You finally make it to Mexico, to a small border town and locate a coyote[1] willing to transport you across the United States border. You hear the others with whom you are planning to cross with discussing the jobs they have lined up in Nebraska at a slaughterhouse. You ask them to tell you more, and they go on about a labor broker[2]

1 A coyote is the colloquial term for a smuggler or smuggling group. Talk of the Nation "Inside the Hidden World of Immigrant Smuggling," National Public Radio, April 12, 2012, https://www.npr.org/2012/04/19/150973748/inside-the-hidden-world-of-immigrant-smuggling.
2 Labor brokers are independent contractors that work with companies to recruit workers and navigate the work visa system. Some labor brokers fail to obtain proper permits and contribute to the employment of workers without proper authorization. Megan Twohey, et al., "Wanted: Foreign Workers—and the Labor Brokers Accused of Illegally Profiting from Them," February 19, 2016, https://www.reuters.com/investigates/special-report/workers-brokers/.

they met in a nearby town making job offers. They talk about the guaranteed work, good pay, and all without the need to show any employment authorization. You decide to tag along with them because it's the first job you've heard of willing to hire immigrants without papers. It seems to be your only choice.

About a month later, you finally arrive in Nebraska. You and the girls you met while being brought over the border find a quick loan service and rent a small apartment together before beginning your first day of work. It's only a matter of time until the job's novelty wears off and your excitement about America dwindles. You sleep, you eat, you work. At work you kill, you sort, you kill. You go home, you watch the news about another immigrant being attacked, beaten, or murdered. And you sleep. And repeat. This is not the American dream you were promised; it is not what you expected. But you are safe, relatively speaking. So, you repeat. It's not that you enjoy the slaughterhouse—it's that it's a necessary part of your day. No one else will hire you, as your bosses remind you of that when they dock your pay and increase the line speed all in the same breath. And when you fall behind, they are quick to mutter that ICE[3] is only a phone call away. You have limited options, continue the slaughter or face immigration enforcement; what will it be, death or deportation?

This story is not attributable to a sole immigrant living in Nebraska, yet the story is familiar to many of those working in immigration law. Our clients come to us, after facing a myriad of hardships, with great hopes of the freedom that America is supposed to offer—especially the promise of economic prosperity. But the reality often varies from the dream. When immigrants arrive to America they face additional abuse, discrimination, racism, and financial and labor exploitation. And sometimes, these harms arise from unexpected places like the animal protection movement.

In the Midwest especially, many immigrants find their first domestic job opportunities in our Nation's meatpacking facilities.[4] Workers in meatpacking

3 Immigration and Customs Enforcement (ICE) is one of three federal agencies charged with immigration enforcement. ICE has three central divisions, the best known of which is the "Enforcement and Removal Operations" responsible for the arrest, detainment, and deportation of immigrants. Ron Nixon and Linda Qiu, "What Is ICE and Why Do Critics Want to Abolish It?," New York Times, July 3, 2018, https://www.nytimes.com/2018/07/03/us/politics/fact-check-ice-immigration-abolish.html. ICE as an agency is the primary force behind workplace raids which are particularly troublesome for many immigrant meatpacking workers. Furthermore, ICE is known for its problematic treatment of immigrants while in their custody with detention facilities being described as "fraught with alarmingly poor conditions, a lack of accountability and a culture of violence that results in system-wide abuses." Silky Shah, "Why America Still Needs to Abolish ICE," NBC News, October 14, 2020, https://www.nbcnews.com/think/opinion/why-america-still-needs-abolish-ice-ncna1243293.

4 This chapter uses the term "meatpacking facilities," meatpacking "refers to the process of turning livestock into meat, including slaughter, processing, packing and

facilities face many occupational risks, everything from the potential of debilitating physical injuries to the animosity workers face from the animal protection movement. Media attention by animal-activists on the conditions of the
meatpacking industry often places the blame on individual workers for the
violent conditions and animal abuse.[5] Furthermore, activists often push for
criminal enforcement of animal abuse laws against workers instead of pushing
for corporate liability and systemic change. For immigrant laborers working in meatpacking facilities this activism poses a unique threat—leading to
potentially harsh immigration consequences.

This chapter is divided into two sections: the first section provides an
overview of the extent of immigrant labor in meatpacking plants in the state
of Nebraska and a general discussion of the dangers of meatpacking. The
second section tackles the ways in which the animal protection movement has
affected immigrant laborers to date, the potential immigration consequences
that meatpackers face in light of animal activism, and a proposed pathway
forward.

Immigrant Labor in Nebraska: Meatpacking Plants, Rural Populations, and Labor Risks

The abuse of immigrant laborers in meatpacking facilities is not a new
problem.[6] Criticism of the inhumane treatment of immigrant workers by

distribution." "Meatpacking and Slaughterhouses," FoodPrint, May 22, 2023,
https://foodprint.org/issues/meatpacking-and-slaughterhouses/. Meatpacking
facilities include dedicated slaughterhouses. FoodPrint, "Meatpacking." While
meatpacking traditionally focuses on the slaughter of animals like cows and pigs,
in this chapter, the term is assumed to also cover poultry processing. This chapter uses the term "immigrant" in the colloquial sense to refer to people that move
with the intent to live in another country permanently. This contrasts with the legal
definition of immigrant: "any person lawfully in the United States who is not a
U.S. citizen, U.S. national, or a person admitted under a nonimmigrant category as
defined by the INA [Immigration and Nationality Act] Section 101(a)(15)." Office
of Immigration Statistics, "Reporting Terminology and Definitions," Department
of Homeland Security, accessed June 17, 2023, https://www.dhs.gov/immigration-
statistics/reporting-terminology-definitions#8. This chapter does not use the term
undocumented immigrant; the term does not have a legal definition and is often
used in the colloquial sense to refer to a variety of immigration statuses. Instead, this
chapter uses the term "without authorization," or "without work authorization," to
refer to laborers who do not have legal permission to be working for U.S. employers.

5 Please read Ellyse Winter's chapter for further discussion on this point.
6 For context, in 2021, Nebraska performed the most commercial slaughter of cattle
   in the United States for a total of 7,091,600 head of cattle. "Nebraska Top National
   Rankings," Nebraska Department of Agriculture, accessed June 17, 2023, https://

meatpackers can be traced back as far as the early 1900s,[7] when central and eastern European immigrants staffed America's kill floors.[8] Presently, meatpacking plants largely employ workers from Latin America, Africa, and Southeast Asia;[9] as a result, laborers face an even more complex-form of xenophobia, one that includes racial-based discrimination.[10]

In Nebraska,[11] and in the larger Midwest where meatpacking facilities are highly concentrated, there is a promise of financial stability and freedom for many immigrants coming to the United States. While rural America is proportionally less diverse than the rest of the Nation, in the Midwest, rural communities have become home for many immigrants.[12] In fact, many rural towns in Nebraska are comprised of large immigrant populations because of meatpacking and the promised "American Dream."[13]

nda.nebraska.gov/facts.pdf. Overall, the state boasts the top three beef cow counties in the United States. "Nebraska: The Beef State," Nebraska Beef Council, accessed June 17, 2023, https://www.nebeef.org/raising-beef/state-national-facts.

7 Anna Williams Shavers, "Welcome to the Jungle: New Immigrants in the Meatpacking and Poultry Processing Industry," *Journal of Law Economics & Policy* 5 (2009): 32.

8 "The Speed Kills You: The Voice of Nebraska's Meatpacking Workers," Nebraska Appleseed 2009, 19, https://neappleseed.org/wp-content/uploads/downloads/2013/01/the_speed_kills_you_100410.pdf.

9 Nebraska Appleseed, "Speed Kills". According to the 2021 Nebraska Meatpacking Industry Workers Bill of Rights Annual Report, the most common language spoken at meatpacking facilities in Nebraska is Spanish. Manuela Benne, "Nebraska Meatpacking Industry Worker's Bill of Rights 2021 Annual Report," Nebraska Department of Labor, December 1, 2021, https://nebraskalegislature.gov/FloorDocs/107/PDF/Agencies/Labor__Department_of/76_20211201-154145.pdf.

10 Xenophobia refers to the "fear and hatred of strangers or foreigners." "Xenophobia," Merriam-Webster Dictionary, accessed June 17, 2023, https://www.merriam-webster.com/dictionary/xenophobia.

11 As of April 25, 2023, Nebraska has 39 U.S.D.A. recognized rendering and slaughterhouses (collectively meatpacking facilities). Animal and Plant Health Inspection Service, "Listed Slaughter and Rendering Establishments," United States Department of Agriculture, April 25, 2023, https://www.aphis.usda.gov/aphis/ourfocus/animalhealth/sa-epidemiology-animalhealth-ceah/btc/main/index.

12 Naomi Starkman, "On the Rural Immigrant Experience: 'We Come with a Culture, Our Own History, and We're Here to Help'," Civil Eats, April 14, 2022, https://civileats.com/2022/04/14/on-the-rural-immigrant-experience-we-come-with-a-culture-our-own-history-and-were-here-to-help/.

13 This is in contrast the world of meatpacking from the early 1900s when facilities were located in large rail hubs like Chicago, Kansas City, and St. Paul; From the 1970s onward, meatpacking has undergone ruralization and processing facilities are now located closer to where the animals are raised. Michael J. Broadway, *Any Way*

Cargill, one of the largest meatpacking companies, has a plant located in Schuyler,[14] Nebraska where, according to the 2020 U.S. Census, a staggering 54.4% of the population identified as foreign born.[15] This is in contrast to the fact that Nebraska as a whole only has a 7.4% foreign born population.[16] The statistic is all the more surprising when one considers that the percentage of immigrants living in towns like Schuyler, is likely much higher than reported because immigrants present in the United States without authorization frequently fail to fill out the census out of fear of the United States Government.[17] In Lexington, Nebraska where there is both a Tyson and an IBP meatpacking facility,[18] the census found that 41.4% of the population was foreign born.[19] And in Dakota County, Nebraska where there is yet another Tyson meatpacking facility,[20] 22.9% of the population identified as foreign born.[21]

Life in these small towns in Nebraska is anything but easy for immigrants.[22] Work at meatpacking facilities comes with many

You Cut It: Meat Processing and Small-Town America (University Press of Kansas, 1995), 17–38.

14 Animal and Plant Health Inspection Service, "Approved Immediate Slaughter Facilities," United States Department of Agriculture, May 9, 2023, https://www.aphis.usda.gov/aphis/ourfocus/animalhealth/animal-and-animal-product-import-information/immed-slaughter-list/animal-slaughter-list.

15 "Quick Facts: Schuyler City, Nebraska," U.S. Census Bureau, Accessed June 17, 2023, https://www.census.gov/quickfacts/fact/table/schuylercitynebraska/PST040222.

16 "Quick Facts: Nebraska," U.S. Census Bureau, Accessed June 17, 2023, https://www.census.gov/quickfacts/fact/table/NE,US/POP645221.

17 The foreign-born category for the U.S. Census measures all persons born outside of the states, it does not ask persons to indicate their immigration status and does not pair census data with identifying information, therefore making it safe for immigrants without status to complete the paperwork. Yet many immigrants are not aware of this information. "Frequently Asked Questions (FAQs) About Foreign Born," U.S. Census Bureau, accessed June 17, 2023, https://www.census.gov/topics/population/foreign-born/about/faq.html; "Immigrant Undercount," National Network for Immigrant and Refugee Rights, accessed June 17, 2023, https://nnirr.org/immigrant-undercount/.

18 APHIS, "Approved Immediate Slaughter Facilities."

19 "Quick Facts: Lexington City, Nebraska," U.S. Census Bureau, accessed June 17, 2023, https://www.census.gov/quickfacts/lexingtoncitynebraska.

20 APHIS, "Approved Immediate Slaughter Facilities."

21 "Quick Facts: Dakota County, Nebraska," U.S. Census Bureau, Accessed June 17, 2023, https://www.census.gov/quickfacts/fact/table/dakotacountynebraska/HCN010217.

22 This is not to say that immigrant populations are not thriving in rural America. In fact, in towns like Lexington, Nebraska, first- and second-generation immigrants

unanticipated and unspoken risks.[23] The dangers are vast, including every-thing from the risk of debilitating physical injuries[24] to the psychological damage[25] that comes from the trauma associated with animal slaughter.[26] And on top of the general risks associated with meatpacking labor, immigrant meatpackers face additional risks like oppressive and preda-tory child labor,[27] political animosity,[28] and immigration enforcement

have contributed significantly to economic development; many families have gone on to open restaurants and retail stores. However, the large contributions that immi-grant populations provide is not met in kind with resources and support the way that U.S. Citizens are supported. Starkman, "On the Rural Immigrant Experience."

23   Human Rights Watch has a report dedicated to detailing and investigating the risks associated with working at meatpacking and slaughterhouse facilities. For more infor-mation on the comprehensive risks of such jobs, access the report online. "Blood, Sweat, and Fear: Workers' Rights in U.S. Meat and Poultry Plants," Human Rights Watch, 2004, https://www.hrw.org/report/2005/01/24/blood-sweat-and-fear/workers-rights-us-meat-and-poultry-plants.

24   There are numerous kinds of physical injuries experienced at meatpacking facilities; these include injuries from repetitive motions as well as traumatic injuries due to hazards like slippery floors and electric knives. Nebraska Appleseed, "Speed Kills", 1; Appleseed, "Speed Kills", 22.

25   Jessica H. Leibler, et al., "Prevalence of Serious Psychological Distress among Slaughterhouse Workers at a United States Beef Packing Plant," *Work* 57, No. 1 (2017): 105–109.

26   At least one Nebraska meatpacker employee stated the psychological impact of the work goes beyond the safety concerns, it includes humiliation and dehumanization. Nebraska Appleseed, "Speed Kills", 4. This employee, surveyed for a report evaluat-ing the state of Nebraska meatpacking plants, stated that after supervisors screamed at the workers a few employees had urinated and defecated in their pants, only to be further laughed at by the supervisors. Nebraska Appleseed, "Speed Kills", 4.

27   A recent 2022 Department of Labor Investigation of Packers Sanitation Services (PSSI), a meatpacking sanitation company, uncovered systemic illegal employment of children, as young as age 13, at slaughterhouses and meatpacking facilities in Nebraska and Minnesota. Estimates are that of the children discovered working in violation of federal labor laws, around 100 or so are also immigrants to the United States. Yamily Habib, "Migrant Child Labor: The Dark Reality of Hundreds of Children in the United States," Mitu, April 14, 2023, https://wearemitu.com/wearemitu/news/migrant-child-labor/. Migrant child labor is especially common in U.S. industries, everything from clothing production to auto parts manufacturing is affected. Habib, "Migrant Child Labor."

28   For instance, during the COVID-19 Pandemic, the Nebraska State Governor Pete Ricketts announced that the state's "illegal immigrant" meatpackers would not be eligible for the state's vaccination program. While Rickett's later recanted, his state-ment reflects some of the xenophobia immigrant meatpackers face. Azmi Haroun, "Nebraska Gov. Ricketts Says He 'Doesn't Expect' Undocumented Workers in Meatpacking Plants Will be Part of State's Vaccination Plans," Business Insider,

raids.[29]

All of these aforementioned dangers, and the dangers elaborated on in other chapters of this book, have arisen despite the fact that there is a Nebraska Meatpacking Industry Workers Bill of Rights.[30] The Bill of Rights is codified into Nebraska state law and includes "the right to a safe workplace."[31] The statute requires the appointment of a meatpacking industry workers rights coordinator.[32] Despite the codification of this Bill of Rights into law in 2000,[33] dangers have continued to arise in Nebraska.

January 6, 2021, https://www.businessinsider.com/nebraska-gov-ricketts-undoc umented-people-not-included-vaccine-rollout-2021-1.

29 Because of the high rates of employment of immigrants without work authorization, meatpacking facilities are a common target of immigration enforcement "workplace raids," by Immigration and Customs Enforcement (ICE). Workplace raids are incredibly traumatic to communities and are the most "visible and harmful" immigration enforcement tactic. "Worksite Immigration Raids," National Immigration Law Center, January 2020, https://www.nilc.org/issues/workersrights/works ite-raids/. During these raids, unannounced federal agents physically enter facilities using militaristic force to arrest workers. NILC, "Immigration Raids." Federal agents block off exists to make arrests and then transport workers to detention facilities for processing. NILC, "Immigration Raids." In the end, very few workers are ever charged with a crime, and meatpacking facilities responsible for the hiring of employees without authorization rarely face any consequences. "Few Prosecuted for Illegal Employment of Immigrants," Transactional Records Access Clearinghouse Immigration, May 30, 2019, https://trac.syr.edu/immigration/reports/559/. What does happen is workers are violated by racial profiling, unlawful searches, denial of medical treatment, harassment, and separation from family. NILC, "Immigration Raids." Unfortunately, a 2022 Supreme Court case overturned 50 years of legal precedence and closed off the pathway for immigrants to recover from ICE agents that violated their constitutional rights. Shaw Drake & Katie Hoeppner, "Four Things to Know Abou the Supreme Court's Ruling in Egbert v. Boule," ACLU, June 27, 2022, https://www.aclu.org/news/civil-liberties/four-things-the-supreme-court-ruling-egbert-v-boule-ice.

30 Neb. Rev. Stat. § 48-2213. This Bill of Rights was codified into Nebraska law in 2001 when the Nebraska Unicameral passed the Non-English Speaking Workers Protection Act. Nebraska Appleseed, "Speed Kills", 21. The act is designed to aid the non-English speaking workforce in understanding the terms and conditions of their employment. Nebraska Appleseed, "Speed Kills", 21.

31 Neb. Rev. Stat. § 48-2213(2)(b).

32 Neb. Rev. Stat. § 48-2213(1); According to a 2009 report by Nebraska Appleseed, while a little over half of meatpackers were aware of the Meatpacking Industry Workers Bill of Rights, very few of them knew of the workers' rights coordinator. Nebraska Appleseed, "Speed Kills". Knowledge of and access to the meatpacking workers right coordinator is a key resource for employees that have questions and concerns they want addressed. Nebraska Appleseed, "Speed Kills."

33 Benne, "Annual Report," 2.

One reason why the Meatpacking Bill of Rights has been ineffective at addressing the continuing and new dangers at meatpacking facilities is that the law does not permit the Bill of Rights Coordinator to actually "impose any consequences for noncompliance of the Meatpacking Bill of Rights."[34] As such, even when the Bill of Rights Coordinator makes suggestions and conducts investigations, "several facilities have been reluctant to respond to the Coordinator's recommendations, or do not respond at all."[35]

Animal Activism, Immigration Consequences, and a Few Paths Forward

All the above-mentioned dangers and xenophobia faced by immigrant meat-packers in Nebraska and beyond, is compounded by harms attributable to the animal protection movement. The movement's increasing carceral approach[36] to animal protection has led to a desire for criminal enforcement and punishment comparable to the war on drugs.[37] This carceral approach has led animal activists and the animal protection movement to become entwined with anti-immigration sentiments and has even led to partnerships with anti-immigration groups.[38]

The animal protection movement's dedication to the concept of "political neutrality," has led leaders to forgo considerations of co-abuse of humans and animals in the industrial animal complex; presently animal protection groups lack knowledge and context of the labor abuses, racism, xenophobia, psychological impacts, and physical harms associated with dangerous meatpacking jobs. The movement chooses to villainize workers instead of questioning why and what kinds of policies and workplace environments lead workers treat animals the way they do.[39]

34 Benne, "Annual Report," 5–6.
35 Benne, "Annual Report," 5–6.
36 For a fuller discussion of the carceral turn of Animal Rights and possible solutions please read Hailey Huget's chapter. *See also,* Michael Swistara, "What Comes After Defund? Lessons From Police & Prison Abolition for the Animal Movement," *Animal Law* 28, No. 1 (2022): 89–116, 90–98.
37 Swistara, "Defund," 93–95; Justin Marceau and William Dewey, "Friends of Every Friendless Beast Carceral Animal Law and the Funding of Prosecutors," University of Denver Sturm College of Law, *Legal Research Paper Series*, Working Paper No. 19–15, 237–238; Justin Marceau, *Beyond Cages: Animal Law and Criminal Punishment* (Cambridge University Press, 2019).
38 Marceau, *Beyond Cages*, 158–159.
39 It is well established that supervisors at meatpacking plants have long threatened their immigrant workers with calling immigration authorities if they refuse to comply with work demands or if workers begin labor organizing. Human Rights Watch

Anti-immigration Sentiments and Anti-immigration Actions

The animosity towards immigrant workers in meatpacking facilities can be tied, in large part,[40] to the way animal activist media chooses to portray meatpacking work. For instance, as discussed further in Ellyse Winter's chapter, when animal activist groups release undercover investigative footage of slaughterhouse conditions, the common reaction is "outrage and disgust with the workers abusing the animals."[41] While the response appears reasonable at a superficial level, it lacks the context of the co-abuse occurring at meatpacking facilities.[42] When animal groups produce videos detailing animal abuse in meatpacking, they do not discuss the poor pay, the pressure of line speeds, the overworking of employees, the structural discrimination that these workers face in society, the pressure to provide for children and elders, and the harassment of workers by supervisors as contributing factors to the violence towards animals.[43] Instead, these videos convey a narrative where animals are victims and workers are the villains,[44] and the culpability of the producers themselves is ignored. Furthermore, the snap-shot presentation of abuse investigations invite the viewer to "let flow all internal xenophobic urges."[45] Animal protection groups ask viewers to engage in outrage, directing this anger at the individual laborer's facing incredible pressures rather than targeting the production companies that create the violent meatpacking conditions in the first place.[46]

"Blood, Sweat, and Fear." One worker stated "They have us under threat [bajo amenaza] all the time. They know most of us are undocumented–probably two-thirds. All they care about is getting bodies to the plant. My supervisor said they say they'll call the [Immigration Enforcement] if we make trouble." Human Rights Watch, "Blood, Sweat, and Fear."

40 Other sources of animosity toward immigrant workers can be traced to the narratives of cultural superiority. Marceau, *Beyond Cages*, 84. Within the animal rights community there is a belief that other cultures outside of the United States are inherently less concerned with animal welfare and animal abuse. Marceau, *Beyond Cages*, 84.

41 Ashley Capps, "Slaughterhouses Prey on the Most Vulnerable Humans and Nonhumans Alike," Free from Harm, accessed June 17, 2023, https://freefromh arm.org/animal-products-and-ethics/slaughterhouses-prey-on-vulnerable-humans-and-animals/.

42 Capps, "Slaughterhouses Prey."

43 Capps, "Slaughterhouses Prey."

44 For more on this concept, read Ellyse Winter's chapter on undercover investigations and carceral veganism.

45 Capps, "Slaughterhouses Prey."

46 Capps, "Slaughterhouses Prey."

There are a few other specific examples of how the animal protection movement has harbored anti-immigration sentiments and partnered with anti-immigration groups that goes beyond how groups portray the meat-packing industry in the media.[47] First, some animal groups actively advocate for the deportation of immigrants convicted of animal abuse;[48] animal protection groups call on prosecutors to convict immigrants of animal abuse, assist them in prosecution, and "file briefs in support of efforts by federal immigration officials to secure deportation."[49] Animal activists have begun to view the deportation of immigrant workers as a demonstration of the rising status of animals under United States' law.[50] Additionally, groups have used the immigration status of those accused of committing animal abuse to increase media attention.[51]

While no animal protection organization has outright and publicly supported restrictions on immigration policies to date, some groups have publicly partnered with anti-immigration activists on certain efforts.[52] In Nebraska in particular, the animal activists partnered with outspoken anti-immigration community members to prevent the opening of a Costco chicken plant in 2017.[53] The coalition of anti-Costco protestors called themselves Nebraska Communities United and the local campaign they launched was successful in stopping the opening of the plant, in part based on inflammatory xenophobic comments from the movement's coalition partners.[54] This is one example of how the animal protection movement has been "complicit in amplifying

---

47 It is worth noting that some animal protection groups, like the Animal Legal Defense Fund, have coordinated with other nonprofits to educate people on the safety and health hazards that agricultural immigrant workers face. Marceau, *Beyond Cages*, 84–85. But this does not make the organization a leader in terms of labor considering recent allegations of union-busting and other labor violations. Alexandra Martinez, "Former Animal Legal Defense Fund Staffers Accuse Organization of Transphobia, Union-Busing, and More," Prism Reports, June 26, 2023, https://prismreports.org/2023/06/26/animal-legal-defense-fund-toxic-workplace/.
48 Marceau, *Beyond Cages*, 35, 83–85.
49 Marceau, *Beyond Cages*, 35.
50 Marceau, *Beyond Cages*, 35.
51 Marceau, *Beyond Cages*, 85.
52 Marceau, *Beyond Cages*, 158.
53 Ted Ganoways, "Compromise: A Group of Small-Town Environmentalists Wanted to Stop a Potentially Toxic Costco Chicken Plant. How Did They End Up Fighting Alongside Anti-Muslim Xenophobes?," The New Republic, December 6, 2017, https://newrepublic.com/article/145924/fighting-toxic-waste-worth-collaborating-islamophobes; Marceau, *Beyond Cages*, 158.
54 Ganoways, "Compromise"; Marceau, *Beyond Cages*, 158–159.

a racist message," by aligning themselves with locals keen on emphasizing islamophobia and anti-immigration beliefs.[55]

Immigration Consequences

There are immigration consequences to the animal protection movement's anti-immigration associations and actions. Specifically, the animal protection movement's support for criminal prosecution of immigrants for animal abuse have profound consequences that depend on the individual's immigration status. Conviction of a crime related to animal abuse is particularly significant in the immigration context because the Bureau of Immigration Appeals found that animal cruelty is categorically a "crime involving moral turpitude."[56] Crimes involving moral turpitude or CIMT's can, in certain circumstances, lead to the deportation of immigrants or prevent an immigrant from receiving benefits.[57]

Crimes involving moral turpitude can be both an inadmissibility ground,[58] and a ground of deportation under the Immigration and Nationality Act.[59] Grounds of inadmissibility apply to noncitizens who either (1) want to enter the United States temporarily or permanently, or (2) to persons wanting to apply for certain immigration statuses that have not been admitted to the United States.[60] In the case where a noncitizen is present in the United States

---

55 Ganoways, "Compromise"; Marceau, *Beyond Cages*, 158–159.

56 Matter of Ortega-Lopez, 26 I&N Dec. 99 (BIA 2013).

57 Please note the below explanation of immigration law does not touch on all the exceptions contained within the Immigration and Nationality Act and does not discuss all the ways in which animal protection groups advocating for 'deportation' can affect an immigrant's status. For instance, this section does not discuss immigrants who have already been ordered to leave the country and are under Orders of Supervision (OSUPs). People under an OSUP are individuals who have already had a removal case launched against them and were found either to be inadmissible or deportable and the government has been unable to obtain travel documents to return the immigrant to their home country (for reasons like natural disasters or civil unrest, etc.). People with OSUPs, oftentimes, are not kept actively in custody for the entire time they are awaiting removal, and therefore the government can grant them work authorization while they wait. If an immigrant with OSUP were to be arrested for an animal cruelty offense, it could be the basis for the government to take the individual back into custody until such time they can be removed. Hillel R. Smith, "The Law of Immigration Detention: A Brief Introduction," Congressional Research Service, September 1, 2022, https://crsreports.congress.gov/product/pdf/IF/IF11343.

58 8 U.S.C. § 1182(a)(2)(A)(i)(I).

59 8 U.S.C. § 1227(a)(2)(A)(i).

60 Note, admission in the legal context means that they entered the country using a visa or other sort of documentation that gave them a right to enter the country. Those

without having been admitted, the grounds of inadmissibility can make that noncitizen "removable."[61]

The grounds of deportability apply to noncitizens that have already been admitted to the United States that have some sort of immigration status.[62] The persons affected by this category include U visa recipients, Asylees, T visa recipients, Legal Permanent Residents, Special Immigrant Juveniles, H-2B visa recipients, persons with student visas, and others.[63] The grounds of deportability can lead to a noncitizens removal or the denial of further immigration benefits.[64]

If a noncitizen commits a CIMT, like animal abuse, and is convicted, DHS may place the person in removal proceedings in Immigration Court, which may lead to their ultimate deportation or removal.[65] In a case where the noncitizen is subject to the grounds of inadmissibility, the burden is on the person to convince the judge that they are still admissible to the United States,[66] and if their argument is not persuasive, the judge will order the noncitizen to be removed.[67] If the noncitizen is subject to the grounds of deportability, the DHS attorney has to prove to the court that the noncitizen is deportable. If the DHS attorney presents persuasive evidence, then the immigrant will be ordered removed (deported) from the United States.[68]

Even if a noncitizen is not ordered removed from the United States, the existence of a CIMT will hinder the immigrant's chances of obtaining immigration benefits. For instance, if the immigrant is a Legal Permanent Resident and they want to apply to naturalize and become a U.S. Citizen, they will not be able to do so because an applicant "who is convicted of or admits to

who have entered the country without inspection or without presenting documentation fall under the non-admitted category.

61 Immigrant Legal Resource Center Staff Attorneys, *A Guide for Immigration Advocates*, 21st ed. (Immigrant Legal Resource Center, 2018), 1-8–1-9.

62 8 U.S.C. 1227(a).

63 David Weissbrodt and Laura Danielson, "Chapter 8: Grounds of Inadmissibility and Removal," University of Minnesota Human Rights Library, 2004, http://hrlibrary. umn.edu/immigrationlaw/chapter8.html.

64 Weissbrodt, "Grounds of Inadmissibility"; 8 USC 1227(a).

65 ILRC, "Guide for Immigration Advocates," 1-8–1-9.

66 To convince the judge that the noncitizen is admissible to the United States, they must either argue (1) that the criterion that DHS claims makes them ineligible does not apply to them, or (2) that they qualify for a waiver for that ground of inadmissibility.

67 8 U.S.C. § 1229a(c)(2) (INA 240(c)(2)); ILRC, "Guide for Immigration Advocates," 1–9.

68 8 U.S.C. § 1229a(c)(3) (INA 240(c)(3)); ILRC, "Guide for Immigration Advocates," 1–9.

committing one or more CIMTs during the statutory period cannot establish [good moral character] for naturalization" ultimately preventing them from becoming a citizen.[69]

These immigration consequences of animal activism do not just affect the immigrants themselves. Oftentimes immigrants come to the United States alone and work to obtain immigration status and save up money to pay for their families to eventually join them in the United States.[70] Other immigrants move to the U.S. with the intent of obtaining an immigration benefit that allows them (1) to sponsor other family members to come to the states,[71] or (2) include their family members as derivative applicants on immigration benefit applications.[72] In these instances deportation, removal, or the denial of benefits hurts the entire immigrant's family unit and often punishes persons who have not committed any animal abuse whatsoever.

Possible Pathways Forward

The current issue plaguing the animal protection movement's approach to the meatpacking industry is the singular focus on the health and wellbeing of the animals.[73] The problem of the abuse of humans and animals should not

69 8 U.S.C. § 1101(f)(3) (INA 101(f)(3)); "Policy Manual: Chapter 5 – Conditional Bars for Acts in Statutory Period," U.S. Citizenship and Immigration Services, June 14, 2023, https://www.uscis.gov/policy-manual/volume-12-part-f-chapter-5#:~:text=An%20applicant%20who%20is%20convicted,the%20statutory%20period%20as%20well.

70 Dilip Ratha, "Remittances: Funds for the Folks Back Home," International Monetary Fund, accessed June 13, 2023, https://www.imf.org/en/Publications/fandd/issues/Series/Back-to-Basics/Remittances.

71 "Sponsored Immigrants and Benefits," National Immigration Law Center, February 8, 2021, https://www.nilc.org/issues/economic-support/sponsored-immigrants-and-benefits/; "How do I Financially Sponsor Someone Who Wants to Immigrate?," U.S. Citizenship and Immigration Services, October 2013, https://www.uscis.gov/sites/default/files/document/guides/F3en.pdf.

72 "Filing for Permanent Residence Based on a Family Petition," U.S. Citizenship and Immigration Services, accessed June 13, 2023, https://www.uscis.gov/sites/defaP ult/files/document/foia/Permanent_Residents_Fam.pdf.

73 Some animal activists are doing an incredible job at taking an intersectional approach to their work—approaching the animal protection movement from a wider perspective. Vegan Activist Aph Ko frequently discusses the interconnectedness of racism and speciesism and has published a few texts examining the interaction of white supremacy and animal oppression. Elyse Jacobson, "Aph Ko on Speciesism as an Extension of White Supremacy," Animal Voices, October 18, 2019, http://animalvoices.org/2019/10/aph-ko-on-speciesism-as-an-extension-of-white-supremacy/. Dr. A. Breeze Harper is another vegan expert on equity and justice, she has hosted quite a few trainings discussing systemic racism and anti-Black sentiments that have

pit animals against exploited workers. Instead, the animal protection movement needs to evaluate and consider the intersection and co-abuse of meatpacking workers and animals.[74] By focusing solely on animal well-being and abuse,[75] activists miss the opportunity for high level change that is presented by concepts found in human-based law like labor and employment law.[76] In

become embedded in animal activism. "Biography," accessed July 1, 2023, https://www.abreezeharper.com/bio; Luis C. Rodrigues, "White Normativity, Animal Advocacy and PETA's Campaigns," *Ethnicities*, 20(1) (2020): 71, 87; "Books and Other Publications," accessed July 1, 2023, https://www.abreezeharper.com/booksabreezeharper. Aryenish Birdie is an animal activist dedicated to creating a more diverse and inclusive animal rights movement, she was the driving force because a collection of 16 essays discussing antiracism in animal advocacy. Christopher Sung, "Areynish Birdie Discusses Anti-Racism in Animal Advocacy," Yale Law School, October 29, 2021, https://law.yale.edu/yls-today/news/aryenish-birdie-discusses-anti-racism-animal-advocacy. Julia Feliz is another activist who has written extensively on anti-oppression veganism, they also co-authored the Vegan Bill of Consistent Anti-Oppression aimed at creating a more inclusive and welcoming vegan movement. "The Importance of Consistent Anti-Oppression. Interview with Julia Feliz," The Vegan Rainbow Project, September 23, 2020, https://www.the-vegan-rainbow-project.org/post/interview-with-julia-feliz; Julia Feliz, "The Vegan Bill of Consistent Anti-Oppression," Sanctuary Publishers, accessed July 1, 2023, https://www.consistentantioppression.com/?page_id=218. Attorney Michael Swistara has also written on this topic. *See*, Swistara, "Defund," 100.

74 S. Marek Muller, "Zombification, Social Death, and the Slaughterhouse: U.S. Industrial Practices of Livestock Slaughter," *American Studies*, 57, No. 3 (2018): 83, https://www.jstor.org/stable/45217115.

75 There is no problem in specializing in an area of the law, in fact most practitioners do so. Where the problem lies in the animal protection law movement is that this prioritization of animal rights has led lawyers to ignore other intersecting oppressions. Marceau, *Beyond Cages*, 163–164.

76 Focusing on the co-abuse of animals and humans could lead animal protection organizations to consider using alternative areas of the law. For instance, In the meatpacking industry, animal protection groups may choose to consider lawsuits using the tort concept of negligence per se for violations of the Occupational Safety and Health (OSH) Act of 1970. Rory T. Skowron, "Treating OSHA Violations as Negligence Per Se", *Boston College Law Review* 61 (2020): 3046. Negligence per se "enables courts to hold a defendant negligent as a matter of law when that defendant's violation of a statute or regulation results in injury to another." Skowron, "OSHA Violations," 3043. The OSH Act requires employers to provide their workers "a place of employment free from recognized hazards to safety, and health." 29 U.S.C. § 654(a)(1). Arguably, many meatpacking facilities violate this standard of care by having incredibly fast line speeds that result in high rates of repetitive motion injuries, traumatic injuries, and mental trauma for workers as well as high rates of animal abuse. Note: Courts disagree on if the concept of negligence per se can apply when "a defendant is alleged to have violated regulations implemented by federal agencies, such as the Occupational Safety and Health Administration." Skowron,

addition to increasing the variety of legal arguments that animal protection groups may make, taking an intersectional approach to the law more fully addresses the harms that meatpacking facilities create. When the movement focuses solely on holding individual worker's responsible for animal abuse, the source of the abuse, the culture of violence, that harms both animals and humans goes unaddressed and unresolved, leaving the situation ripe to repeat itself time and time again.[77]

The effect of the animal protection movement's sole focus on animal abuse and resulting desire for individual carceral punishment compounds the abuses that workers suffer in the meatpacking industry. By being set on punishing meatpacking workers for animal abuse, animal protection groups miss the opportunity to attack the predatory practices of the meatpacking industry that contribute to abuse occurring in the first place. If animal protection groups focused their energy on the root causes of animal abuse instead of individual punishment, there is a far greater chance to prevent harm on a much larger scale.[78]

The above proposal, for animal protection groups to consider co-abuse of animals and humans in their actions, is based on the combination of two concepts. First the proposal is based on the public health concept known as "One Health." The American Veterinary Medical Association (AVMA) defines One Health as: "two related ideas: First, it is the concept that humans, animals, and the world we live in are inextricably linked. Second, it refers to the collaborative effort of multiple disciplines working locally, nationally, and globally to attain the optimal health for people, animals, and the environment."[79] The effect of implementing the concept of One Health into animal activism is that it requires advocates for animal protection groups to recognize and account for the impact of their actions on behalf of animals on the human population and the broader natural world. Per the One Health theory then, advocates should not take actions to benefit animals that simultaneously harm humans or the environment.

"OSHA Violations," 3043. Nevertheless, the point being that labor and employment law present additional legal pathways for animal protection groups where the benefit extends to both animals and humans.

77 Muller, "Zombification," 82.
78 In Michael Swistara's article "What Comes After Defund?," he discusses the lessons that the animal protection movement can learn from the anti-carceral social justice movements, this is one example of policies that have the potential to address greater harm and benefit animals in a more significant manner than focusing on individualized carceral punishment. Swistara, "Defund," 104–116.
79 "One Health", AVMA, accessed July 1, 2023, https://www.avma.org/resources-tools/one-health.

The second concept that is the basis for the above proposal is the theory behind Restorative Justice (RJ) practices. Restorative Justice practices tell us that the central obligation that arises out of a crime is to right the wrongs that have occurred. To right a wrong, one must address both the harm and the causes of the harm. It is just like in medicine, if the doctor treats the symptoms of a disease instead of the underlying disease itself, they are simply putting a band aid on the situation. In the context of animal abuse in meatpacking facilities, the symptom is animal abuse, but the main remedy cannot simply promote the arrest and prosecution, and deportation, of exploited meatpacking workers; this approach does not end animal abuse, particularly when the meatpacking industry itself suffers no significant penalty other than the inconvenience of replacing deported workers. Instead, the movement needs to look at the root cause; workers are not abusing animals because they wish to, with the rare exception, they are doing so because of the system that meatpacking companies have built.[80]

In combining these two concepts, the solution to the co-abuse of meatpackers and animals is clear: addressing the predatory meatpacking industry standards of operation will help to prevent future harm befalling humans and animals alike in a way that individual carceral punishment alone cannot.

Imagine. An animal protection organization reaches out to you and a handful of other workers at your meatpacking facility. They tell you that they want to interview you and the other workers to discuss the ways in which you've experienced harm at the hands of the meatpacking corporation. You're a bit skeptical at first, because animal groups don't have the best reputation when it comes to working with immigrants. But you decide to give them a chance because they tell you that they are anonymously surveying workers to get a better understanding of the policies in place and the culture of the meatpacking facility. They ask you about what the managers like, how much you know about your labor rights, if you have ever been threatened, how fast the line speeds are, and have you ever been injured.

They explain how they intend to use the results of their interview. They want to identify the areas that can be improved to prevent harm to both workers and animals.

The animal protection group then drafts a report detailing the co-abuse of animals and workers occurring at meatpacking facilities throughout the Midwest. And they begin planning for impact litigation and legislative lobbying. They invite you and your fellow workers to provide anonymous quotes about your experiences to support their campaign, making sure to not put you at more risk than you already are.

---

80 The "system" generally refers to the high pressures present in the meatpacking industry: the consistent threats to call immigration enforcement, the fast line speeds without regard for worker safety, the inadequate breaks, the overworking of employees, the poor compensation, the harassment of workers on a variety of bases, and more.

Eventually, you watch their campaign flourish, and their lawsuits succeed. And little by little, conditions start to improve, for both you and the animals.

References

Animal and Plant Health Inspection Service, "Approved Immediate Slaughter Facilities," United States Department of Agriculture, May 9, 2023, https://www.aphis.usda. gov/aphis/ourfocus/animalhealth/animal-and-animal-product-import-informat ion/immed-slaughter-list/animal-slaughter-list.

Animal and Plant Health Inspection Service, "Listed Slaughter and Rendering Establishments," United States Department of Agriculture, April 25, 2023, https:// www.aphis.usda.gov/aphis/ourfocus/animalhealth/sa-epidemiology-animalhealth-ceah/btc/main/index.

Benne, Manuela. "Nebraska Meatpacking Industry Worker's Bill of Rights 2021 Annual Report," Nebraska Department of Labor, December 1, 2021, https://nebraskalegi slature.gov/FloorDocs/107/PDF/Agencies/Labor__Department_of/76_20211 201-154145.pdf.

"Biography," accessed July 1, 2023, https://www.abreezeharper.com/bio.

"Blood, Sweat, and Fear: Workers' Rights in U.S. Meat and Poultry Plants," Human Rights Watch, 2004, https://www.hrw.org/report/2005/01/24/blood-sweat-and-fear/workers-rights-us-meat-and-poultry-plants.

"Books and Other Publications," accessed July 1, 2023, https://www.abreezeharper. com/booksabreezeharper.

Broadway, Michael J. *Any Way You Cut It: Meat Processing and Small-Town America* (University Press of Kansas, 1995), 17–38.

Capps, Ashley. "Slaughterhouses Prey on the Most Vulnerable Humans and Nonhumans Alike," Free from Harm, accessed June 17, 2023, https://freefromharm.org/animal-products-and-ethics/slaughterhouses-prey-on-vulnerable-humans-and-animals/.

Drake, Shaw and Hoeppner, Katie. "Four Things to Know about the Supreme Court's Ruling in Egbert v. Boule," ACLU, June 27, 2022, https://www.aclu.org/news/civil-liberties/four-things-the-supreme-court-ruling-egbert-v-boule-ice.

Feliz, Julia. "The Vegan Bill of Consistent Anti-oppression," Sanctuary Publishers, accessed July 1, 2023, https://www.consistentantioppression.com/?page_id=218.

"Few Prosecuted for Illegal Employment of Immigrants," Transactional Records Access Clearinghouse Immigration, May 30, 2019, https://trac.syr.edu/immigration/repo rts/559/.

"Filing for Permanent Residence Based on a Family Petition," U.S. Citizenship and Immigration Services, accessed June 13, 2023, https://www.uscis.gov/sites/defa ult/files/document/foia/Permanent_Residents_Fam.pdf.

"Frequently Asked Questions (FAQs) About Foreign Born," U.S. Census Bureau, accessed June 17, 2023, https://www.census.gov/topics/population/foreign-born/about/faq.html

Ganoways, Ted. "Compromise: A Group of Small-Town Environmentalists Wanted to Stop a Potentially Toxic Costco Chicken Plant. How Did They End up Fighting Alongside Anti-Muslim Xenophobes?," The New Republic, December 6, 2017, https://newrepublic.com/article/145924/fighting-toxic-waste-worth-collaborating-islamophobes.

Habib, Yamily. "Migrant Child Labor: The Dark Reality of Hundreds of Children in the United States," Mitu, April 14, 2023, https://wearemitu.com/wearemitu/news/migrant-child-labor/.

Haroun, Azmi. "Nebraska Gov. Ricketts Says He 'Doesn't Expect' Undocumented Workers in Meatpacking Plants Will Be Part of State's Vaccination Plans," Business Insider, January 6, 2021, https://www.businessinsider.com/nebraska-gov-ricketts-undocumented-people-not-included-vaccine-rollout-2021-1.

"How Do I Financially Sponsor Someone Who Wants to Immigrate?," U.S. Citizenship and Immigration Services, October 2013, https://www.uscis.gov/sites/default/files/document/guides/F3en.pdf.

Immigrant Legal Resource Center Staff Attorneys, *A Guide for Immigration Advocates*, 21st ed. (Immigrant Legal Resource Center, 2018), 1-8–1-9.

"Immigrant Undercount," National Network for Immigrant and Refugee Rights, accessed June 17, 2023, https://nnirr.org/immigrant-undercount/.

Jacobson, Elyse. "Aph Ko on Speciesism as an Extension of White Supremacy," Animal Voices, October 18, 2019, http://animalvoices.org/2019/10/aph-ko-on-speciesism-as-an-extension-of-white-supremacy/.

Leibler, Jessica H. et al. "Prevalence of Serious Psychological Distress among Slaughterhouse Workers at a United States Beef Packing Plant," *Work* 57, No. 1 (2017): 105–109.

Marceau, Justin. *Beyond Cages: Animal Law and Criminal Punishment* (Cambridge University Press, 2019).

Marceau, Justin and Dewey, William. "Friends of Every Friendless Beast Carceral Animal Law and the Funding of Prosecutors," University of Denver Sturm College of Law, *Legal Research Paper Series*, Working Paper No. 19–15, 237–238.

Marek Muller, S. "Zombification, Social Death, and the Slaughterhouse: U.S. Industrial Practices of Livestock Slaughter," *American Studies*, 57, No. 3 (2018): 83, https://www.jstor.org/stable/45217115.

Martinez, Alexandra. "Former Animal Legal Defense Fund Staffers Accuse Organization of Transphobia, Union-Busing, and More," Prism Reports, June 26, 2023, https://prismreports.org/2023/06/26/animal-legal-defense-fund-toxic-workplace/.

Matter of Ortega-Lopez, 26 I&N Dec. 99 (BIA 2013). "Meatpacking and Slaughterhouses," FoodPrint, May 22, 2023, https://foodprint.org/issues/meatpacking-and-slaughterhouses/.

Neb. Rev. Stat. § 48-2213.

"Nebraska: The Beef State," Nebraska Beef Council, accessed June 17, 2023, https://www.nebeef.org/raising-beef/state-national-facts.

"Nebraska Top National Rankings," Nebraska Department of Agriculture, accessed June 17, 2023, https://nda.nebraska.gov/facts.pdf.

Nixon, Ron and Qiu, Linda. "What Is ICE and Why Do Critics Want to Abolish It?," New York Times, July 3, 2018, https://www.nytimes.com/2018/07/03/us/polit ics/fact-check-ice-immigration-abolish.html.

Office of Immigration Statistics, "Reporting Terminology and Definitions," Department of Homeland Security, accessed June 17, 2023, https://www.dhs.gov/immigration-statistics/reporting-terminology-definitions#8.

"One Health", AVMA, accessed July 1, 2023, https://www.avma.org/resources-tools/one-health.

"Policy Manual: Chapter 5 – Conditional Bars for Acts in Statutory Period," U.S. Citizenship and Immigration Services, June 14, 2023, https://www.uscis.gov/policy-manual/volume-12-part-f-chapter-5#:~:text=An%20applicant%20who%20is%20convicted,the%20statutory%20period%20as%20well.

"Quick Facts: Dakota County, Nebraska," U.S. Census Bureau, Accessed June 17, 2023, https://www.census.gov/quickfacts/fact/table/dakotacountynebraska/HCN010217.

"Quick Facts: Lexington City, Nebraska," U.S. Census Bureau, accessed June 17, 2023, https://www.census.gov/quickfacts/lexingtoncitynebraska.

"Quick Facts: Nebraska," U.S. Census Bureau, Accessed June 17, 2023, https://www.census.gov/quickfacts/fact/table/NE,US/POP645221.

"Quick Facts: Schuyler City, Nebraska," U.S. Census Bureau, Accessed June 17, 2023, https://www.census.gov/quickfacts/fact/table/schuylercitynebraska/PST040222.

Ratha, Dilip. "Remittances: Funds for the Folks Back Home," International Monetary Fund, accessed June 13, 2023, https://www.imf.org/en/Publications/fandd/iss ues/Series/Back-to-Basics/Remittances.

Rodrigues, Luis C. "White Normativity, Animal Advocacy and PETA's Campaigns," *Ethnicities*, 20(1) (2020): 71, 87.

Shah, Silky. "Why America Still Needs to Abolish ICE," NBC News, October 14, 2020, https://www.nbcnews.com/think/opinion/why-america-still-needs-abolish-ice-ncna1243293.

Skowron, Rory T. "Treating OSHA Violations as Negligence Per Se," *Boston College Law Review*, 61 (2020): 3046.

Smith, Hillel R. "The Law of Immigration Detention: A Brief Introduction," Congressional Research Service, September 1, 2022, https://crsreports.congress.gov/product/pdf/IF/IF11343.

"Sponsored Immigrants and Benefits," National Immigration Law Center, February 8, 2021, https://www.nilc.org/issues/economic-support/sponsored-immigrants-and-benefits/

Starkman, Naomi. "On the Rural Immigrant Experience: 'We Come with a Culture, Our Own History, and We're Here to Help'," Civil Eats, April 14, 2022, https://civile ats.com/2022/04/14/on-the-rural-immigrant-experience-we-come-with-a-cult ure-our-own-history-and-were-here-to-help/.

Sung, Christopher. "Areynish Birdie Discusses Anti-Racism in Animal Advocacy," Yale Law School, October 29, 2021, https://law.yale.edu/yls-today/news/aryenish-bir die-discusses-anti-racism-animal-advocacy.

Swistara, Michael. "What Comes After Defund? Lessons From Police & Prison Abolition for the Animal Movement," Animal Law, 28, No. 1 (2022): 89–116, 90–98.

Talk of the Nation "Inside the Hidden World of Immigrant Smuggling," National Public Radio, April 12, 2012, https://www.npr.org/2012/04/19/150973748/inside-the-hidden-world-of-immigrant-smuggling.

"The Importance of Consistent Anti-oppression. Interview with Julia Feliz," The Vegan Rainbow Project, September 23, 2020, https://www.the-vegan-rainbow-project. org/post/interview-with-julia-feliz

"The Speed Kills You: The Voice of Nebraska's Meatpacking Workers," Nebraska Appleseed 2009, 19, https://neappleseed.org/wp-content/uploads/downloads/ 2013/01/the_speed_kills_you_100410.pdf.

Twohey, Megan, et al. "Wanted: Foreign Workers—and the Labor Brokers Accused of Illegally Profiting from Them," February 19, 2016, https://www.reuters.com/inves tigates/special-report/workers-brokers/.

Weissbrodt, David and Danielson, Laura. "Chapter 8: Grounds of Inadmissibility and Removal," University of Minnesota Human Rights Library, 2004, http://hrlibrary. umn.edu/immigrationlaw/chapter8.html.

Williams Shavers, Anna. "Welcome to the Jungle: New Immigrants in the Meatpacking and Poultry Processing Industry," Journal of Law Economics & Policy, 5 (2009): 32.

"Worksite Immigration Raids," National Immigration Law Center, January 2020, https://www.nilc.org/issues/workersrights/worksite-raids/.

"Xenophobia," Merriam-Webster Dictionary, accessed June 17, 2023, https://www.merr iam-webster.com/dictionary/xenophobia.

8 U.S.C. § 1101(f)(3).

8 U.S.C. § 1182(a)(2)(A)(i)(I).

8 U.S.C. § 1227(a).

8 U.S.C. § 1229a(c).

29 U.S.C. § 654(a)(1).

Laboring for Nonhumans: An Autoethnography of an Animal Rights Non-Government Organization

Drew Robert Winter

Introduction

My department director wore a concerned look at our first meeting. I had been coughing, non-stop, for about 40 seconds. I couldn't stop coughing long enough for him to finish a sentence uninterrupted. It was my second week in the organization, and I'd developed an upper respiratory infection. But when I asked my supervisor if I could leave, he told me (sympathetically) that I'd not yet accrued enough sick hours to leave. So I sat on a park bench outside our headquarters with my department head, and wheezed him into silence. After about five minutes of false starts, he mercifully resolved to get me out of the office—the rules be damned.

"What a rule!" I thought to myself—I am putting other employees at risk, and preventing them from focusing, because sick time is something I need to earn?

This was my first lesson in the nonprofit world's corporate culture—even at organizations radical enough to criticize society's use of other species for food, entertainment, and research. Even here, I was an employee subject to maxims of productivity and bureaucratic governance. The experience taught me a lot about the structure and operation of nonprofit logic, which attempts to turn every action into measurable productivity, and treats its donors—rather than those it's meant to help—as the bottom line.

In the early 2010s I became employed with a large animal rights non-profit headquartered on the East coast. After 13 months, I left feeling burned out; although organizing and activism for animals had consumed my life until I became professionalized, I did not do any animal-related activities for approximately one year following my departure from this organization. Subsequently, I pursued my PhD in cultural anthropology, and studied (among other things) animal rights and environmental nonprofits. While writing my doctoral dissertation in 2018, a colleague suggested I apply an anthropological lens to my experience as a professional activist in the form of an "autoethnography." Anthropologists primarily conduct research in the method known as "ethnography"—a long-term holistic study and explanation of a particular group, with focus on belief systems and patterns of behavior. An "autoethnography" is a form of ethnography in which the anthropologist is also an "insider" from the population studied.

In this chapter, I provide an account of my time at this nonprofit. I've chosen to act on this suggestion for the benefit of the animal rights movement as a whole; I hope that my retelling will encourage reform among activists and organizers, and add to the growing anthropological data on NGOs. Based on this recounting, combined with growing literature about the trends in today's nonprofit world, I argue that many animal rights nonprofits—like the one I worked for—are part of what is called the Nonprofit Industrial Complex: mimicking strategies used by for-profit and government institutions, nonprofits depress wages, avoid solidarity with groups and movements not directly related to their own cause, and quantify every aspect of work for measurement that harms its workforce. I argue that this method of pursuing social change has questionable benefits to animals, but accomplishes much in the way of raising the social status of donors, and even preventing more effective means of achieving animal liberation. I then explain how this emphasis on donor satisfaction, small reforms, and productivity-based corporate logic is part of a global trend known as "neoliberalism"—a socioeconomic philosophy that emerged in the 1980s that treated profit and markets as self-evidently good, and welfare and government regulation self-evidently bad. Neoliberalism became so commonplace that its values and logic seeped into the nonprofit and government world, and even organizations devoted to something as radical as animal liberation were contaminated by it.

I conclude by advising employees of animal rights nonprofits to actively organize their workplaces: to fight for better pay, shorter hours, and recognition of human injustices both outside and inside their organizations—with a long-term aim to create more democratic organizations.

Working at FAR: Money, Organization, Culture

FAR is an animal *rights* (not welfare) organization based on the East coast of the United States, but with satellite offices in multiple countries across the globe. I do not know its exact budget, but it is over $1 million annually, and derived its funding primarily through donations. "Development" as it is called in nonprofit parlance, was extremely important to the organization. Larger donors were given annual tours of our offices, and development officers spent the majority of their time building and maintaining relationships with wealthy donors—going to lunch with them, asking them about their family, etc. Sometimes, large donors would allocate funds to specific projects they found useful. On at least one occasion, this forced my team to effectively drop what we were doing to shift gears for two months, since this project represented new money that would not otherwise be spent.

I became affiliated with FAR as a result of my animal activism in college. After going vegan in 2006 I quickly threw my energy into animal advocacy work on campus. With an undergraduate population of over 40,000 and a prominent agricultural college, there were plenty of opportunities to agitate and create controversy. Co-founding Students Promoting Animal Rights (SPAR) at Michigan State University with a number of others, we campaigned to stop animal circuses on campus, revealed deaths of animals in university research labs, argued for more vegan options in school cafeterias, and brought multiple high-profile speakers to campus.

We eventually got into contact with Luke, a FAR employee with the group's college outreach division. He provided me with some of my most valuable mentorship in activism tactics and strategy. My efforts earned me a "Top 30 activists under 30" award from VegNews magazine. I was tireless, full of purpose, and irritated people with my "born-again" zeal.

Upon graduation, with no real job prospects, I volunteered with a pro-vegan organization that handed out leaflets on college campuses. With an employee and one of my SPAR co-founders, we handed out tens of thousands of brochures about industrial agriculture and switching to a plant-based diet. We drove my car since the vehicle owned by my colleague (a paid employee) was unsafe and he couldn't afford repairs. We stretched out our per diems by sleeping on the floors of generous volunteers and eating garbanzo beans out of a can (Taco Bell was our indulgence meal).

While on the road, I found out that I'd been hired at FAR to work directly under Luke. It absolutely felt like I was ascending to do what I was meant to do—I couldn't think of a better job than "fighting for the animals" full time. The pay would be meager at $27,000 per year, but it offered health insurance. After all, wasn't this far better than what the animals were experiencing? I heard rumors from a few different activists that FAR was a poor place to work—specifically, employees developing depression on the job and suffering under poor management, resulting in high turnover rates. But it was an opportunity to get out of my parents' house and live my dream, and I took it.

I found an apartment with another FAR employee, and quickly realized that there was an intense drive to create community at FAR. Based in a relatively conservative city, FAR employees—especially the young contract employees—stood out, but we were large enough to provoke ample plant-based options in the local restaurants. I was immediately scooped up by Luke and others to hang out after work at these establishments. The social groups I experienced were pretty insular—everyone was a FAR employee or former FAR employee. And everyone seemed to mostly want to talk about food—where the best vegan country-fried steak was (Chicago Diner), where to get vegan food if you're following Warped Tour and in Selma, Texas, etc.

The effort to create community stood in stark contrast to rumors and secrecy around management decisions; my first week on the job, our department received an email titled "Some News" with a body text saying simply "Friday was [name]'s last day at FAR." As an hourly employee, I had to leave the office at 5 pm sharp to avoid overtime, but salaried employees my age would frequently stay for 2–3 hours more to avoid falling behind with their ever-accumulating workload. I was told early on at FAR that "you need to learn to say 'no' because people will pile on as much work with you as you can handle." Although this might sound reasonable, this adage doesn't account for the social pressure we were all under. With employees habitually working past normal hours and the organizational emphasis on "dedication," turning down assignments felt to me like letting down my colleagues, and privileging myself over "the animals." What's more, the focus of my attention had to constantly shift based on new projects—the President would decide that an event or emergency required our focus to shift, and so every department had to rapidly re-prioritize our projects and daily responsibilities; I often felt that I spent as much time re-organizing my tasks as I did actually completing them, and the work kept piling up. The completion of one task often yielded no discernible effects, and the constant reshuffling of priorities made focus extremely difficult. My attention was so dictated by the rapidly-shifting agenda of the organization and the micromanagement from my supervisor that I felt no ownership over my own work: I didn't feel passionate about what I was doing because I felt I had almost no control over what I did or how I did it, but I still constantly felt like I was not doing enough.

In addition to the duties in our job description, employees were encouraged to volunteer with the organization after work and on weekends: at 5 pm many of us would go upstairs and—alongside non-employee volunteers—"stuff" envelopes that would be sent out to members, usually to request donations. On weekends we could volunteer with the Rescue department, to take a truck out to the poor rural neighborhoods adjacent to the city, where we would drive slowly down streets looking for dogs on chains without adequate shelter or needing some other kind of assistance. When we found one (several on each block), we offered free dog houses (sturdy and warm, built by FAR employees) and gave elementary pet care advice. Most owners received us politely, seemed familiar with our services, and were grateful for our contributions. Workers did not pass judgment on clients, nor did they have a punitive attitude, and provided unconditional material assistance. In one instance, we found a pit bull puppy attached via leash to an extremely heavy chain, with a plastic garbage container on its side as their only shelter. We gave the owner recommendations on leash weight that wouldn't injure the small animal and scheduled to have a doghouse delivered.

These extracurricular duties functioned to incorporate employees into the group's social network beyond their direct coworkers. I welcomed these actions at first, to be the most dedicated activist possible. But, as I will argue in the conclusion, these actions take place within a context that can reinforce material and moral disparities across race and class lines. The Rescue department provided emergency response to individual animals in need, as opposed to larger social and political campaigns. It consisted of employees who handled animal emergencies, crimes, and adoption. Although FAR did not operate a shelter, it would accept surrenders in dire circumstances. Rescue would often both find out about animal cruelty cases from concerned citizens, and repeatedly prod the (typically reluctant) police forces to action. In some cases, they would enlist the help of local FAR members to corroborate the conditions of animals. As I will argue in the next section, these more direct methods of intervention demonstrate the limitations (and dangers) of today's nonprofit model.

Demographically, the organization was overwhelmingly white, but relatively balanced in gender. There were no out transgender employees, and most people of color were white-passing. One black woman on my team was hired to act as an ambassador for a project that compared animal exploitation to slavery, apartheid, and the Holocaust. Leadership at the time (vice presidents and the president) was entirely white, majority female. Although most entry-level positions were filled by "believers" some positions—especially Legal—hired based on talent and not conviction. In effect, the "bottom layer" of the organization (entry level advocacy and operations positions) were 20-something activists recruited from the Youth Department's volunteer lists. Tour activists usually lived on the road, spent days standing, walking, and talking in the sun, and had to put together and take down their mobile tents.

Although they were representatives of the organization, instructed, directed, and limited in their behavior by FAR, FAR classified them as independent contractors. This meant they were not given benefits or PTO, and reduced the tax burden on FAR—although doing so may violate the IRS tax code. Leadership positions were held by veteran activists who had been with the organization for decades.

Political views at the organization seemed to span from radical left to conservative, with most employees probably self-identifying as "liberal." Many of the older employees were staunch liberals: supporters of gay marriage and racial equality, opponents of hunting, and skeptical of US military intervention—but averse to the political radicalism to which vegans were often associated. This is important, because although "compassion" was a central concept for FAR employees, worker solidarity was not. "Compassion" extended towards oppressed identities, but I saw little, if any, indication that this extended to the labor sphere.

One belief that was never vocally expressed within the organization was unionizing. One member of Human Resources at FAR told me over dinner that unions have no place because "that is what HR is for." While checking out at the local food co-op, the cashier (a former FAR employee) suggested that FAR needed unionization. I suggested that union organizing might not be needed at a nonprofit where the focus should be on animals. "I think it's *more* needed there," my cashier said. The work culture was indeed problematic—several managers were known for verbally abusing their employees, and I suffered this on at least one occasion myself. Firings and quitting were extremely common.

For the first few months, I felt positive about my job, which revolved around sending and answering emails, as well as sending letters to the editor of student newspapers to spark or continue discussions of animal rights. I took on many of Luke's responsibilities mentoring college student activists, so that he could begin to grow our division. My most committed student correspondents were a joy to work with—I could immediately identify with their verve and purpose, and they looked up to me the way I had looked up to Luke.

But discord would occur when groups would rebuff our invitations to collaborate. On at least one occasion, I was told to back off by a faculty advisor after sending additional emails at Luke's insistence. FAR's college outreach was designed with a top-down, standardized approach meant to create policy changes that would survive the dissipation of a particular student group; this was not a bad strategy per se, but it meant that my job was to help homogenize animal rights on college campuses, often with student groups critical of or uninterested in FAR's approach. In addition to my duties sending students stickers and answering their emails on how to organize, I fielded all questions from students directed at the organization. Oftentimes, this would include letters from students asking for an interview for a report or writing a letter in protest of FAR's activities and methods. I could respond personally or with a form letter—usually my level of sympathy for the criticism dictated how much I retouched the form letter—when I thought they were right, I'd send the form letter without any personalization, whereas I'd happily write a short manifesto if I believed in what we were doing. Later on, I started ghostwriting op-eds for the group's vice presidents to appear in student newspapers, and traveling to campuses to "create buzz" in anticipation of an event.

Within six months I felt so overwhelmed and burned out that I would spend hours staring at my laptop at the office, unable to bring myself to complete even simple tasks. I received a mixed performance review, and planned to find another job. I met with Luke to inform him of my decision, and offered to stay on as long as was necessary to help facilitate the transition to a new employee to fill my post.

Shortly thereafter, HR informed me that I would not be getting two organization-wide days off that had been promised me, because I had formally given notice. I inquired into the employee handbook and found no mention of days being removed for giving notice, and was told that these were not officially-sanctioned "holidays" but an "act of kindness" by the president given at their discretion, therefore not subject to any rules in the handbook. Contesting this, HR set up a meeting with me and my department head, who told me it was not his decision to make and he therefore could not negotiate, but refused to tell me whose decision it was. In keeping with the rules of employee grievance, I then emailed the president directly. I later received an email from HR in which they offered to give me back one of these two vacation days if I would drop the matter.

This incident itself is not important for its banal content, so much as its protocol: unclear rules, antagonistic and secretive relationships between management and employees, and a resolution process lacking transparency. For my giving advanced notice in a show of good will to an organization I believed in, I was subjected to punitive action without written precedent, and my attempts to negotiate it met with obfuscation and opposition. I believed that this organization, with its desire to foster community and common cause of justice—specifically a form of justice we all agreed was hypocritically left out of the mainstream—would mean that my co-workers and supervisors would prioritize my well-being and value my transparency. This was not the case, but to explain what I witnessed as an individual error—as malice, poor managers, or unclear rules—would avoid the larger socioeconomic climate in which nonprofits operate, and which create the values that drive managers to act as they do. Policies that attempt to maximize employee labor and punish disloyalty are products of larger economic forces that drive individual supervisors to act in ways that they may find uncomfortable or even objectionable. That coercion is why feelings towards individuals—whether sympathy or vengeance—cannot resolve labor disputes. So, what are the logics and values that animate these kinds of decisions, and where do they come from?

Analysis: Neoliberalism and Its Impact on NGOs

What I experienced and witnessed at FAR is not unique. In fact, scholars have extensively documented how the economic and social changes happening around the world since the early 1980s have had a consistent and measurable effect on the nonprofit world. Those changes are called "the neoliberal turn." The neoliberal turn represents the stage of the capitalist economic system currently dominating the world. No single event triggered the transition to neoliberalism, but scholars often begin their analyses with the elections of Ronald Reagan in the US and Margaret Thatcher in the UK. Neoliberalism is a form of capitalism that rejects the "Keynesian" approach of the mid-20th century. Keynesian economics—named after economist John Maynard Keynes—views the state as a tool to close the gaps in public welfare left by private enterprise. Keynesian economics is not opposed to markets, working for a wage, or the accumulation of profits that characterizes capitalism. But Keynes—like his predecessor Adam Smith—emphasized that the profit motive does not always lead to optimal outcomes. Keynes thus argued for regulation of private companies, government intervention into markets, and funding programs for the common good. Keynes' vision motivated the New Deal in the United States: a massive public investment meant to create jobs and bolster the middle class. Neoliberalism, by contrast, is supposedly a form of market fundamentalism in which government is considered wasteful by definition, and its influence must therefore be minimized to the project of supporting markets (chiefly through cutting social services and "opening markets" with military interventions). I say "supposedly" because, despite rhetoric of cutting government spending and reducing waste, neoliberal policymakers actually tend to increase both—but in ways that siphon funds to the richest citizens and away from public services (Harvey, 2006).

Due to this "belt tightening" from austerity measures and a general opposition to the state caring for its citizens, the burden of meeting the needs of the sick, poor, and otherwise marginalized increasingly falls to what academics call nongovernmental organizations (NGOs), funded by mixtures of private donors and state grant funds, to administer these services. The neoliberal logic is that, untethered from "government"—an institution considered needlessly bureaucratic—these organizations can more efficiently administer care. The sociocultural aspect of this cannot be understated: this is not simply a claim about policy, but a value judgment about a host of social ills. Crime and poverty, most notably, are explained by individual failings, bureaucratic overreach, lack of markets, and "cultures" of poverty. So rather than investing directly in providing social services through government welfare agencies, government funding is increasingly spent on law enforcement and "market" solutions. In sum, NGOs—as products of neoliberal capitalism—serve the same interests as for-profit companies attempting to concentrate wealth in fewer hands. Neoliberalism is a culture-wide belief that the accumulation of wealth either can help (as indicated by the increasing privatization of the healthcare sector) or is unrelated to increasing poverty and abuse; the role of NGOs is for the "lucky" ones to generously demonstrate their beneficence by creating charitable organizations that "give back." Therefore, maximizing income, rather than care, is the first order of business.

This hollowing out and commodification of our sense of social justice and community care has a name: The Nonprofit Industrial Complex (NPIC). The NPIC is a process and a culture that turns community action into a profession, restructures care organizations and worker relationships to resemble for-profit companies, and restrains them to funding available from wealthy individuals and corporations seeking to polish their image (Incite! Women of Color Against Violence, 2007). At the same time that neoliberalism changes the way care is administered, it disempowers those employed to do the work: with unionization rates far lower in the nonprofit sector than government (37 percent to 15 percent in the US Gallop, 2019)– neoliberalism's systematic shifting of care and justice work from the state to private nonprofits helps to drive down wages and bargaining power for employees.

FAR's direct outreach work, delivering doghouses and drawing on networks to pressure police to act, represents the neoliberal alternative to resolving social issues: animal neglect and cruelty are defined as problems *by those who lead nonprofits*. Naturally, this means that problems are defined disproportionately by middle- and upper-class members of the population, who—predictably—locate those problems disproportionately in lower-class neighborhoods. Aid is thus provided by outsiders who do not share the community's values and are not accountable to the community's concerns. Neoliberal charity is a form of "voting with one's dollar" by turning social policy into private charity, which reinforces the very hierarchies it claims to oppose in the act of giving; residents are given supplies and information, but these provisions do not help residents become self-sufficient or empower them to communicate their own values and needs. Rather, it perpetuates cycles of dependency for which the recipient is made to deserve pity. Those found to reject the values of NGOs entering their communities may be targeted by police notified by the NGO, and subjected to incarceration and fines that only deepen poverty and emotional trauma. This system is considered a replacement to publicly-funded and more evenly-distributed social services. Furthermore, it runs on neoliberal *logic* that rejects the possibility that neglect or abuse is based on unequal distribution of social resources. While the individuals working for a nonprofit can usually exercise some level of personal judgment, their ability to take punitive action is far greater than their ability to build alliances and long-term solutions that transcend the single issue of animal suffering. So while all of my personal experiences in the dog outreach campaign were polite interactions by nonjudgmental staff with appreciative residents, the impact is fundamentally short-term and interpersonal. Furthermore, an aid system of outsiders surveilling an area for violations of *their own* values—potentially with a threat of law enforcement—is an unequal power dynamic. These invasive practices, no matter how well-intentioned, can place the NGO in tension with the members of communities it means to help. As we will see in the next section, common NGO practices also place their leaders in tension with their own employees.

Neoliberal Logic in the Nonprofit Workplace

Neoliberal thought treats profits as a self-evident good, and nonprofit endeavors to be ancillary ethical matters governed by fundamentally different social mores. To help others is an act of character, and anything is better than nothing. As such, this duty work is understood to be its own reward, in terms of both personal satisfaction and external praise. But donors tend to see their donations in profit-based terms, and want a maximal return on investment ("ROI"). This means prioritizing program outcomes over employee wellbeing (employees at nonprofits are not here to "make money" after all, otherwise they'd be in a different sector). This nonprofit ROI mindset is formalized in the "effective altruism" (EA) movement, which continues to exert influence over animal rights nonprofits. EA-focused groups advocate for people to either work long hours for low pay within NGOs, or seek jobs that offer large compensation that they can then donate.

To facilitate working long hours for low pay, FAR promoted a "duty" mentality encouraging zealotry. This is an "intrinsic motivator" as opposed to an extrinsic motivator like compensation, and it works as a psychological buffer against low wages and long working hours. It also undermines class consciousness that would promote employee solidarity and unionization: if "we are all in it for the animals" then employees are less likely to see the adversarial relationship between themselves and managers, whose job is to maximize the efficiency of organizational dollars at the expense of employee satisfaction. This will only temporarily mitigate the effects of poor working conditions that will still likely result in burnout, but can help to extend employee tenure and redirect blame for it away from the employer.

Increasingly, the nonprofit world is acknowledging the high rates of "burnout" among employees. Articles and books proliferate on how to create more sustainable and healthy nonprofit workplaces. Such materials recommend employees and leaders at NGOs take personal account of burnout symptoms, and provide strategies for individual and organizational health. These include napping at work, avoiding work on weekends, using vacation time, exercising, setting aside time for hobbies and creative thinking, separating one's life from one's job, and encouraging healthy eating habits.

The first thing many will notice from this list (from a 2017 book on the topic) is that none of these strategies are particularly revelatory. The importance of sleep, diet, exercise, and work/life balance are well known and extensively researched. They were known to me when I worked at FAR. And part of the reason that they are not surprising to most readers is because these recommendations did not originate as solutions to nonprofit burnout, but as tips for increased worker productivity. So while the profit motive is gone from the organization, employees are still understood to be mechanisms for increasing donor ROI, and are therefore still subject to the same rigors as their counterparts in the for-profit sector. Authors of these "healthy nonprofit" publications may not even drop the "productivity" rhetoric from their articles. They do not caution against working 70-hour weeks because it leads to burnout and unhappy employees, but rather because studies found that the extra time in the office didn't actually produce more value for the company, and high turnover rates are costly. Furthermore, these recommendations serve a disciplinary function on the employee: failing to excel in a grueling work environment may be grounds for the employee to take more personal responsibility for their well-being so that they can muster the energy to increase their performance and avoid being fired. So, while regular exercise, a good night's sleep, and proper nutrition are indeed valuable aspects of anyone's life, they can be used as weapons to circumvent an organization's failures, by placing the onus on employees to modify their own lives to become more resilient. Crucially, these practices do not empower employees, but simply increase their capacity to yield ROI.

What often *does* separate nonprofits from government and private sectors is pay. A substantial culprit of stress in nonprofit work is not just the stakes of the job and the insurmountable workload, but the low pay and precarious employment it affords. The authors of the above book do acknowledge this, but fold that issue into "stress" from employees—stress itself becoming the object to combat, rather than the low wages and precarious career itself. Such thinking is no different than the apparent explosion in company pizza parties and wellness seminars across all sectors. But these nonprofit reformers cannot address the issue of wage shortages and overwork head on, because doing so violates the neoliberal principles of what NGOs are meant to do and the way they're allowed to be structured.

Conclusion: Unionizing the Nonprofit Workforce

All wage-providing organizations are subject to what Marx called the "contradiction" of capitalism: the fundamental tension between those who labor to survive, and those with capital who hire labor in their quest for yet more capital. We are meant to think that the employer and employee are working cooperatively, despite the employer benefitting from minimizing what they pay the employee. This was reflected at FAR by relatively low wages across the board, but especially by its extensive use of "contract" employees to carry out its most physically grueling labor. Furthermore, contract workers are hired for specific projects, meaning that there is no agreement for long-term job security. While marketed by employers as "autonomy" this usually means autonomy for the employer, who has power in the hiring process and can therefore easily hire new contract employees if their current staff are overworked and burn out. Crucially, this inherent antagonism between worker and employer does not change under a nonprofit model, because "development" functions as the profit motive. No amount of funding by wealthy donors will resolve this struggle, as it is always preferable from an NGO standpoint to increase output by hiring more underpaid workers to accomplish more tasks, over granting existing employees better pay and benefits. Donors themselves who exert the most power are those with the most to give, meaning they are the most successful under our current economic system; this means they are the likely to see labor as a cost to be minimized—since that is the logic that likely earned them the funds to donate in the first place. You do not attract donors to your organization by advertising that you pay employees a competitive wage and offer generous benefits; you do it by claiming that a maximum amount of every donation goes "directly to the animals" with minimum "administrative" costs—meaning the wages of employees. Nonprofits increasingly advertise this fact about their organization to donors as a feature, to argue that donations are not going to "bureaucratic waste" or "overhead" like employee wages.

Many FAR employees I spoke with complained of unrealistic workloads that seemed to constantly change in their scope, and poor supervision (a combination of unprofessional behavior and overzealous monitoring). This also applied to me, combined with a lack of autonomy: with SPAR, I had worked on every aspect of our campaigns, and at FAR I had virtually no input on what was done or how. These complaints are precisely what Pynes (1996) found to be the most common concerns with employees at nonprofit organizations. These concerns make nonprofits more susceptible to unionization. Supervisors in nonprofit work are just as opposed to unions, if not more so, than supervisors in other sectors. One was even quoted in a study as saying "I am not warm to the idea of workers protecting themselves. If you want to work in nonprofits, it's going to be lumpy" (Peters & Masaoka, 2000, 311). That same study also cited perception of racist management as a salient employee complaint that unions were sought to mitigate.

Longtime animal rights advocate and founder of the Food Empowerment Project, lauren Ornelas, described her experience working in two animal rights organizations in a blog post on unionization:

> And what had been my passion in life, the reason I went to college, ended up being my weakness as I allowed myself to be verbally abused, degraded, and have every ounce of my self-esteem sucked out of me. With my first job in the animal rights movement, I began to have health problems that were directly correlated to my work and the treatment I was facing from the head of the organization. My doctor encouraged me to quit my job as it was obvious when the spikes in my heart monitor were coming up. To me, the doctor did not understand that I was doing this "for the animals."
>
> I quit the other vegan animal rights organization I worked for after four months; I saw the same micromanaging and self-esteem whittling tactics being used (Ornelas, 2021a).

Citing racial wage disparities, sexual harassment, bullying, and making employees feel guilty for requesting higher wages, Ornelas succinctly describes widespread problems in professional settings that are not less true within animal rights organizations. For a movement frequently criticized for being disproportionately white, unionization could create the grounds for effective anti-racist policies that would make people of color better represented in professional animal rights spaces. Furthermore, Ornelas makes the vital point that, as a nonprofit director herself, she is necessarily a boss, and implores other organization leaders to accept the inherent tension of this position and support unionization efforts (Ornelas, 2021b).

There is, fortunately, growing resistance to the neoliberal model in the animal rights movement. In January 2021, a majority of the Animal Legal Defense Fund (ALDF) voted to unionize. They took this decision to ALDF Executive Director Stephen Wells and asked him to recognize their union. Wells both declined and forced a formal vote with the National Labor Relations Board (NLRB), but also hired a law firm notorious for aiding in union-busting, and held small meetings with employees to dissuade them from voting for unionization. Throughout this process, ALDF management emphasized that they were "progressive" and "not anti-union." A major flashpoint for the union formation was the refusal of ALDF leadership to formally endorse the Black Lives Matter movement. That March, a super majority of eligible staff voted in the NLRB elections and joined the Nonprofit Professional Employees Union (NPEU). This instance highlights the resistance of management—even within "progressive" nonprofits—to the democratization of the workplace. Furthermore, it highlights the value in unionization to bring animal rights nonprofits out of the "single issue" tradition and towards a holistic theory and practice integrated with issues of gender & sexuality (McJetters, 2016), racial justice (Kim, 2015), indigenous thought (Robinson, 2014; Dunn, 2019), and disability (Taylor, 2017; Jenkins, Montford, & Taylor, 2020). Building on these insights, groups like Rights for Animal Rights Activists (RARA) emerged to advocate for activists and improve their workplaces.

Since leaving FAR I've often felt at odds with both its critics and its proponents. I met some of the strongest and most dedicated activists at FAR—both those working with activists, and especially those who do the least appreciated work directly with animals and animal cruelty cases: working directly with abused animals likely saved many from further harm, while taking a serious psychological toll on the workers. Furthermore, any professional organization will struggle with a certain level of bureaucracy and conflict. Hierarchies emerge, and decisions must be made that will leave someone less than fully satisfied. And I also still believe in the bulk of the work done at FAR. But the good work done by individuals, or small groups, is constrained within the larger, NPIC-based organization. Even the actions that prove successful cannot be optimally built on because the strategic focus of the organization is so beholden to its donors. Another way forward is possible, against the corporate structure and "charity" model—that relies on human collective action to change social norms and forcefully redistribute the capital needed to create a more just world.

Bibliography

Dunn, Kirsty. 2019. "Kaimangatanga: Maori Perspectives on Veganism and Plant-Based Kai." *Animal Studies Journal* 8 (1): 42–65.

Harvey, David. 2006. "Neo-Liberalism as Creative Destruction." *Geografiska Annaler. Series B, Human Geography* 88 (2): 145–158.

Hayek, F. A. 2005. *The Road to Serfdom: With the Intellectuals and Socialism : The Condensed Version of The Road to Serfdom... as It Appeared in the April 1945 Edition of Reader's Digest.* London: Institute of Economic Affairs.

Incite! Women of Color Against Violence, ed. 2007. *The Revolution Will Not Be Funded: Beyond the Non-Profit Industrial Complex.* Cambridge, MA: South End Press.

Kim, Claire Jean, 2015. *Dangerous Crossings: Race, Species, and Nature in a Multicultural Age.* New York, NY: Cambridge University Press.

Jenkins, Stephanie, Kelly Struthers Montford, and Chloë Taylor, eds. 2020. *Disability and Animality: Crip Perspectives in Critical Animal Studies.* 1st edn. Milton Park, Abingdon, Oxon; New York, NY: Routledge.

McJetters, Christopher-Sebastian. 2016. "Queering Animal Liberation: Why Animal Rights Is a Queer Issue." In London. https://www.youtube.com/watch?v=SkRk e88QKPs.

Ornelas, lauren. 2021a. "Why Vegan Animal Rights Organizations* Should Unionize (Part I of II)." February 5, 2021.

Ornelas, lauren. 2021b. "Why Vegan Animal Rights Organizations* Should Unionize (Part II of II)." February 23, 2021.

Peters, Jeanne B., and Jan Masaoka. 2000. "A House Divided: How Nonprofits Experience Union Drives." *Nonprofit Management and Leadership* 10 (3): 305–317.

Pynes, Joan E. 1996. "The Anticipated Growth of Nonprofit Unionism." *Nonprofit Management and Leadership* 7 (4): 355–371.

Robinson, Margaret. 2014. "Animal Personhood in Mi'kmaq Perspective." *Societies* 4 (4): 672–688.

Taylor, Sunaura. 2017. *Beasts of Burden: Animal and Disability Liberation.* New York: The New Press.

Wark, Julie, and Daniel Raventós. 2018. *Against Charity.* Chico, CA: AK Press.

"What Percentage of U.S. Workers Are Union Members?" 2019. Gallup.Com. August 28, 2019.

Horses of a Different Color: Reckoning with Race in the March for Animal Rights

RAJESH REDDY

Entering the Ranks

When people ask why I chose a career in animal law, what I don't tell them is they got it backwards: animal law chose me. I came to it halfway through an English PhD. Driving my transition to law school and into the ranks of the Animal Rights, or AR world, was a determination to move beyond the academy, to be more vocal, more visible, more on-the-ground in my advocacy. And within weeks of coming to Lewis & Clark Law School, I seized my chance. It was Farm Sanctuary's annual Walk for Farm Animals. A few classmates and I met at Director Park in downtown Portland, where we came upon the organizers and an assortment of signs emblazoned with images of cows, pigs, and chickens and captions like *Animals Are Friends, Not Food* and *Someone, Not Something.*

I'd never been in a march before. Had never marched *for* anything, and as the organizers detailed our route and the calls and responses we'd shout, I felt an unease start to course through me. That's the great thing about academia, which affords you the time to reflect upon, refine, and make your message yours. But it's different with the march. By submitting your voice to the collective, every voice in it speaks on your behalf. And of the half dozen calls and responses they led us on, one in particular stuck with me:

> What do we want?
> *Animal Rights!*
> When do we want them?
> *Now!*
> What do we want?

Animal Rights!

When a Black man stepped out of a coffee shop and called. "What about human rights?" he put to us, to which a white woman from our ranks answered him in time: "Humans are animals."

I'll return to that exchange in a moment, but suffice it to say that in the heat of that moment a new call and response forged in my mind.

What about human rights?

Humans are animals.

It was a refrain I suspected the man knew all too well, and the cadence of it saw me stumble just when I thought I'd found my footing.

The Beat of a Different Drum

Before animal law, my area of focus was postcolonial literature, specifically the representation of human and nonhuman animals in the genre. As to this theme, I think the Cameroonian political theorist Achille Mbembe (2011) put it best: "In the heyday of colonial conquest and occupation," he argued, "humanism was a racially exclusive ideology predicated on the belief that a difference of color was a difference of species." What Mbembe so casually observes is how colonialism necessitated a dehumanization of the Other in order to maintain humanity as the basis for legal rights. To this end, the West branded animal markers into its victims—think "savage," "beast," "barbarian," "brute," and so on—to justify their commodification and exploitation. It would be a mistake to dismiss these labels as idle metaphors, for they weren't just ways of talking about colonized people but a means of keeping them captive within a rigid legal order, one that would define them as objects as opposed to subjects, as legal property as opposed to persons. Underpinning the system was an effective if simple principle: animals had no rights.

What first drew me to literature and why I hold it in such esteem to this day is its ability to illustrate paradigms like these. Take Aravind Adiga's *The White Tiger.* Set in modern-day India, the novel captures a people's internalization of their animality, as well as its ramifications for their perceived relationship to the law. To this end, the narrator notes how on "the day the British left ... the cages had been let open; and the animals attacked and ripped each other apart and jungle law replaced zoo law" (2008, 54). This inflection point in India's past illustrates the logic of colonial-era "zoo laws," which literally barred the colonized from shaping the laws that governed them as wildlife. And although the letting open of these cages might suggest a freedom from the colonial order, the resulting carnage subverts such a reading by calling attention to the legacy of colonialism. Indeed, still branded by the animal markers that justified their exclusion from the law's concern, the subcontinent finds itself reduced to a kind of "jungle law," or the equivalent of a lawlessness state. What the scene as attests to, then, are the consequences of a people's not having being seen in the law's eyes as fully human—both under colonial rule and after.

It was in a postcolonial literature and human rights seminar that I first encountered many of these works and grew uncomfortably aware of the trope that bound them. It was in the face of this pseudospeciation that the protagonists would adopt the language, culture, religion, and traditions of the colonizer. The hope was that by mimicking white humanity, the colonized might prove they'd been misbranded. What that seminar betrayed was a world that aspired to a white center, which enjoyed a kind of gravity designed to attract but never admit those in its orbit. Of course, as Mbembe noted, it could be no other way, for if the humanism of the colonial enterprise cleaved to one principle above all, it was that a difference in color constituted a difference in species.

The tragedy of it all is best captured by Frantz Fanon, the Martinican psychiatrist, philosopher, and revolutionary, who, in his seminal *Black Skin, White Masks*, observes the urge of the colonized to adopt Western markers at the expense of their ethnic and racial identity. Speaking to this impulse within himself, Fanon admits, "Out of the blackest part of my soul, across the zebra striping of my mind, surges this desire to be suddenly white" (2008, 45). Despite being aware of colonialism's false promise of inclusion, the Blackest parts of him—both mind and spirit—prove defenseless against its tug. What the confession likewise pays homage to is the uncanny power of metaphor to capture deeper truths than what its author perhaps intended, for no matter how many white stripes Fanon assumes at the expense of his Blackness, he nevertheless remains an animal in the colonial paradigm, or the ideology that underpins the colonizer's domination over and subjugation of the colonized.

That seminar ended with a study of the Universal Declaration of Human Rights and a debate as to its promise. That is, if this new, universal law could affirm the humanity of marginalized people beyond this historically white center, would that spell the end of colonialism's legacy? But for me, the question implied others as to why a truly universal rights framework should stop there. After all, wasn't the underlying principle that fueled the colonial project that it provided for the exploitation of animals, against whom the Other could be compared? Could we really secure the rights of humans without providing for their interests? And so whether out of ignorance or indignation,

I asked, "What about the animals?" And whether it was my professors or peers, the answer to a person was, "Well, what about them?"

In the literary arts, we often talk about what "haunts," or informs, the way a writer sees the world, and the same, I believe, applies to one's advocacy as well. For me, it was that refrain, What about the animals? *Well, what about them?*, that spurred me to seek out other spheres of thought, the gravity of the animal law field so compelling that I came to believe I'd been chosen. It was that conviction that drove me to enter the ranks of the march that day, when I found myself haunted a second time.

A March Out of Step with Human Rights

The exchange between that white woman and Black man lasted just seconds at the most—for if the logic of the march dictates anything, it's that the march must go on. Yet I found myself saddled by its weight and wondered if others did, too. I wasn't the only person of color in our ranks but one of two or three in sixty. I kept that call and response to myself, however, carried it down new streets and back home, where I attempted to unpack it.

What about human rights?

Humans are animals.

How could I fault her answer? It was benign enough, and true. Humans *are* animals. But it was also true that the retort conveyed more than what was said, for the implicit message was that in marching for animal rights, we were marching for him as well. Of course, it was likewise true that she'd spoken on her own behalf. Yet it was as if she'd taken the words out of my mouth. I'd voiced the same or similar sentiment not long before. And in leaving him to consider the fact that he was taking to the sidelines as his own movement passed him by, we continued to march in what appeared like lockstep with the discourse of human rights.

The intervening years, however, have made me wonder if the march for animals is truly a march for all. Examples of animal advocates targeting marginalized communities to extract animal gains are many. Take, for one, the infamous *Hialeah* Supreme Court case, which saw the Hialeah city council contrive a series of animal protection ordinances targeting the sacrificial practices of Santeríans, a minority religious group, while exempting secular and kosher slaughter, hunting, and more. Although not motivated by racial or religious animus, similar efforts have included the targeting of live animal markets in major cities. Unable to garner enough support to shut down live animal marketplaces in San Francisco, advocates persuaded the council to target sales of mammals, fowl, amphibians, and reptiles—animals predominantly consumed by the city's minoritized Chinese population—while leaving intact sales of fishes, crustaceans, and others consumed by majoritarian groups (Kim, 2015, 78–79). The upshot of similar campaigns is that minority animal-use practices, whether real or just perceived, are characterized as "barbaric" (Boyle, 2017),[1] as seen in the passage of legislation to end the "underground," or non-existent, U.S. cat and dog meat trade (Kelly, 2018).

But the problem is more subtle than questions of discriminatory intent or impact. As those in the legal field know, the law evolves by means of comparison, by taking precedent and analogizing or distinguishing as new facts arise. In this fashion, lines once thought indelible are blurred and new lines are drawn. Perhaps the most notorious of these efforts to reshape the law for animals has been PETA's attempt to apply the Thirteenth Amendment's prohibition of slavery to Tilikum, an orca forced to perform tricks at SeaWorld (Tilikum, 2012, 1259). To be sure, the harms inflicted upon Tilikum merited attention.[2] Yet how should we view the argument for invoking an amendment deemed sacrosanct for affirming the humanity of a long-dehumanized race to free a captive animal, a goal laudable in itself? In an originalist reading, that the authors of the Thirteenth Amendment had intended it to apply to all animals, both human and non-? Or if we read the Constitution as an evolving text, that one's humanity is all but irrelevant for its purposes now? Or does narrowing our discussion to the legal issues that animate *Tilikum* dispose us to miss the point?

Today, I direct the same animal law program I graduated from, and the *Tilikum* case is one I ask my students to interrogate the implications of. Most appreciate the opportunity to assess its merits, but the majority point to it as a distraction and offensive owing both to the nature of the comparison and the overwhelmingly white makeup of the AR movement. To be sure, this species-neutral application of the Thirteenth Amendment exemplifies a

---

1 Boyle's characterization of the practice as "barbaric" is from the previous year's attempt to see the bill passed. In his statement, Boyle contended, "The fact that this legislation is even necessary today is astonishing. It is past time for us to outlaw such a cruel and barbaric practice once and for all." Given the underground nature of the practice, one might wonder how the legislation is actually "necessary." Indeed, backers of the ban argue it will have mostly "symbolic" power (Dewey). Along with the bill, the House passed a resolution urging the countries of China, South Korea, Vietnam, Thailand, the Philippines, Indonesia, Cambodia, Laos, and India, among others, to adopt similar laws (Block). Left out of the moral calculus, of course, are the billions of farmed animals the U.S. subjects to routine cruelties each year.

2 Just a few of these concerned the lack of environmental stimulation, shortened lifespan, and psychological and emotional suffering, among others (1261).

corollary colorblindness at the core of PETA's messaging. One such analogy has been the exploitation of animals to slavery (Kim, 2021, 312). Another is PETA's "Modern-Day Holocaust" ads, which compare the deaths of Jews to the slaughter of animals, with the food for thought it leaves viewers with being that "[t]he Holocaust is on [their] plate" (MacDonald, 2006, 427). Of more recent notoriety is PETA's commercial inspired by the controversy surrounding Colin Kaepernick, the NFL quarterback blackballed by the league for silently taking a knee during the national anthem in protest of police brutality against Black Americans (Moore, 2018). Against the humming of the national anthem, PETA's ad cuts between kneeling cartoon animals before settling on a child who's taken a knee, with the ad's final frames reading, "Respect is the right of every living being" and "#EndSpeciesism" (PETA, 2020). Notwithstanding the ad's having been rejected to air during the Super Bowl, PETA's attempt to lay claim to a stage denied to Kaepernick betrays how the call to address racial injustice has been co-opted to seek gains for animals.

Along these same lines, the AR movement has sought to embrace human rights efforts that directly implicate the animal-use industry. Examples include activists citing the prevalence of slavery in the global fishing sector, the environmental and health toll animal agriculture inflicts upon communities, and the brutal working conditions at meat processing plants (Slater, 2020). With these harms disproportionately falling upon the marginalized and showing how stronger animal protections, if not the disavowal of animal products altogether, would afford relief to all, the AR movement has managed to incorporate racial justice into its discourse without causing offense.

Yet what this intersectional approach signals is that the human wrongs that matter are those that lead to animal rights. Underlying this instrumentalization is a perception of racial injustices not as occasioning change but conduits for it. For a movement that aspires to be seen as being in lockstep with other social justice causes, these avenues offer unparalleled opportunities to convey how human and nonhuman animal oppressions are intimately braided, if not one. This was the tenet imparted to me upon entering its ranks. In marching for animals, I was to know I was marching for humanity, too. But what the limits of intersectional activism has revealed is a white-dominated movement largely content to stand silent in response to broader calls for racial justice. What this silence speaks to is a vision that sees communities of color insofar as their interests align with those of animals, or not at all. These communities, already marginalized, are further so in either case. As Breeze Harper (2010), a critical race theorist in the AR space, notes, such postures fail to surprise given how the rhetoric of animal rights is "often entrenched in whiteness and white privilege that are collectively unacknowledged by white-identifying people engaged in them" (35). As Harper observes, this failure to acknowledge, or even consider, the implications of their advocacy flows from privilege—in this case, of having only ever known the center. In stark contrast, advocates of color bear the burden of advancing efforts that seek to mine the plight of our communities, who wrestle with our complicity in them and the hypocrisy of our critique. Many whom I've commiserated with have since taken to the sidelines, often wondering whether the movement will even realize that they've left. The question presumes, of course, that they were noticed in the first place.

A Reckoning with Race in Our Ranks

I was in my last year of law school and attending the 2016 Animal Law Conference when I first saw the movement addressing the issue of race. Speaking on that panel was Joyce Tischler (2016), who, regarded as the "Mother of Animal Law," had been part of the movement since its inception. What Tischler noted was the mistreatment of minorities in the AR community for their cultural differences, not being vegan enough or not being vegan in the right way. They were welcome to join the march, she noted, but could not enter its ranks as they were. And when people of color did show up, she added, they tended to be exploited. What the movement thought yet never said, she disclosed, was, "You're not one of us, but we need you … for the optics." And assuming a comedic tone to share a secret so open that it could only be expressed through humor, she asked in the voice of animal activists where all the people of color were. Really, she said, where are they? And if you found one, she advised the crowd, don't forget to pull them into a selfie with you.

What Tischler's authority empowered her to voice was an uncomfortable if ironic truth, for what the image betrays—if we examine what it *doesn't* as well as *does* show us—is that minorities are objects, not subjects in the AR movement of today. The practice of pulling people of color into the selfies of a white-dominated movement amounts to exclusion by inclusion, if not erasure. How to answer her question, then, of where people of color are when their entry entails their invisibilization? The logic that drives this "representation rhetoric" in such spaces is that if they "just show more minoritized faces in the white marketplace, then progress is being made" (Ko, 2017, 97). This phenomenon Tischler called attention to is not unique to the AR world. The rarity of minorities in similarly homogenous spheres has been expressed in hyperbolic, even mythological terms, with people of color sometimes referred to as "unicorns" (Le, 2015).

It would be months before I'd reflect upon that panel and be awed yet again by the uncanny power of metaphor to reveal layered truths with time. But at the time I was just a student who knew his name announced his race and that his race held a certain value—and in a field where there are few jobs to come by, I'm more than a little ashamed to admit that I was ready to be drawn into someone else's selfie and cash in on my token value.

Reflecting on it years later, what I've come to learn is that one's token value isn't exchanged but taxed at a certain rate. In one study conducted on the incidence of burnout in the AR movement, researchers found that in addition to experiencing the same stressors as their white counterparts—such as empathizing with the suffering of animals and a self-imposed obligation to prioritize animal suffering over their own, just to name a few—people of color also had to contend with workplace racism, with every minority interviewed pointing to it as a factor in their burnout (Gorski et al., 2018, 10). One respondent confessed feeling "responsible for educating white activists about racism—a task that '[came] at [the] cost' of making her doubly vulnerable as an activist and an activist of color" (10). Another expressed frustration that the AR world is "generally ... a pretty white movement, especially in terms of who gets visibility" (10). This last remark is striking given Tischler's mocking of the question often voiced by animal activists regarding where people of color are in a movement that has absorbed them into its selfies.

How to explain the paradox of their (in)visibility except to say that sometimes what's most striking about a thing is the thing about it that goes unquestioned? And for a unicorn, what we take for granted is its whiteness. To lean on Fanon again, who confessed to wanting to shed his colored stripes, the markers of his identity, to illustrate that he belonged, a similar thing has happened and continues to happen to advocates of color in the march. There is a pressure to not disrupt its calls and responses by questioning the discriminatory intent and impact of animal protection campaigns, the coopting of minority suffering, or the instrumentalization of the marginalized under the banner of intersectional activism. In the stables of the AR movement, there can be no horses of a different color. All stripes must be shed.

And still, some in the field ask me why people of color don't join the march. They ask me why I did.

The answer requires perspective, for the phenomenon represents what I offer is a neocolonial state of mind. What's more is that the force of it is so subtle that I fear it escapes our notice. I admit to missing it myself the first time I taught my International Animal Law course. I'd assigned a reading concerning global developments for the first day of class. In its opening paragraph, the author remarked as to how their native Britain had rejected its "barbaric past" by demonstrating a "new humanity" toward animals (Kean, 2013, 9). What followed were assessments by other contributors as to how formerly colonized nations failed to meet this measure. To perform a comparative reading of the frameworks, the analysis was sound. But the reference to barbarism said more than it was saying. It spoke to a colonial order related to yet different from that of the past. Whereas the humanism of the former era branded people of color as barbarians because they were deemed to be animals, the humanism of the neocolonial present brands them the same for failing to espouse compassion toward animals. What this new framework demands is that formerly colonized states adopt animal protection laws to meet Western measures in order to be regarded as fully human. Indeed, the promise of a full humanity in this new order was so subtle yet so seductive that, drawn by its gravity, I came to believe that I'd been chosen. And in many ways I had. Like Fanon, I had no other choice.

A Call for New Marching Orders

Colleagues I speak with on this issue ask if there aren't any points of hope. But I'm afraid I don't think they exist, at least not once the route has been charted and the march begun. Increasing the diversity in our ranks is critical, but what does it mean if it's realized at the lowest levels of an organization, where marching orders are carried out, not made? Rather, diversity must be braided with values of equity and inclusion. Marginalized voices must be centered by being integrated into and empowered by the planning process, where the routes are planned and the call and responses orchestrated.

Looking back on my first and only animal rights march to date, a part of me would like to repeat that humans are animals. That is, I'd like to believe that the movement cares for the interests of the marginalized beyond the use-value of our aligned interests. But to do so requires an acknowledgment that society has failed to deliver human rights for many human animals and a holding accountable of those in the movement content to apply bestial markers to humanity. To that end, I hope we can revisit, revise, and refine our message.

What do we want?

Animal rights and human rights beyond them.

But when do we want it?

References

Adiga, Aravind. *The White Tiger: A Novel*. New York: Free Press, 2008.

Boyle, Brendan. "Boyle Introduces Dog and Cat Meat Trade Prohibition Act of 2017." March 7, 2017. https://boyle.house.gov/media-center/press-releases/boyle-introduces-dog-and-cat-meat-trade-prohibition-act-2017.

Church of the Lukumi Babalu Aye, Inc., et al. v. City of Hialeah, 508 U.S. 520 (1992).

Dewey, Caitlin. "Congress Doesn't Want You to Eat Your Dog or Cat," April 24, 2018. https://www.washingtonpost.com/news/wonk/wp/2018/04/24/congress-doesnt-want-you-to-eat-your-dog-or-cat. Accessed May 10, 2019.

Fanon, Frantz. *Black Skin, White Masks*, trans. Richard Philcox. New York: Grove Press, 2008.

Gorski, Paul, et al. "'Nobody's Paying Me to Cry': The Causes of Activist Burnout in United States Animal Rights Activists." *Social Movement Studies*, vol. 18, no. 3. (2018): 364–380.

Harper, Breeze A. "Social Justice Beliefs and Addiction to Uncompassionate Consumption: Food for Thought." In *Sistah Vegan: Black Women Speak on Food, Identity, Health, and Society*, ed. A Breeze Harper. New York: Lantern Press, 2010.

Kean, Hilda. "Animal Protection in Britain." In *The Global Guide to Animal Protection*, ed. Andrew Linzey. Illinois: University of Illinois Press, 2013.

Kelly, Erin V. "Eating Dogs and Cats Banned in U.S. in House-passed Bill." September 13, 2018. https://www.usatoday.com/story/news/politics/2018/09/13/eating-dogs-and-cats-banned-house-passed-bill/1288897002. Accessed May 10, 2019.

Kim, Clair Jean. *Dangerous Crossings: Race, Species, and Nature in a Multicultural Age*. Cambridge: Cambridge University Press, 2015.

Kim, Claire Jean. "Moral Extensionism or Racist Exploitation? The Use of Holocaust and Slavery Analogies in the Animal Liberation Movement." *New Political Science*, vol. 33, no. 3 (2011): 311–333.

Ko, Aph. "How Social Media Serves as a Digital Defibrillator for 'the American Dream.'" In *Aphro-ism: Essays on Pop Culture, Feminism, and Black Veganism from Two Sisters*, eds. Aph Ko and Sil Ko. New York: Lantern Press, 2017.

Le, Vu. "Waiting for Unicorns: The Supply and Demand of Diversity and Inclusion." March 2015. https://nonprofitaf.com/2015/03/the-supply-and-demand-of-diversity-and-inclusion.

MacDonald, David B. 2006. "Pushing the Limits of Humanity? Reinterpreting Animal Rights and 'Personhood' Through the Prism of the Holocaust." *Journal of Human Rights*, vol. 5, no. 4 (2006): 417–437.

Mbembe, Achille. "Collision, Collusion, and Refractions: Reflections on South Africa After Liberation." May 26, 2011. Oxford, England.

Moore, Jack. "At Least the NFL Isn't Pretending It's Not Blackballing Colin Kaepernick," April 13, 2018. https://www.theguardian.com/sport/2018/apr/13/kaepernick-reid-blackballed-nfl-kneeling-anthem.

PETA. "The Award-Winning PETA Ad the NFL Squashed: 'Don't Stand for Injustice,'" January 31, 2020. https://www.youtube.com/watch?v=2XbCoOIEJ7s.

Slater, Bronwyn, "Worker Exploitation in Agriculture – the Cost of Cheap Food," May 29, 2020. http://vegansustainability.com/worker-exploitation-in-agriculture-the-cost-of-cheap-food.

Tischler, Joyce. "Gender and Race within the Animal Protection Movement." Presented at the Animal Law Conference at Pace University, New York City, NY, October 2016.

Section 3 Moving towards Multispecies Liberation

Abolish the Meat Industry: A Roadmap for Transforming Animal Liberation from a Single-Issue Cause into a Mass Movement

Hailey Huget

Traditionally, the animal liberation movement has gone to great lengths to distance itself from other movements for social justice. For example, during the last several decades, animal protection organizations have invested in a "tough on crime" strategy when it comes to prosecuting animal cruelty, advocating for harsh jail sentences and funneling money into prosecutors' offices in an attempt to send a largely symbolic message about the moral wrongness of animal cruelty (Marceau, 2019). This trend has been met, and rightly so, with resistance and anger from racial justice activists and police/prison abolitionists who view tough-on-crime policies as perpetuating systemic and institutional racism (Marceau, 2019). The animal liberation movement has also had an openly hostile relationship with workers in animal agriculture and the labor movement as a whole, using tactics like "undercover investigations," which—even when they succeed in exposing animal cruelty on factory farms—can come at the cost of getting low-wage, frequently immigrant, workers on those farms fired, jailed, or deported (Mercy for Animals, 2019; Nunez, 2017; Bangert, 2019).[1] Nonprofit animal protection organizations[2] and vegan food companies have also gone to great lengths to oppose union drives among their employees, further alienating the movement from labor organizations and the cause of workers' rights more broadly (Nolan, 2021; Starostinetskaya, 2021). In sum, it seems that the dominant strategy of the

1 Ellyse Winter piece in Handbook.
2 Drew Robert Winter piece in Handbook.

movement has been to advocate for non-human animals in ways which come at the expense of human ones.

At the same time, animal activists have also questioned the value of framing animal liberation as a single-issue cause, isolatable from and even in tension with other social justice causes. Morally, insofar as animal liberation is a philosophy that values compassion and justice over cruelty, domination, and exploitation, it seems that consistency demands we fight with humans who are also victims of these forces, rather than against them. Activists and theorists who make these kinds of arguments and seek to transcend a single-issue framing of animal liberation typically call themselves *total liberationists* and/ or describe their approach as *intersectional* (Pendergrast, 2018).[3] Advocates of these approaches understand the root causes of all oppression, whether based on race, gender, class, sexual orientation, species, etc., to be linked to one another (see, e.g. Best, 2014).

While I agree with the moral arguments for these intersectional/total liberationist approaches, here I focus on the strategical question of *how we win* animal liberation in a practical sense. I will argue that the movement's insistence on remaining a single-issue fight is a strategic disaster, one which prevents us from heeding lessons from other successful social movements, such as the labor movement, Civil Rights movement, and various antiwar movements. I'll discuss some important lessons we can learn from these movements in Section 1. These lessons involve choosing our targets more carefully, giving more entry points into the movement, and expanding our menu of tactics.

I'll argue that, if we are to learn from these other movements, one thing we need to do is critically examine the animal liberation movement's current strategy of placing central importance, and almost total focus, on convincing consumers to go vegan. While I am vegan and personally agree that being vegan is, morally speaking, the right thing to do, the central place that this demand holds within our movement is a strategic mistake that holds us back from building coalitions with many natural allies engaged in anti-oppression work in the domains of racial justice, workers' rights, immigrant rights, environmental justice, and more. I'll argue that there is a different kind of demand and strategic agenda available to us that allows us to follow in the footsteps of other social justice movements and better forge alliances with these movements. This approach can be summed up in the slogan: "abolish the meat industry." I'll explain this alternative strategic framework and make a provisional case for it in Section 2. Then, in Section 3, I will shift my focus

3 Boisseau piece in Handbook.

to explain how, even though this agenda emphasizes institutional change over individual action, it still nonetheless has implications for individual choices and for veganism, and can illuminate a path forward for reconciling animal rights organizations with the broader left.

Learning from Other Social Movements: More Reasons; More (and Better) Tactics; Fewer, Carefully Chosen Targets

Other movements, like the labor movement, various antiwar movements, and the Civil Rights movement,[4] have succeeded where they have followed several key strategic principles: proliferate reasons someone might adopt to enter and become active in the movement; proliferate tactics; and choose targets carefully. I'll explain each of these in greater detail below, while also assessing the degree to which the mainstream animal rights movement follows these principles.

Proliferate Reasons

It is easier to build a mass movement in support of a cause if you allow a wide range of reasons for participation in the movement. A fundamental insight of labor organizing, for example, is that not everyone is motivated to make big changes or sacrifices for the same reasons, at least not right away. One worker may be motivated to take action because they want a wage increase, another because of harassment or racism in the workplace, another because they want more control over their schedule, another because of the need for better childcare benefits or lactation spaces, etc. Labor unions mobilize workers to take action by allowing them to bring many different reasons to the table for doing so—trying not to assume that one worker's reason for participating in

---

4 I want to acknowledge, in invoking the Civil Rights movement here, that mainstream animal rights organizations frequently make misguided and thoughtless comparisons to this movement as well as to racial justice struggles more broadly. As Marceau (2019), discusses, animal rights organizations will often analogize the plight of animals to the struggles of racial minorities while simultaneously advocating for pro-carceral policies which directly undermine the goals of racial justice organizations. The animal rights movement, in other words, "wants it both ways when it comes to histories of racism—it seeks to analogize to the suffering of black bodies when it is useful, and to ignore it when it is inconvenient" (Marceau, 2019, 153). Here, I hope to avoid this kind of unhelpful, damaging analogy by focusing throughout on making a case for why animal rights organizations must cultivate racial justice groups as allies rather than enemies (and so cannot "have it both ways" when analogizing the cause of animal rights to racial justice struggles).

a strike or for voting "yes" on union representation is the same as another's. Likewise, participants in various antiwar movements in the US and abroad, which have mobilized some of the largest numbers of protestors globally to date (Lamb & Roos, 2012), brought many different reasons to the table for getting involved. These ranged from religious objections, to secular pacifist moral commitments, to racial justice concerns, to political positions like opposition to imperialism or support of leftist governments abroad, to name just a few (Zimmerman, 2017).

While movements like the labor movement and antiwar movement have mobilized supermajorities to take action by proliferating the number of reasons someone can bring to the table for participating, the animal rights movement has gone in the opposite direction and has sought to limit the number of entry points into the cause. Mainstream animal rights organizations have spent the last several decades attempting to combat animal cruelty by cozying up to prosecutors, advocating for mandatory minimum sentences, and generally adopting "tough on crime" approaches. In addition to having questionable success at actually improving animal welfare (Marceau, 2019), such approaches alienate people of color from the movement and prevent people from realizing that racial justice concerns can actually be an entry point into animal rights, as some black vegans have argued (Ko & Ko, 2017). Likewise, the animal liberation movement frequently alienates itself from the labor movement and workers' rights causes by pursuing "undercover investigation" tactics that—in an effort to expose the catastrophic cruelty of factory farming—end up getting animal agriculture workers fired, jailed, and sometimes deported. In addition to the fact that these tactics have limited impact upon the operations of factory farms themselves—once workers are fired, they're replaced with new workers who have the same incentives to engage in animal abuse—they also ignore the fact that the interests of animal agriculture workers and animal rights activists are, in reality, much more aligned. As I've argued elsewhere, animal agriculture workers are uniquely positioned to sabotage the operations of factory farms—even better positioned than activists outside of the industry—and may even have compelling motivations to do so, ranging from the majorly exploitative conditions of their jobs to the likelihood of getting PSTD due to the inherently dangerous and upsetting nature of their work (Huget, 2021). In this way, concern for workers' rights and safety could be potential entry point into goals that animal liberationists share, like ending factory farms. But the way the mainstream movement operates today, that entry point is closed off.

So with concerns for racial justice and workers' rights largely off the table as entry points into the mainstream animal rights' movement, we are left with, essentially three entry points: health, animal rights or welfare, and the environment. But why should we think that this is a sufficient number of entry points into the movement? Consider the central demand of this tunnel-vision approach: going vegan or vegetarian. Only a tiny percentage of people in the US, and a tiny percentage of people globally are vegan or vegetarian. In the US, less than 0.5% of people are vegan; that number is also less than 1% globally (Meyer, 2021). It is probably safe to assume that an even smaller percentage are active participants in the animal liberation/rights movement and in movement organizations, even if we construe "active participant" broadly to include donors to animal rights organizations and sanctuaries as well as people who participate in direct actions like protests. Given this state of affairs, we have strong reason to believe that we are not providing enough entry points or reasons to care about the cause and need to rethink some fundamental aspects of our movement's strategy.

More (and Better) Tactics

At the moment, the animal rights movement is centrally invested in tactics that engage consumers in various ways and ask them to change their consumption choices. Our main, central effort is focused on getting people to be vegan. While there is debate about whether veganism is a consumer boycott or a different type of action (Roberts, 2021; Dickstein et al., 2020), there is no question that the demand to "go vegan" targets consumers. Many tactics used in the service of this overall agenda focus on persuading consumers, such as, for example, Anonymous for the Voiceless's tactic of standing in public places and holding up gruesome footage of factory farms (Leenaert, 2018), or PETA's frequent use of provocative costumes and imagery in various public demonstrations (South Florida Sun-Sentinel, 2014). While it would be unfair to argue that mainstream animal liberation organizations focus *only* on consumers—PETA, for example, does spend some money on political lobbying (Willis, 2017)—it is fair to say that the movement is most associated with a call to change one's consumption habits, specifically to be vegan.

Consumer and citizen boycotts (if that is how ethical eating practices are to be understood) have a long and respectable history as social justice tactics, which should not be ignored. However, consumer and citizen boycotts tend to be more successful when paired with other tactics, in the context of a broader strategy that is capable of engaging large numbers of people. For example, the success of the Montgomery Bus Boycott cannot be understood outside of the larger context of the Civil Rights movement, which included many other kinds of tactics such as marches, civil disobedience, political lobbying and engagement, as well as deep organizing—a slow, careful process of relationship-building that prioritizes listening, above all else, to people impacted by the issue you are focusing on (Payne, 1995). Labor unions typically use consumer boycotts as part of an escalation strategy in a workplace fight. And when unions use this tactic, it is typically timed carefully to occur in conjunction with other actions, like strikes or slow-downs. As veteran labor organizer and thinker Jane McAlevey argues, further, tactics such as supermajority strikes are nearly impossible to pull off without engaging in deep organizing (2016). To take another example, in the Palestinian struggle to end Israeli apartheid, it is no coincidence that that the tactic of boycotting certain Israeli products and companies is coupled with the further tactics of divestment and sanctions (BDS Movement, 2016). The problem, then, is not with the consumer boycott itself, but with the fact that we do not seem to be using the tactic as wisely as we could be—as part of a broader strategy that includes many other effective tactics.

There are also strong reasons to think that we *must* diversify our tactics beyond those that merely target consumers in order to succeed as a movement. The COVID era has revealed ways in which mass animal death and suffering sometimes comes apart from consumer demand for animal products. In the early days of the COVID crisis in the US, so many meatpacking workers were out sick that farmers had a "backlog of pigs" that were ready for slaughter but had "nowhere to go." This resulted in farmers gassing and shooting hundreds of thousands of pigs without them being processed into food (Corkery & Yaffe-Bellany, 2020). These pigs were killed not because consumers wanted to eat them, but because of how factory farms are designed. As institutions that are tightly calibrated to maximize efficiency while keeping costs low, they have very little wiggle-room to adjust their operations when shocks and disruptions occur (Reynolds et al., 2021). So when a major crisis like COVID-19—or even more minor crises like cyberattacks (Creswell, Perlroth, & Scheiber, 2021)—occur, it has major ripple effects that can shut down enormous portions of the industry and lead to needless waste like mass killing of farmed animals (Smith, 2021). In this sense, mass animal slaughter and consumer demand for animal products can come apart. So while tactics that engage consumers may be important levers of change in the animal liberation fight, they cannot be our sole focus, as consumer demand is not the only problem here—the corporations responsible for producing and selling animal products and how they structure their supply chains also play a huge role.

The movement's myopic focus on consumers and consumer-tactics also obscures the fact that our system of industrial animal agriculture impacts many other groups and constituencies. These are whole communities who could be motivated to take part in struggles to end industrial animal agriculture—bringing with them new options to add to our menu of tactics. This is one way that the strategic imperatives of "proliferate entry points" discussed above and "use a wider array of more-thoughtfully chosen tactics" are related to one another and can support one another. Workers in animal agriculture and the members of communities that house these industries' farms and meatpacking plants are more directly impacted by these industries than most consumers. They are directly impacted by the industry's enormous, ugly cost. For example, in addition to bearing responsibility for massive environmental degradation (Flesher, 2020), union-busting (McAlevey, 2019), other labor abuses (Treisman, 2021; McConnell, 2019), and exploitation of immigrants (Leonard, 2014), major meat and dairy companies also contribute to higher rates of mental illness (Nagesh, 2017; Leibler, Janulewicz, & Perry, 2017) and aggression/violence among meatpacking workers (Richards, Signal, & Taylor, 2013). What possibilities would open up if, instead of focusing almost exclusively on persuading consumers, we invested in deep organizing approaches to engaging workers and communities impacted by animal agriculture? A slow process of relationship-building might reveal not only new reasons or entry points to animal liberation but also new tactics we can use. For example, engaging animal agriculture workers in our struggle opens up the possibility of using tactics like work slow-downs or strikes to shut down the industry's operations.

When our approach to animal liberation focuses almost exclusively on the consumer, we leave power at the table: the power workers hold and the power their communities hold. When we focus more broadly on worker-power and community-power, in addition to consumer-power, we generate new options for tactics.

Choosing Targets Carefully

Successful campaigns in other movements for social justice typically have another feature in common: they focus on a small, manageable number of targets, such as specific corporations, governments, or employers. Focusing energy and resources on fighting one or a few carefully chosen targets prevents participants' efforts from being spread too thin, where minimal impact is made on each target while requiring greater effort from each individual participant. Consider again, for example, the Montgomery Bus Boycott, which was targeted at a single public transit organization (Burns, 1997). Likewise, a bedrock aspect of labor organizing is that you organize people who work for a specific employer, so that you can bring the power of a united workforce to bear on that single target. Similarly, the Palestinian-led Boycott, Divestment, and Sanctions movement does not ask consumers to boycott every single Israeli company; they only ask consumers to boycott the ones that are most egregious in their violations of Palestinian rights. Despite the fact that almost every Israeli company is guilty of violating Palestinian rights, the BDS website states that they nonetheless "focus our boycotts on a small number of companies and products for maximum impact. We focus on companies that play a clear and direct role in Israel's crimes and where we think we can have an impact" (BDS Movement, 2022).

Meanwhile, the animal liberation movement's focus on veganism and on changing consumption habits in general necessitates that we spread our targets out in a completely un-strategic fashion: to all consumers and producers of animal products. For example, the demand "go vegan" targets the person who raises chickens for eggs in the backyard, or the Indigenous cattle rancher, or the minority religious group engaged in animal sacrifice as part of a religious practice, in the same breath as it targets the massive corporations that do the vast majority of the harm to non-human animals, the planet, and human communities. While it may well be the case that all uses of animals are morally wrong—including raising backyard chickens, engaging in animal sacrifice for religious reasons, etc.—that does not mean targeting every use of animals is a recipe for a winning movement. We must search for ways to focus the energy of our movement's participants as well as our movement's material resources on a more carefully-chosen set of targets.

Changing Direction

I have argued that the mainstream animal liberation movement, at least in the status quo, (a) gives potential activists too few entry points into the cause; (b) over-utilizes consumer-focused tactics, when we should be working to expand the menu of tactics available to us; and (c) has an extremely large number of poorly chosen targets.

If you agree with these arguments, you may feel as though there is no way out for animal liberation—that we are, in some sense, doomed to be a painfully small movement that use its limited resources ineffectively. However, I see no need to accept this kind of fatalism. There is another approach available to us. In the next section, I will argue that shifting our strategy away from our myopic focus on consumer practices and toward prioritizing institutional targets and institutional change will allow us to build a far wider-reaching and potent movement for animal liberation.[5] As I explain below, I sum up this alternative approach under the umbrella phrase "abolish the meat industry." I begin in by explaining what "abolish the meat industry" means in greater detail, before moving on to explain why I think this alternative strategic agenda better incorporates the lessons from other social movements described above.

Defining Our Terms: "the meat industry" and "abolition"

Despite the appearance of variety in the meat and dairy aisles at your grocery store, the vast majority of meat in the United States is in fact produced by just a small handful of companies (Suozzo et al., 2021). JBS, Cargill, Smithfield, Tyson, and a small handful of others now are responsible for almost all of the meat products in the United States (Leonard 2014). The intense degree of corporate consolidation in meatpacking has led the Biden administration to pursue antitrust action against the top four players (Deese, Fazili, & Ramamurti, 2021). While consolidation is a major trend throughout agriculture, the dairy industry is consolidating at a faster rate than almost all other agricultural sectors (Jones, Bhutada, & Deshmukh, 2020). In Wisconsin, one of the top dairy-producing states in the US, the amount of milk being produced is increasing while the number of farms that produce it is decreasing; 3% of farms now produce about 40% of the state's milk (Sewell, 2021). This had led some small Wisconsin dairy farmers to say that there is "no future" in the industry for them (Sewell, 2021). And though the global aquaculture industry is arguably less consolidated than the meat and dairy industries, the last decade in aquaculture has also been marked by trends toward ever-greater consolidation as well as meat processing giants branching out into aquaculture. This consolidation has "blurred the lines between aquaculture, fisheries, processing and feed companies, with giants such as Norway's Austevoll Seafood diversifying across the full value chain" (IntraFish, 2019). Likewise, the meat industry giant Cargill has made major, multi-billion-dollar investments into acquiring fish feed companies in recent years (Kelloway, 2019). As in the dairy and meat industries, this consolidation harms small, local fisheries, which also (not coincidentally) tend to use more sustainable practices (Miles, 2020). As Patty Lovera, the Assistant Director of Food & Water Watch puts it, local fish farmers cannot "get those fish to market if they're

---

5 The Sentience Institute also finds that institution- rather than individual-focused messaging is a more effective way of advocating for animals (https://www.sentien ceinstitute.org/foundational-questions-summaries#individual-vs.-institutional-interventions-and-messaging).

being undercut by ... Big Feed players dealing with Big Aquaculture players dealing with Big Processing players, who are maybe vertically integrated into one player" (Kelloway, 2019).

It is these giant companies—these mega-conglomerates—across the increasingly-interconnected meat, dairy, and aquaculture industries that I refer to when I use the term "the meat industry" in the rest of this discussion. Crucially, this definition allows us to see what the meat industry is *not*: it is not people who raise chickens in their backyard, or the Indigenous cattle rancher who operates a local farm on sustainable principles, or the small fisherman or dairy farmer. Instead, the meat industry is a tiny handful of companies who hold a huge amount of power and ever-increasing market shares in their respective sectors.

Now let's turn to the concept of abolition. In its most general sense, "abolition" refers to stopping or ending something. But this general idea tends to take at least two different, more specific forms in our political discourse, which I will call *practice abolition* and *institutional abolition*. For an example of the former, we can stick to our topic of animal rights: Gary Francione advocates abolition of all animal use, arguing that *practices* of eating, using, wearing, abusing, and experimenting on animals are all morally unacceptable because they depend upon a fundamentally indefensible idea—that non-humans are appropriately treated as human property (2008). Meanwhile, the best examples of *institutional* abolition can be found within contemporary racial justice movements.[6] For example, movements to abolish prisons, police, immigration enforcement agencies like ICE, etc. would all count as "institutional abolitionisms" because they take institutions of policing, prisons, etc. rather than practices as their target.

While institutional and practice abolitionism are often deeply related to one another and commitments about institutional abolition can have implications for practice-abolition, as I'll discuss in greater detail in Section 3, they are in principle distinguishable. For the Black Panther Party, for instance, their demand to abolish police was not necessarily to abolish *practices* of policing but to abolish the specific institutions of policing in our society—namely, state and municipal police departments. This institutional demand was, for the Party, still compatible with the existence of community- or citizen-led

---

6 Though I would be remiss not to mention that there have been some arguments for institutional-abolition already advanced by animal liberation scholars, but focusing on a different type of institution: the US Department of Agriculture (https://newr epublic.com/article/164874/abolish-department-agriculture). Like other institutional abolitionisms, this proposal the USDA should be replaced by an alternative institution: the Department of Food.

safety patrols, or practices of "policing the police" as some have described them (Gross, 2015). Policing as a *practice* may be acceptable if said practice is carried out by alternative institutions, like the Party's own community patrols, rather than problematic government-funded institutions of policing.

Because I am advocating for abolishing the meat industry—which, again, refers to an interconnected set of corporate institutions—I consider it to be a form of institutional abolition, rather than practice abolition. This makes my approach different from the way in which the term "abolition" has primarily been used in the animal liberation movement, which has tended to refer to abolishing practices of animal use.[7] While I am sympathetic with the position of authors like Francione that practices of animal use are morally indefensible, no movement—and especially not one as small and resource-limited as ours—can succeed by targeting every instance of moral wrongdoing. Instead, I will argue that focusing our energy on abolishing the worst institutional actors, rather than on abolishing all practices of animal use, will not only have major strategic payoffs, but can also do more to advance the goals of practice abolitionists.

How "abolish the meat industry" Better Incorporates Strategic Lessons from Other Social Movements

When it comes to non-human animals, practice-abolition focuses on targeting all producers and consumers of animal products—an approach that, as I've already pointed out, turns figures who are more sympathetic in the eyes of the public, like the small dairy farmer, into enemies. Meanwhile, institutional abolition of the meat industry focuses on ridding our society of a handful of enormous mega-corporations that many more people, including that small dairy farmer, has reason to dislike, or even to hate.

Because the tiny handful of companies that comprise the meat industry are also responsible for a litany of social ills, from environmental damage to racial discrimination to union-busting to price-fixing to increasing mental illness to oppressing immigrants to the creation of new pandemics (McAlevey, 2016; Leonard, 2014; Marceau, 2019; Levitt, 2020; Sebo, 2022), to name just

---

7 Best (2014) objects to Francione's approach by pointing out that his version of abolitionism does not include a substantive, sustained critique of capitalism. Instead, Best calls for a "richer and more radical concept of abolitionism" that "returns to and renews" the "radical roots, pluralist tactics, and alliance politics orientation" of anti-slavery abolitionism in the US (47). I am sympathetic with this critique and take what I am offering here to be a proposal for a strategic vision that can accomplish said renewal.

a few, naming the meat industry as our target allows us to provide many more entry points into our cause than the "go vegan" or practice-focused demand. Any constituencies that are negatively impacted by the meat industry—such as labor and immigrant rights groups, racial justice groups, environmental groups, communities in places where meatpacking plants operate, and groups focused on public health and combatting violence—could be brought on board as potential allies in a fight for meat industry abolition. In fact, we can see the viability of this kind of coalition when we look at the extensive and diverse list of animal rights/welfare, labor, faith, public health, environment, and other groups which have endorsed the US Farm System Reform Act (2020), an act which aims to phase out factory farms or concentrated animal feeding operations (CAFOs) by 2040 and replace them with a food system that is better for animals, farmers, communities, and the environment.

With more entry points for workers, community groups, etc., we also expand the menu of tactics available to us, transcending our myopic focus on leveraging consumer-power and pursuing tactics that also use worker-power, community-power, and citizen-power. This can look like mobilizing voters to support legislation like the Farm System Reform Act, or organizing in workplaces and communities impacted by the meat industry to build toward actions like strikes or boycotts. Furthermore, focusing on the corporate institutions of meat industry gives us a straightforward way to choose our targets more carefully. For example, we can focus upon turning mega-corporations like Nestlé into the enemy, rather than the small dairy farmer. Targeting Nestlé is a better bet because most people, regardless of their attitude toward non-human animal liberation, can be moved to oppose Nestlé for some reason or another—whether for their role in environmental degradation (Grossman, 2014), use of child labor in their supply chains (Balch, 2021), etc.—while the small independent dairy farmer is more likely to garner a sympathetic public response.

At this point one might object that taking "abolish the meat industry" as our strategic frame, rather than focusing on changing consumer choices and individual practices of animal use, will backfire because without changing consumer practices first, consumers will revolt at the idea of the meat industry going away. This would be a worry for this approach if the demand "abolish the meat industry" meant that those institutions needed to disappear overnight. But institutional abolition, as prison/police abolitionists have argued at length, is not about getting rid of an institution overnight. It is rather about embarking upon a gradual process of transforming society in such a way that it no longer needs the institution in question to accomplish the goal that institution supposedly serves. In the case of police and prison abolition, activists argue that while police and prisons claim to serve the goal of "keeping the public safe," they fail spectacularly in doing so, and instead are responsible for *threatening* and *undermining* the safety of large swaths of the public, particularly black, brown, immigrant, and LGBTQ+ communities (Davis, 2003; Kaba, 2021). Police and prison abolitionists argue that the goal of "public safety" can be better achieved with entirely different institutions that better address the root causes of violent crime. By divesting funds from institutions of policing and prisons and re-investing those funds in things like our education system, health and mental health care, and in fulfilling, well-paid, unionized jobs, we can make more progress toward the goal of protecting public safety than we can with our current approach, which seems to take "more policing" and "expanding prisons" to be the default answer to all public safety issues. But, crucially, establishing and supporting alternative institutions that could address the root causes of threats to public safety is a long game. It's not simply about getting rid of police forces and prisons today, but transforming our society in such a way that these institutions become obsolete (Davis, 2003; Kaba, 2021). For this reason, while police/prison abolitionists take abolishing these institutions to be their "north star" or long-term goal, they focus in the near- and medium- term on public demands to defund those institutions and reinvest those funds in alternatives—on reducing our reliance upon these institutions as a society.

In the same vein, "abolish the meat industry" does not imply that the meat industry must vanish overnight. Rather, we need to think about the social function that the meat industry serves and ask whether that function can be better served, with less human, non-human, and environmental cost, by different institutions. Currently the goal the meat industry serves in our society is simple—providing food. But is the meat industry well-positioned to achieve this goal? In addition to all of the damage the meat industry has inflicted upon humans, non-humans and the planet, the industry is also beset by some fundamental inefficiencies that seem like they cannot be addressed through reform. In order to produce the enormous amount of meat, dairy, and fish that these companies produce today, our societies expend a huge amount of resources into growing feed for livestock and fish farms. Of all the soy grown in the United States, for example, 70% is grown specifically for livestock and fish feed (USDA, 2015). This contributes to deforestation, which in turn contributes to climate change and also to creating pandemics (Sebo, 2022). Furthermore, attempts to reform the meat industry in the US over the last several decades have consistently failed.[8] What if, instead of

---

8 One example is the Obama administration's attempt to reform the industry early

subsidizing these industries—which resist any kind of oversight or reform—with massive amounts of taxpayer dollars, we advocated for a divest/reinvest approach to those funds? Instead of US taxpayer money going into the pockets of top executives at companies like Tyson Foods (Leonard, 2014), we can take our cue from the demands articulated by police/prison abolitionists and advocate for public funds to be diverted from the industry and invested into local and sustainable food production.

In addition to allowing us to expand entry points into the animal liberation movement, this alternative approach to animal liberation also invites us to articulate and forge concrete connections to other movements for institutional abolition—such as the movements for police/prison abolition and abolition of immigration enforcement agencies like ICE (Immigration and Customs Enforcement) in the US. It invites mainstream animal liberationists, who have tended to view their cause as isolatable from these other movements, to consider showing up in solidarity for these movements and building bridges between them and the cause of animal liberation. This approach—of cultivating other movements and groups fighting for institutional abolition as allies, rather than enemies—makes even more strategic sense when we realize the fundamental interconnections between the institutions of policing, prisons, immigration enforcement, and the meat industry. One way that meat industry giants like Smithfield, for example, are able to maintain control over their workforces and successfully bust organizing efforts among workers is by threatening them with ICE raids (McAlevey, 2016). In addition, in recent years judges in the US have been increasingly diverting defendants from prison by sending them to "rehabs," which in reality are "little more than lucrative work camps for private industry" (Harris & Walter, 2017). One industry where judges send defendants is chicken processing, where defendants say that "they work you to death" *without pay* (Harris & Walter, 2017; see also Reese & Carr, 2020). So once we start to consider animal agriculture workers as potential allies to the animal rights movement, and start to see immigration enforcement like ICE as well as the criminal legal system as roadblocks to worker organizing, it can provide a strategic reason for us

in his presidency (Leonard, 2014). We can also point to a long legacy of failures to reform the industry on animal welfare grounds; for example, Marceau (2019) discusses the many ways in which the meat industry has managed to carve itself out of animal welfare and animal cruelty legislation with "standard industry practice exemption" clauses over the last several decades. As a January 2022 op-ed in the New York Times discussed, the industry has managed to evade many attempts at environmental regulation as well. (https://www.nytimes.com/video/opinion/1000 00008091680/climate-sustainability-agriculture-lobby.html) to show up in solidarity with groups and coalitions fighting to abolish these institutions.

Once we begin to see the various institutions in our society that are dedicated to caging, killing, torturing, and exploiting as fundamentally interconnected and dependent upon one another, the possibilities for collaboration and solidarity with movements to abolish these institutions are virtually endless.

Resituating Veganism

Where does all of this leave the practice of veganism? I do not mean to claim, as some leftists who foreground institutional change over individual choice do, that individual choices are simply irrelevant to the project of building a better world for non-human animals. However, I do think that by adopting an approach that foregrounds institutions we can start to *resituate* rather than abandon veganism as an animal liberation tactic.

While various forms of institutional abolition will, of course, center demands about divesting from and eventually abolishing institutions, they can also have implications for individual choice. For example, a police and prison abolitionist who is the victim of a grave wrongdoing should make every possible effort not to address that wrongdoing through the infrastructure of the criminal legal system but rather through alternative transformative justice approaches (Kaba, 2021). Someone who believes we should abolish ICE should not call that agency to deport their undocumented neighbors. Those who think we should abolish a given institution should, in general and wherever possible, try not to use or call upon the institution that they think should not exist. Those who want to abolish certain institutions, in other words, may think of themselves as having obligations as individuals to *prefigure* the world as we want it to exist in the future, without the institution in question. This involves making some individual choices so that one relies upon these institutions less or, ideally, not at all.

Likewise, someone who agrees that the meat industry should be abolished should make every possible effort to withhold support from that institution by using or purchasing its products: animal flesh and secretions. Since 99% of meat in the United States comes from factory farms (Anthis, 2019), which are operated by the major meat industry players, someone who agrees with the position of meat industry abolition should try their best to cut out 99% of their meat consumption. So even though I have argued that we should center an institutional demand, this institutional focus can result in a *de facto* endorsement of diets that are largely if not entirely vegetarian or vegan, given that these diets are how one can opt-out completely from supporting the meat industry. Encouraging people who agree that the meat industry must be abolished to adopt vegan diets, to the greatest extent they can, can also help us prefigure the world we want—a world without the meat industry. When people go vegan or greatly cut down on their consumption of animal products, it can help them realize that, rather than being joyless and austere, a world where everyone consumes far fewer or no animal products can joyful and abundant. It can be a world where people still enjoy eating, where they can still prepare cultural foods, and much more.

This approach gives people more entry points, not only into the idea of animal liberation, but into the practice of veganism itself. To see this, imagine the following scenario. A major animal rights organization invests, in partnership with worker-led and community-led organizations, in deep organizing in a community surrounding a Tyson Foods slaughterhouse facility. As a result of this deep organizing approach, the community starts to realize that Tyson's presence in their town harms them all—from workers, to workers' families, to non-human animals, to the environment in the community at large. They determine that they will pressure their government to divest from Tyson by withholding taxpayer subsidies, and also that they will boycott products made by Tyson Foods. Because Tyson Foods makes a huge share of the meat and dairy products on the market, a Tyson Foods boycott could be a way for people to try out reducing their consumption of animal products. Once they succeed in cutting out, say, 15% of their animal product consumption and realize they in doing so they didn't get sick or turn eating into a joyless activity, maybe the idea of cutting out a larger share of animal products wouldn't seem so impossible or scary. In this way, boycotts focused on specific industry players communities have many reasons to dislike could be an easier entry point into veganism as a practice. This shows how, in shifting our strategic focus away from the idea of practice-abolition and toward institutional-abolition, we can still make progress on the goals practice-abolitionists like Francione hold. The major players in the meat industry are responsible for promoting practices of animal use; they are, by leaps and bounds, the biggest promoters of those practices. So focusing our energy upon these players will end up doing more to end practices of animal use than the practice-abolitionist approach, which—mistakenly—foregrounds the moral imperative of ending all animal use as a practical strategy.

Resituating veganism in this way illuminates the kind of role that animal rights activists and vegans can play in a broader coalition which advocates for meat industry abolition, and why leftists should care about forging relationships with animal rights advocates and organizations. The meat industry, at

least in the US, has shown itself to be very adept at evading any sort of regulation, oversight, or reform. It has consolidated its influence in US politics
like few other industries and spends incredible amounts of money per year on
lobbying.[9] The fact that the major titans of this industry are deep-pocketed
and well-connected means advocating successfully for the industry's abolition will be very difficult without a mass movement behind the demand. Of
course, animal rights organizations, like any other coalition group, can bring
much-needed numbers to add to that movement. But there are also reasons
why the broader left should *specifically* want to work with animal rights activists and organizations in advancing an agenda of meat industry abolition.

To see this, let's consider what will happen if a bill like the Farm System
Reform Act starts to gain serious political momentum. We know exactly what
the major meat industry players will say, because they've already said it about
legislation like the Green New Deal—that the bill's sponsors and advocates
want to "take away your hamburger."[10] And even if this is not correct about
the Green New Deal, it is about Farm System Reform Act: if the bill achieves
its goal of phasing out CAFOs by 2040, the average person will not be able
to indulge in anywhere close to their current consumption of animal products.[11] So when the meat industry attempts to provoke outrage around this
point, they, unfortunately, will succeed in turning many people away from
the cause of meat industry abolition if we have not done the work to convince people that eating far fewer animal products is not going to make your
life worse (and may even make it better). Thankfully, this is something that
vegans and animal rights activists already do: they engage the communities
around them and ask them to take steps toward using fewer animal products.
In other words, in a broader agenda of meat industry abolition, there will be
a need for conversations about why and how one must greatly reduce one's
animal product consumption – conversations that animal rights activists are
already having. And while I have argued that these consumer-focused tactics
must be unseated from their central, almost totalizing place in animal rights
advocacy, that does not mean there is no place for them at all. If animal
rights activists continue to advocate for eating far fewer animal products—
specifically in the service of the alternative political vision I have suggested,
which has broader appeal and more entry points—perhaps we can succeed in
the project of building a mass movement to take on the meat industry that
does not immediately fall apart when the industry bombards consumers with

9 https://www.nytimes.com/video/opinion/100000008091680/climate-sustain
   ability-agriculture-lobby.html
10 https://newrepublic.com/article/153187/potency-republicans-hamburger-lie
11 https://sentientmedia.org/what-would-happen-if-the-u-s-banned-factory-farming/

messaging about their favorite foods disappearing.[12] So resituating veganism, in this way, can illuminate a path for how we can make animal liberation organizations and activists central and indispensable to a strategic vision that also appeals to the broader left.[13]

One might object that this "resituated veganism" is not applicable to other areas of animal exploitation such as the clothing industry, animal-based entertainment industries or animal experimentation industries, among others. But this is exactly the point. As I argued in section 1(c), a crucial mistake the movement currently makes is that, rather than focusing all of our energy the worst industries that do the vast majority of the harm to non-humans, humans and the planet, we spread our energy and resources out in an unstrategic fashion, attempting to mobilize against every violation of animal rights. The strategy that I advocate for here involves honing in on the biggest and

12 Understood this way, as one piece of an overall struggle to abolish the meat industry that involves taking on these industry's capitalist giants, vegans can help non-vegans develop a "critical engagement" with and an anti-capitalist perspective upon the food we eat, as Angela Davis, a prison abolitionist and vegan, suggests here:

I usually don't mention the fact that I'm vegan but I think it's the right time to talk about it because it's part of a revolutionary perspective...People don't think about the horrendous suffering that those animals endure simply to become food products to be consumed by human beings. And I think that the lack of critical engagement with the food that we eat demonstrates the extent to which the commodity form has become the primary way in which we perceive the world...And so I think that would really be revolutionary: to develop a kind of repertoire, a habit, of imagining the relations, the human relations and the nonhuman relations behind all of the objects that constitute our environment. (Davis, 2012, qtd. in Dickstein et al., 2020, p. 6).

13 The ways in which some AR organizations advocate for veganism may need to change in order to be helpful in advancing this agenda, however. Vegan advocacy in the context of this agenda needs to start from an acknowledgment that perfection in one's consumption choices is rarely possible. It should acknowledge that the dominant institutions of our society often constrain and shape the choices that we are able to make and the practices we are able to engage in. The person who lives in a food desert, for example, and who supports a family on a very low income and/or with multiple jobs, will likely not have many options for buying vegan food, or time to learn how to prepare that food. Our attitude toward people in this situation should not be to blame or shame—but rather stem from an understanding that we have collectively failed in creating alternative institutions outside of the meat industry upon which they can rely for food. Thus the remedy is not to wag our finger at this person and accuse them of not being committed to the cause, but rather to work with them and others who are similarly situated to develop institutions for food production outside of the meat industry.

worst actors, rather than targeting every use of animals. While this would, of course, leave morally unacceptable forms of animal exploitation untouched, what is worse—spreading ourselves too thin, so we have an impact nowhere, or concentrating all of our energy and resources on the worst violators, so that we have a real shot at making a difference for and with non-human animals? I think the answer is clear.

Conclusion

For those who are still persuaded by the idea that animal liberation should remain a single-issue cause, I invite you to reflect upon what we have accomplished for non-human animals after decades of treating animal liberation as a single-issue fight. What I see when I look at the movement as it stands today is a tiny handful of people standing within a big, mostly empty tent. And rather than spending our time recruiting more people to enter it, we instead spend time demanding greater purity from the tiny group of people clustered together in the tent. While this "purity" may make us feel good about ourselves, as we praise one another for our self-sacrificial commitment to non-humans, what do "pure" and self-sacrificing motives have to do with winning animal liberation? The dairy cow who suffers daily under a regime of meat industry exploitation does not care about the purity of your motives; she cares about her suffering coming to an end. The approach I suggest here gives us a roadmap for ending that suffering. In fact, it gives us a roadmap for ending an enormous amount of animal suffering; today's factory farms are responsible for the most animal suffering that has ever occurred in human history (Animal Equality, 2016).

But to follow this roadmap, we must admit that we need a mass movement in order to fight and win against the meat industry's most powerful players. Thankfully, mass movements have been built before, and we can learn from their successes. An important lesson from these movements is that a single-issue framing is a dead end. Foregrounding an agenda of meat industry abolition will better help us transcend single-issue framing and win a better world for us all, humans and non-humans alike.

Works Cited

Animal Equality. "Why Factory Farming Is the Largest Cause of Animal Abuse in History." animalequality.org, February 3, 2016. https://animalequality.org/news/why-factory-farming-is-the-largest-cause-of-animal-abuse-in-history/.

Anthis, Jacy Reese. "US Factory Farming Estimates." *Sentience Institute.* www.sentien ceinstitute.org, April 11, 2019. https://www.sentienceinstitute.org/us-factory-farm ing-estimates.

Balch, Oliver. "Mars, Nestlé and Hershey to Face Child Slavery Lawsuit in US." *The Guardian.* www.theguardian.com, February 12, 2021. https://www.theguardian. com/global-development/2021/feb/12/mars-nestle-and-hershey-to-face-landm ark-child-slavery-lawsuit-in-us.

Bangert, Dave. "Fair Oaks Farms Animal Abuse: Ex-worker Bonds Out, Never Leaves Jail as ICE Steps In." *Journal and Courier.* www.jconline.com. Accessed January 15, 2022. https://www.jconline.com/story/news/2019/07/24/fair-oaks-farms-ani mal-abuse-ex-worker-bonds-out-never-leaves-jail-ice-steps/1812523001/.

BDS Movement. "What Is BDS?" bdsmovement.net, April 25, 2016. https://bdsmovem ent.net/what-is-bds.

BDS Movement. "Get Involved." bdsmovement.net, January 14, 2022. https://bdsm ovement.net/get-involved/what-to-boycott.

Best, Steven. *The Politics of Total Liberation.* New York: Palgrave, 2014.

Burns, Stewart. *Daybreak of Freedom: The Montgomery Bus Boycott.* Chapel Hill, NC and London, UK: University of North Carolina Press, 1997.

Corkery, Michael, and David Yaffe-Bellany. "Meat Plant Closures Mean Pigs Are Gassed or Shot Instead." *New York Times,* www.nytimes.com, May 14, 2020. https://www. nytimes.com/2020/05/14/business/coronavirus-farmers-killing-pigs.html.

Creswell, Julie, Nicole Perlroth, and Noam Scheiber. "Ransomware Disrupts Meat Plants in Latest Attack on Critical U.S. Business." *New York Times,* www.nytimes.com, June 1, 2021. https://www.nytimes.com/2021/06/01/business/meat-plant-cybe rattack-jbs.html.

Davis, Angela Y. *Are Prisons Obsolete?.* New York: Seven Stories Press, 2003.

Deese, Brian, Sameera Fazili, and Bharat Ramamurti. "Addressing Concentration in the Meat-Processing Industry to Lower Food Prices for American Families." *The White House.* www.whitehouse.gov, September 8, 2021. https://www.whitehouse.gov/ briefing-room/blog/2021/09/08/addressing-concentration-in-the-meat-process ing-industry-to-lower-food-prices-for-american-families/.

Dickstein, Jonathan, Jan Dutkiewicz, Jishnu Guha-Majumdar, and Drew Robert Winter. "Veganism as Left Praxis." *Capitalism Nature Socialism* (2020). Doi: https://doi. org/10.1080/10455752.2020.1837895

Flesher, John. "Factory Farms Provide Abundant Food, But Environment Suffers." *PBS NewsHour.* www.pbs.org, February 6, 2020. https://www.pbs.org/newshour/econ omy/factory-farms-provide-abundant-food-but-environment-suffers.

Francione, Gary. *Animals as Persons: Essays on the Abolition of Animal Exploitation.* New York: Columbia University Press, 2008.

Gross, Terry. "'Policing The Police': How the Black Panthers Got Their Start." *WBUR.* www.wbur.org, September 23, 2015.https://www.wbur.org/npr/442801731/direc tor-chronicles-the-black-panthers-rise-new-tactics-were-needed.

Grossman, Elizabeth. "As Dairy Farms Grow Bigger, New Concerns about Pollution." *Yale E360*. e360.yale.edu, May 27, 2014. https://e360.yale.edu/features/as_dairy_farms_grow_bigger_new_concerns_about_pollution.

Harris, Amy Julia, and Shoshana Walter. "They Thought They Were Going to Rehab. They Ended Up in Chicken Processing Plants." *The World from PRX*. theworld.org, October 10, 2017. https://theworld.org/stories/2017-10-10/they-thought-they-were-going-rehab-they-ended-chicken-processing-plants.

Huget, Hailey. "How the Animal Rights Movement Hurts Its Own Cause." *Current Affairs*.www.currentaffairs.org, 2021. https://www.currentaffairs.org/2021/04/how-the-animal-rights-movement-hurts-its-own-cause.

IntraFish. "Business Intelligence Report: The World's 150 Largest Seafood Companies Now Account for $120 Billion in Sales." www.intrafish.com, August 26, 2019. https://www.intrafish.com/news/business-intelligence-report-the-worlds-150-largest-seafood-companies-now-account-for-120-billion-in-sales/2-1-655808.

Jones, Katie, Govind Bhutada, and Anshool Deshmukh. "MegaMilk: Charting Consolidation in the Dairy Industry." *Visual Capitalist*. www.visualcapitalist.com, August 21, 2020. https://www.visualcapitalist.com/megamilk-charting-consolidation-in-the-u-s-dairy-industry/.

Kaba, Mariame. *We Do This 'Til We Free Us*. Chicago, IL: Haymarket Books, 2021.

Kelloway, Claire. "Big Ag Eyes Big Aquaculture." *Food & Power*. www.foodandpower.net, February 28, 2019. https://www.foodandpower.net/latest/2019/02/28/big-ag-eyes-big-aquaculture.

Ko, Aph, and Syl Ko. *Aphro-Ism: Essays on Pop Culture, Feminism, and Black Veganism from Two Sisters*. Brooklyn, NY: Lantern Publishing, 2017.

Lamb, Robert, and Dave Roos. "What Was the Largest Protest in History?" *HowStuffWorks*. people.howstuffworks.com, October 5, 2012. https://people.howstuffworks.com/largest-protest.htm.

Leenaert, Tobias. "Thoughts on the 'Cube Of Truth' and Anonymous for the Voiceless." *The Vegan Strategist*. veganstrategist.org, July 16, 2018. http://veganstrategist.org/2018/07/16/thoughts-on-the-cube-of-truth-and-anonymous-for-the-voiceless/.

Leibler, Jessica H., Patricia A. Janulewicz, and Melissa J. Perry. "Prevalence of Serious Psychological Distress among Slaughterhouse Workers at a United States Beef Packing Plant." *Work* 57, no. 1 (2017): 105–109.

Leonard, Christopher. *The Meat Racket: The Secret Takeover of America's Food Business*. New York: Simon & Schuster, 2014.

Levitt, Tom. "Covid and Farm Animals: Nine Pandemics That Changed the World | Environment." *The Guardian*. www.theguardian.com, September 15, 2020. https://www.theguardian.com/environment/ng-interactive/2020/sep/15/covid-farm-animals-and-pandemics-diseases-that-changed-the-world.

Marceau, Justin F. *Beyond Cages Animal Law and Criminal Punishment*. Oxford, UK: Cambridge University Press, 2019.

McAlevey, Jane F. *No Shortcuts: Organizing for Power in the Gilded Age*. New York: Oxford University Press, 2016.

McConnell, Matt. "Workers' Rights Under Threat in US Meat and Poultry Plants." *HRW*. www.hrw.org, September 4, 2019. https://www.hrw.org/report/2019/09/04/when-were-dead-and-buried-our-bones-will-keep-hurting/workers-rights-under-threat.

Mercy For Animals. "Chilliwack Cattle Sales Workers to Be Jailed for Animal Cruelty." *Cision Canada*, 21 Dec. 2018, https://www.newswire.ca/news-releases/chilliwack-cattle-sales-workers-to-be-jailed-for-animal-cruelty-623012574.html.

Meyer, Mandy. "This Is How Many Vegans Are in the World Right Now (2021 Update)." *The VOU*. thevou.com, January 17, 2021. https://thevou.com/lifestyle/2019-the-world-of-vegan-but-how-many-vegans-are-in-the-world/.

Miles, Kathryn. "Entrance of Large-Scale Fisheries and Aquatic Farms Could Hamper Maine Aquaculture Industry." *US News and World Report*, https://www.usnews.com/, Oct. 14 2020. https://www.usnews.com/news/best-states/articles/2020-10-14/growth-of-large-scale-fisheries-could-hamper-maine-aquaculture-industry

Nagesh, Ashitha. "The Psychological Effects of Killing Animals on Slaughterhouse Workers." *Metro News*, metro.co.uk, December 31, 2017. https://metro.co.uk/2017/12/31/how-killing-animals-everyday-leaves-slaughterhouse-workers-traumatised-7175087/.

Nolan, Hamilton. "The Animal Legal Defense Fund Is Busting Its Union with a Smile." *In These Times*, January 13, 2021. https://inthesetimes.com/article/animal-legal-defense-fund-busting-union-labor.

Nuñez, Lissette. "Undercover Investigation Reveals Animal Cruelty in Tyson Farm." *47abc*. www.wmdt.com, December 14, 2017. https://www.wmdt.com/2017/12/undercover-investigation-reveals-animal-cruelty-in-tyson-farm/.

Payne, Charles M. *I've Got the Light of Freedom: The Organizing Tradition and the Mississippi Freedom Struggle*, Berkeley and Los Angeles, CA: University of California Press, 1995.

Pendergrast, Nick P. "PETA, Patriarchy and Intersectionality." *Animal Studies Journal* 7, no. 1 (2018): 59–79.

Reece, Ashanté M., and Randolph Carr. "Overthrowing the Food System's Plantation Paradigm." *Civil Eats*, civileats.com, June 19, 2020. https://civileats.com/2020/06/19/op-ed-overthrowing-the-food-systems-plantation-paradigm/

Reynolds, Maura, Sean McMinn, Janaki Chadha, and Renuka Rayasam. "America's Meat Supply Is Cheap and Efficient. Covid-19 Showed Why That's a Problem." *Politico*, www.politico.com, September 23, 2021. https://www.politico.com/news/2021/09/23/coronavirus-cheap-meatpacking-513559.

Richards, Emma, Tania Signal, and Nik Taylor. "A Different Cut? Comparing Attitudes toward Animals and Propensity for Aggression within Two Primary Industry Cohorts—Farmers and Meatworkers." *Society & Animals* 21, no. 4 (2013): 395–413.

Roberts, Spencer. "Boycotting Animal Products as a Collective Act of Protest." *Current Affairs*. www.currentaffairs.org, March 4, 2021. https://www.currentaffairs.org/2021/03/boycotting-animal-products-as-a-collective-act-of-protest.

Sebo, Jeff. *Saving Animals, Saving Ourselves: Why Animals Matter for Pandemics, Climate Change, and Other Catastrophes*. New York: Oxford University Press, 2022.

Sewell, Summer. "Small Farms Vanish Every Day in America's Dairyland: 'There Ain't No Future In Dairy' | Food | The Guardian." *The Guardian*. www.theguardian.com, July 21, 2021. https://www.theguardian.com/environment/2021/jul/21/small-farms-vanish-every-day-in-americas-dairyland-there-aint-no-future-in-dairy.

Smith, Georgie. "What the Pandemic Revealed about the Meat Supply Chain." *Fortune*. fortune.com. Accessed January 15, 2022. https://fortune.com/2021/06/24/what-the-pandemic-revealed-about-the-meat-supply-chain/.

South Florida Sun-Sentinel. "Photos: Sexy PETA Protests Around the Globe." www.sun-sentinel.com, July 23, 2014. https://www.sun-sentinel.com/features/sfl-petaprotests.pg-photogallery.html.

Starostinetskaya, Anna. "VegNews Exclusive: The Story Behind No Evil Foods and Its Major Labor Controversy." VegNews.com, August 14, 2020. https://vegnews.com/2020/8/vegnews-exclusive-the-story-behind-no-evil-foods-and-its-major-labor-controversy.

Suozzo, Andrea, Maryam Jameel, Michael Grabell, and Bernice Yeung. "Your Free-Range Organic Chicken May Have Been Processed at a Large Industrial Poultry Plant." *ProPublica*. www.propublica.org, December 28, 2021. https://www.propublica.org/article/your-free-range-organic-chicken-may-have-been-processed-at-a-large-industrial-poultry-plant?utm_source=twitter&utm_medium=social.

Treisman, Rachel. "Meatpacking Companies, OSHA Face Investigation Over Coronavirus in Plants." NPR.org. www.npr.org, February 1, 2021. https://www.npr.org/sections/coronavirus-live-updates/2021/02/01/962877199/meatpacking-companies-osha-face-investigation-over-coronavirus-in-plants.

US Department of Agriculture (USDA). "USDA Coexistence Factsheets: Soybeans." Office of Communications, https://www.usda.gov/sites/default/files/documents/coexistence-soybeans-factsheet.pdf

Willis, Derek. "Lobbying by PETA." *ProPublica*. projects.propublica.org, February 27, 2017. https://projects.propublica.org/represent/lobbying/300924814.

Zimmerman, Bill. "Opinion | The Four Stages of the Antiwar Movement (Published 2017)." *New York Times*, www.nytimes.com, October 24, 2017. https://www.nytimes.com/2017/10/24/opinion/vietnam-antiwar-movement.html.

Animal Liberation, Class and Direct Action for Total Liberation

WILL BOISSEAU

"The struggle should be unified", Magaly Licolli, the co-founder of labour rights organisation Venceremos tells me, "we have to be in unity to fight against these systems that are oppressing humans, that are oppressing the animals and that are destroying our environment".[1] Venceremos is a worker-based organization in Arkansas whose mission is to ensure the human rights of poultry workers; the group was founded in 2019 by workers, predominantly women and Black Brown Indigenous People of Color (BBIPOC). Throughout the Covid-19 pandemic Venceremos organised poultry workers to take on the might of multination food giant Tyson Foods. During the pandemic workers in processing plants feared for their lives as they were faced with cramped, unsanitary working conditions and unsafe line speeds. In 2020 Venceremos organised the first strike of poultry workers in Arkansas and achieved a historic victory in forcing Tyson to maintain staggered shifts which increased social distancing for workers.[2] Licolli explains that there has been some support for the poultry workers from the animal advocacy movement, including the mainstream animal protection group the Humane League who were targeting Tyson from an animal welfare perspective and offered Venceremos support in promoting their online campaigns and media outreach. However, Licolli believes that there is still a lot of work to be done in building solidarity alliances between workers and advocates for animals:

> There's a lot of work to do especially amongst the white [animal rights] community... to really unpack the racism and classism when talking about workers. The workers in meat processing plants are also victims of the system, and if we don't

1 Interview with Magaly Licolli, February 2022.
2 Ibid.

understand this then we are always going to be fighting against each other and not against our common enemy which is the [meat] companies and the system.[3]

Magaly believes that campaigns that unite labour organizations and animal rights advocates will focus on transforming our food systems to a way of life that is: "better for our wellbeing, our environment and everything". Such campaigns would highlight the exploitation of both workers and animals under capitalism. This chapter explores the relationship between the animal protection movement and workers in animal exploiting industries, particularly in slaughterhouses, and asks how we can build social justice campaigns that seek to protect workers, animals and the environment.

This chapter takes a Critical Animal Studies and Anarchist Studies approach to explore the precarious class position of workers in the animal-industrial complex in relation to direct action for animal liberation. The animal-industrial complex refers to the totality of economic exploitation of animals which is intertwined with the capitalist system in multiple ways, from the meat and dairy industries, to animal testing, medicine, clothing, work animals and transport, breeding for pets, and entertainment. The precarious class position, or precariat, refers to an emerging class caused by neo-liberal policies in which people, including migrant employees, are "living and working precariously, usually in a series of short-term jobs, without recourse to stable occupational identities or careers, social protection or relevant protective regulation".[4]

Through an intersectional class analysis we can learn a great deal about direct action for total liberation. It is worth defining three key terms here: intersectional class analysis, direct action and total liberation. The concept of intersectionality relates to Kimberlé Crenshaw's approach which outlines the way that different social categories of power such as gender, race and class function in an overlapping way or rely on the same groundings such as dismissal of the "other".[5] Intersectionality could theoretically show how categories such as gender, race and class overlap, or focus on how intersectionality is experienced by an individual who is oppressed in a variety of ways. Intersectionality has been developed by BBIPOC theorists such as Amie

---

3 Ibid.
4 M. Savage, *Social Class in the 21st Century* (London: Penguin Random House, 2015), p. 351.
5 K. Crenshaw, *On Intersectionality: Essential Writings* (New York: New Press, 2019). Intersectionality emerged from black feminists and highlighted the lived experience of oppression, it has since been used by (white) social movement activists who campaign against different forms of oppression but without an awareness of lived experience.

Breeze Harper and the Sistah Vegan network; Harper's work reveals how racism and sexism operate within the animal rights movement and frames veganism "in an intersectional way [...] that is inclusive and inviting to a majority of non-white people who are trying to survive through and fight against systemic racism".[6] An intersectional class analysis focuses on these connections and is intended as a corrective to earlier forms of (Marxist) class analysis which ignored intersecting oppressions such as race and gender. Direct action is an "action without intermediaries, whereby an individual or a group uses their own power and resources to change reality in a desired direction" and which demands "taking social change into one's own hands, by intervening directly in a situation rather than appealing to an external agent (typically a government) for its rectification".[7] Direct action has a long association with animal liberation and animal liberation activists rightly take pride in this connection. Total liberation is an activist philosophy that simultaneously campaigns for human, animal and Earth liberation and aims "to advance an anti-capitalist and, more generally anti-hierarchical politics" that seeks to "dismantle all structures of exploitation, domination, oppression, torture, killing, and power in favour of decentralising and democratizing society".[8] This is important because through a total liberation framework, inspired by intersectionality, animal liberation activists will no longer engage in single issue campaigning for animals that ignores other forms of oppression.

The chapter is divided into four sections: the first section briefly considers the current conditions for workers in the animal-industrial complex, notably in slaughterhouses, in which precarious workers are exploited and subjected to appalling health and safety conditions. The second section considers the traditional response to slaughterhouse workers by groups such as the Animal Liberation Front (ALF) and Stop Huntingdon Animal Cruelty (SHAC), who regarded these workers as enemies in the struggle for animal rights. The material in this section is derived from my PhD research, which explored the relationship between the direct action and legislative wings of the animal rights movement in the UK, in which I interviewed over fifty animal

---

6 A. Breeze Harper, "Veganism Should Always 'Trump' Intersectionality: Make Veganism Great [and White] Again!" May 21, 2016, http://www.sistahvegan. com/2016/05/21/veganism-should-always-trump-intersectionality-make-vegan ism-great-and-white-again/

7 U. Gordon, *Anarchy Alive!: Anti-authoritarian Politics from Practice to Theory* (London: Pluto Press, 2008), p. 17.

8 S. Best, A. J. Nocella II, R. Kahn, C. Gigliotti, L. Kemmerer, 'Introducing Critical Animal Studies', *Animal Liberation Philosophy and Policy Journal*, Vol. 5, No. 1. (2007), p. 5.

rights activists. In the third section I discuss an approach in which vegan activists link the exploitation of workers in the animal-industrial complex to the exploitation of animals as a key reason to boycott the meat and dairy industries, an example of such a group is the Food Empowerment Project. The conclusion of the chapter will point to ways that animal liberationists can build solidarity and take diverse forms of direct action that promotes total liberation and social justice.

I argue that coercive or violent actions against individual workers are contradictory to the ideals of total liberation. However, other activists will agree with American ecophilosopher and anarcho-primitivist Derrick Jensen's assertion that "anybody's freedom from being exploited will *always* come at the expense of the oppressor's ability to exploit".[9] Jensen stipulates that the "freedom" of animals "to survive will come at the expense of those who profit" from their destruction.[10] In the chapter I do not aim to provide all the answers, but rather aim to provoke a discussion which I hope will be useful for vegans, animal liberationists and trade unionists (members of a trade union, organizations set up to protect and advance the interests of the working class) who want to build coalitions based on total liberation as we work towards a world free from human and animal oppression. When I talk about a lack of intersectionality amongst animal rights activists, I am talking about activists groups which are "overwhelmingly white and privileged, insensitive to class oppression and the lack of diversity within their movements".[11] It is important to note that many BBIPOC scholar-activists such as Aph and Syl Ko, Julia Feliz, Christopher Sebastian, and Amie Breeze Harper have been doing intersectional advocacy work for decades.[12]

This chapter focuses on animals and humans who are exploited by the meat and dairy industry, this is partly due to word length limitations. However, the meat and dairy industry is also an appropriate entry point for these discussions because of the hyper exploitation of workers in the meat industry which is cause by the workers' precarious class position. Animal

---

9 D. Jensen, 'Preface', in W. Churchill, M. Ryan, *Pacifism as Pathology: Reflections on the Role of Armed Stuggle in North America* (Edinburgh: AK Press, 2007), p. 22.

10 Ibid.

11 S. Best, *The Politics of Total Liberation: Revolution for the 21st Century* (Basingstoke: Palgrave Macmillan, 2014), p. 85.

12 A. Breeze Harper (ed.), *Sistah Vegan: Black Female Vegans Speak on Food, Identity, Health, and Society* (New York: Lantern Books, 2010); S. Ko, A. Ko, *Aphro-Ism: Essays on Pop Culture, Feminism and Black Veganism from Two Sisters* (New York: Lantern, 2017); J. Feliz, 'Racialized Speciesism?', August 29, 2018, https://medium.com/@jd.feliz/racialized-speciesism; J. Feliz Brueck, *Veganism in an Oppressive World: A Vegans-of-Colour Community Project* (Sanctuary, 2017).

advocates have raised the issue of workers' rights in other spheres of animal oppression, for instance even SHAC were prepared to highlight the poor working conditions at Huntingdon Life Sciences, which included underqualified employees being forced to miss breaks and work overtime.[13] That said, in the animal experimentation industry the highly educated and highly paid status of (some) workers makes them less obvious recipients of class solidarity. For instance, one ALF activist asked:

> Have you ever come across a poor vivisector? Go into the ultra-wealthy areas of either town, city or country, find the most expensive properties… and there you will find the average vivisector.[14]

Of course, debates about the merits of solidarity and the class position of different groups of workers based on their wealth, status and perceived educational background will take place amongst animal rights activists and there are no easy answers to these dilemmas.

I should also note that in the chapter I discuss exploited animals as distinct from exploited workers, but I take on board the long held view of animal activists, such as Henry Salt, that "the labour of animals has been interwoven with the labour of man [sic] in the fabric of human society, it seems wiser to claim for animals their due rights, as a part of that organisation": members of the working class.[15]

Human Workers in the Animal-Industrial Complex

The animal-industrial complex has many different aspects and features (it encompasses all sectors in which animals are used for profit) and conditions will vary greatly for humans and other animals. Most animals caught in the animal-industrial complex do not simply have limited life chances but are bred into existence in ways which best serve the industries that exploit them, their very existence is based on their use as a resource, they are tortured, turned into living commodities and killed for consumption. In this section I will briefly consider workers in the meat industry, where conditions for human workers have been particularly poor. Such a consideration helps us to see that humans and animals are exploited in overlapping ways by these

---

13 SHAC Newsletter, No. 42, July/August 2006.
14 *ALF Supporters' Group Newsletter*, No. 6, August 1983, p. 7.
15 H. S. Salt, 'Have Animals Rights?', *Human Review*, January 1908, Vol. 8.

industries, and that the exploitation of humans is a factor that animal liberationists should consider when engaging in campaigns against the meat industry.

In Europe the meat industry employs around 1 million workers, many of these are precarious workers on agency contracts, with zero-hours contracts and no statutory sick pay.[16] Because of these poor working conditions and job insecurity, accidents are common and bullying and harassment by management is rife.[17]

A 2010 Equality and Human Rights Commission report found instances of widespread mistreatment and exploitation of workers in the UK meat industry, including demeaning abuse from managers and sexual harassment.[18] A fifth of workers reported being physically abused by managers, a third of workers had experience or witnessed bullying and harassment. Sexual harassment was rife, including mistreatment of pregnant workers which led directly to miscarriages.[19] During the Covid-19 pandemic it was clear that the crammed unsanitary conditions for slaughterhouse workers meant that such buildings became Covid-19 super spreading hotspots.[20]

The meat industry in the UK and Europe has traditionally hired cross-border and migrant workers to take advantage of their precarious status.[21] Many of those employed in the meat industry in Western Europe come from Central and Eastern Europe, they are then employed by agencies who deduct wages for accommodation, transportation and equipment.[22] Workers

16 E. McSweeney, H. Young, "'The whole system is rotten': Life Inside Europe's Meat Industry", *Guardian*, September 28, 2021, https://www.theguardian.com/environment/2021/sep/28/the-whole-system-is-rotten-life-inside-europes-meat-industry

17 F. Lawrence, K. McVeigh, "'I'm not a slave, I just can't speak English'—Life in the Meat Industry", *Guardian*, March 13, 2010, https://www.theguardian.com/society/2010/mar/13/life-meat-industry-report-ehrc

18 F. Lawrence, K. McVeigh, "'I'm not a slave, I just can't speak English'—Life in the Meat Industry", *Guardian*, March 13, 2010, https://www.theguardian.com/society/2010/mar/13/life-meat-industry-report-ehrc

19 Ibid.

20 European Federation of Food Agriculture and Tourism Trade Unions, Covid-19 outbreaks in slaughterhouses and meat processing plants: State of affairs and demands for action at EU level (EFFAT, September 7, 2020), https://effat.org/wp-content/uploads/2020/09/Covid-19-outbreaks-in-slaughterhouses-and-meat-processing-plants-State-of-affairs-and-demands-for-action-at-EU-level-7.09.2020.pdf

21 Ibid.

22 ibid

are housed in overcrowded accommodation which is often owned by the employer.[23]

Despite these difficult circumstances, trade unions such as Unite the Union in the UK, Services Industrial Professional and Technical Union in Ireland and the Gewerkschaft Nahrung-Genuss-Gaststätten (Food, Beverages and Catering union) in Germany have been organizing within the meat industry. In 2020 there were walk outs by workers to protest against the lack of safety measures and lack of social distancing during the Covid pandemic.[24] The League of United Latin American Citizens in the USA called for a boycott of the meat industry in 2020 to protect workers from Covid.[25] The poor conditions for workers is directly linked to the cost and demand for cheap meat. In 2020 during the Covid pandemic there was a demand for cheap meat in the UK as people started to panic buy, this led to a 40% increase in "production levels" in the meat industry.[26] The link between the increased demand for meat and the poor conditions for workers is something that activists should bear in mind as they encourage veganism, promote boycotts of certain employers, and even engage in economic sabotage—such campaigns would increase the cost of meat which could have beneficial implications for these workers leading to "win-win" campaigns in which the bargaining conditions for workers improve as demand for meat decreases. However, as Raj Reddy explains in a chapter in this volume, this presents a further danger in that intersectionality can be used in a way in which the oppression of workers is only raised to the extent that the interests of workers (and other marginalized groups) are seen to align with the interests of the animals.

Single Issue Direct Action Approach

In this section I briefly explore the approach of the Animal Liberation Front (ALF) and Stop Huntingdon Animal Cruelty (SHAC), these are two significant groups to consider because they are perhaps the most well-known

23 Ibid.
24 European Federation of Food Agriculture and Tourism Trade Unions, Covid-19 outbreaks in slaughterhouses and meat processing plants: State of affairs and demands for action at EU level (EFFAT, September 7, 2020).
25 A. Starotientskaya, 'Latino Civil Rights Group Calls for Meat Boycott to Protect Workers from Covid 19', *Veg News*, May 1, 2020, https://vegnews.com/2020/5/latino-civil-rights-group-calls-for-meat-boycott-to-protect-workers-from-covid-19
26 European Federation of Food Agriculture and Tourism Trade Unions, Covid-19 outbreaks in slaughterhouses and meat processing plants: State of affairs and demands for action at EU level (EFFAT, September 7, 2020).

animal rights groups in Europe and North America in terms of the amount of direct action undertaken, however they have traditionally failed to take an intersectional approach because they have ignored the oppression of human workers in the animal-industrial complex. ALF and SHAC have traditionally taken a negative view of workers in animal abusing industries, typically viewing them as outside the scope of solidarity[27] and even legitimate targets of coercive direct action. Examples of coercive direct action allegedly carried out by the campaign movement inspired by SHAC included: "razor blade letters, bomb threats or bomb attacks, arson, harassment, death threats, and physical assaults", typically against companies who did business with SHAC.[28] Such tactics ignore the concept of total liberation because by targeting individual workers who are in precarious positions, animal rights groups fail to recognize that workers are also exploited by the meat industry.

SHAC took a negative view of human workers in the animal-industrial complex. One SHAC activist told me that it is not the case that all animal rights activists would support all exploited workers and if groups "perceive that person [or group of workers] to be an oppressor they lose our solidarity"; for instance, the police, prison officers and slaughterhouse workers may not be appropriate candidates for solidarity (interview with anonymous SHAC activist). This is problematic because it ignores the fact that humans working in the meat industry are also exploited and work in extremely poor and unsafe conditions, and the exploitation of these workers relies on the fact that they are often BBIPOC, often immigrants, undocumented or otherwise precarious workers. This means that the predominantly white animal rights movement has chosen to deny BBIPOC workers solidarity and therefore closed the door to building social justice movements that combine human and animal rights.

Another ALF and SHAC activist told me: "we wouldn't really have sympathy for workers in slaughterhouses, just like we wouldn't have sympathy with Nazi officers campaigning for better conditions while they gas people". One SHAC activist linked the campaign against Huntingdon Life Sciences and its associates with freedom fighters who resisted the holocaust:

> In Germany during the war there were [concentration] camps… and there were people not working directly in the camps, but working indirectly with them,

---

27 Such solidarity could involve offering moral and material support to those who directly struggle against their own oppression.

28 S. Best, A. J. Nocella II, 'Behind the Mask: Uncovering the Animal Liberation Front', in S. Best, A. J. Nocella II (eds.), *Terrorists or Freedom Fighters? Reflections on the Liberation of Animals* (New York: Lantern Books, 2004), pp. 34–36.

supplying food or whatever at the camp or just outside and being paid by the Nazis and my view is the same as that really, I wouldn't support them. The same as I wouldn't support someone working in a slaughterhouse no matter what (interview conducted by the author).

Such comparisons with the holocaust, and indeed with slavery, are dangerous because they instrumentalist the suffering of racialized groups without any sense of solidarity with those groups. As law professor Justin Marceau explains, in the case of slavery analogies "the [animal rights] movement wants it both ways when it comes to histories of racism—it seeks to analogize the suffering of black bodies when it is useful, and to ignore it when it is inconvenient".[29] Scholar-activist Christopher Sebastian McJetters has explained that in such situations BBIPOC experiences become a prop for "Neo-liberal white guilt" and instead of making such incendiary comparisons, animal rights activists should "amplify the voices of marginalized people" and "attempt to understand how layered oppressions impact different groups to maximize our impact and build a broader, more inclusive community".[30]

People for the Ethical Treatment of Animals (PETA) have also drawn comparisons between the animal-industrial complex and the holocaust and in doing so have inappropriately used holocaust imagery.[31] PETA's campaign has alienated potential allies in other social justice movements and can be seen as anti-Semitic.[32] Clearly, PETA and the activists quoted above use the concept of speciesism, which suggests that harming an animal and harming a human are morally equivalent. Perhaps in this instance the concept of speciesism is somewhat contradictory to the concept of total liberation, because it means that activists will deny solidarity to a group of workers who are exploited by an intersecting form of oppression. Dismissing workers in the animal-industrial complex as the moral equivalent of Nazi collaborators seems grossly exaggerated and could cause deep and unnecessary offence. Such an approach would negate the spirit of total liberation which focuses on the intersectionality of oppression and on overarching systems of domination

29 J. Marceau, *Beyond Cages: Animal Law and Criminal Punishment* (Cambridge: Cambridge University Press, 2019), p. 153.
30 C. Sebastian McJetters, "The Prop of Black People in White Self Perceptions: Revisiting the Slavery Comparison", <u>Sistah Vegan, December 28, 2015, http://sistahvegan. com/2015/12/28/the-prop-of-black-people-in-white-self-perceptions-revisiting-the-slavery-comparison-guest-post-christopher-sebastian-mcjetters/</u>
31 PETA, "PETA Germany's Holocaust Display Banned", March 27, 2009, https:// www.peta.org/blog/peta-germanys-holocaust-display-banned/
32 D. Teather, "'Holocaust on a plate' Angers US Jews", *Guardian*, 3 March 2003, https://www.theguardian.com/media/2003/mar/03/advertising.marketingandpr

that include the marginalization, exploitation and oppression of dominated groups. Animal activists who dismiss slaughterhouse workers as the moral equivalent of concentration camp guards would contribute to the marginalization of these workers, and it would therefore neglect intersectional issues. Comparing animal slaughter to human genocide also uses the experiences and feelings of genocide victims and survivors instrumentally as a resource for animal rights campaigns. Finally, if animal activists are willing to make a comparison between slaughterhouse workers and concentration camp guards, then they must also accept their own position as the equivalent of Nazi collaborators, because they exist in a society that continuously perpetuates the abuse of animals.

I quote from the above ALF and SHAC activists not in any way to downplay the significance and bravery of the direct action undertaken by these activists, who in some instances received lengthy prison sentences for their courageous animal liberation activism, but to contribute to a conversation about how we can better promote animal liberation through total liberation. The example of PETA using holocaust and slavery imagery shows that mainstream animal advocacy groups, in perusing single issue campaigns, have ignored the experiences and struggles of BBIPOC which has meant that such animal advocacy campaigns have not followed an intersectional approach which takes into account the oppression of human workers in animal abusing industries.

Intersectional Approaches

There are signs that the mainstream and predominately white animal rights movement has begun to take on board the examples and experiences of the intersectional scholarship and activism carried out by BBIPOC vegans;[33] in recent years there has also been a shift away from traditional direct action for animal liberation towards an invitational vegan outreach approach. Vegan outreach means encouraging people to adopt a vegan diet by providing sample vegan food, often at "vegan festivals" such as VegFest UK but also as part of wider political campaigns such as Food Not Bombs (who provide vegan food to those who need it), McLibel (the anti-McDonalds campaign), Anarchist Teapot (who provide vegan meals at protest sites). The move towards a vegan outreach approach has concurrently led to a movement away from regarding workers in the animal-industrial complex as legitimate targets of coercive

---

33 Vegans of Color, "About", https://vegansofcolor.wordpress.com/about/; Sistah Vegan, http://sistahvegan.com

forms of direct action to viewing them as potential allies and victims of an interrelated form of oppression. This does not mean that animal rights activists will ignore the horrors that animals are put through or stop campaigning against all forms of animal abuse. Animal activists must also avoid denying agency to workers in animal abusing industries. There is a danger that animal rights activists morally infantilize workers in animal abusing industries, for instance by suggesting that because they are oppressed or marginalized they have no moral agency to choose whether to engage in certain practices. It is simply about recognizing that that the meat industry exploits both animals and workers in intersecting ways. As the vegan strategist Tobias Leenaert argues:

> The fact that what animals go through is worse, does not mean we shouldn't have compassion for the workers themselves. This isn't about some suffering-competition, but about seeing the problems of the system as a whole. I believe the horrible working conditions at slaughterhouses can in some cases be a helpful argument for people who don't get the "animal message".[34]

Leenaert believes that slaughterhouse workers "shouldn't be called 'evil' or 'bad people'... [because] the core problem is the animal-industrial complex, the system of exploiting animals which also has negative effects on the workers in the system".[35] There are numerous other examples of animal rights groups raising concern and awareness of the conditions of workers in the animal-industrial complex. An article on the vegan website *Surge* discusses slaughterhouse workers who experience post-traumatic stress disorder.[36] Vegan Canada list the animal rights benefits of veganism, the health and environmental benefits before asking: "How about after learning the tremendous amount of pain and suffering slaughterhouse workers have to endure? Is this a good reason to start to care?"[37] UK animal advocacy group Animal Aid have highlighted the fact that in the UK an average of two slaughterhouse

---

34 T. Leenaert, "Slaughterhouse Workers: The Meat Industry's Other Victims", August 5, 2016, http://veganstrategist.org/2016/08/05/slaughterhouse-workers-the-meat-industrys-other-victims/

35 Ibid.

36 A. Gough, "The Disturbing Link between Slaughterhouse Workers and PTSD", *Surge*, January 24, 2021, https://www.surgeactivism.org/articles/slaughterhouse-workers-and-ptsd

37 Vegan Society of Canada, "Strengthening Our Motivation: Compassion and Protecting the Health of Animal Agriculture Workers", February 6, 2019, https://www.vegancanada.org/news/article/2019/02/06/motivation-compassion-slaughterhouse-worker.html

workers per week suffer serious industries.[38] Katie Pevreall, the first LGBTQ+ employee at vegan news site LIVEKINDLY, has argued that slaughterhouse workers "represent a portion of the, often forgotten, human victims of the meat industry".[39] The move amongst animal rights activists to considering the conditions and experiences of workers in animal abusing industries is in part caused by the rise of an intersectional approach within animal rights. This can be a genuinely beneficial approach for workers and animal rights activists if joint campaigns are organised with the involvement of workers in the industry; on the other hand the conditions of workers could be mentioned by animal rights groups in a tokenistic way which makes no attempt to engage with the needs and interests of the workers.

It is right that vegan activists use everything in their arsenal to encourage people to stop consuming meat and dairy. However, there needs to be something deeper at work to avoid instrumentalizing the oppression of workers for other ends. PETA, who have a history of denying solidarity to other marginalized groups (for instance by running sexist ad campaigns),[40] launched a programme to train slaughterhouse workers to make vegan meat.[41]

BBIPOC scholar-activists, have critiqued the way that white social justice activists—including vegans—have used intersectionality in a tokenistic way. Aph and Syl Ko explain that "Intersectionality may be a fun word to toss around, but people are scared to make connections in their movements because they will have to create new blueprints for their activism".[42] Aph and Syl Ko explain that whilst intersectionality remains a useful tool to navigate current systems of oppression, it does little to help dismantle these oppressive systems:

> Intersectionality maps out the world that has been imposed on us; it doesn't begin the process of mapping out the future. More importantly, intersectionality deals with the external conditions of racism and oppression that impact our lives, but doesn't speak to the internal struggles that arise after colonization.[43]

38 Animal Aid, "Covid-19 Outbreaks in Slaughterhouses: Yet Another Reason to Opt for Cruelty-free Food", June 26, 2020, https://www.animalaid.org.uk/covid-19-slaughterhouses/

39 K. Pevreall, "Slaughterhouse Workers: The Forgotten Victims of the Meat Industry", *LiveKindly*, https://www.livekindly.co/slaughterhouse-workers-victims-meat-industry/

40 M. Deckha, "Disturbing Images: Peta and the Feminist Ethics of Animal Advocacy", *Ethics and the Environment*, Vol. 13, No. 2 (Autumn 2008), pp. 35–76.

41 L. Pritchett, "Former Slaughterhouse Workers Will Be Trained to Make Vegan Meat", https://www.livekindly.co/former-slaughterhouse-workers-make-vegan-meat/

42 S. Ko, A. Ko, *Aphro-Ism: Essays on Pop Culture, Feminism and Black Veganism from Two Sisters* (New York: Lantern, 2017), p. 30.

43 Ibid., pp. 131–132.

In order to be a genuinely intersectional campaign, PETA's retraining programme would need to be led by the workers or done with workers involvement, animal rights activists will need to go a long way to build trust and solidarity with exploited workers in the animal-industrial complex, and PETA has not engaged in this trust-building work. Animal rights activists also need to understand that the precarious situation of many of workers in the animal-industrial complex means that they are not in a position to simply retrain as vegan artisan chefs as PETA suggest.

There are many examples of these types of intersectional campaigns including in July 2020 the Animal Legal Defense Fund launching a whistle blower campaign to report Covid-19-related abuses towards animals and humans.[44] Also in 2020, the animal advocacy and environmental group Food and Water Watch formed a solidarity alliance with the poultry worker rights group Venceremos to file a complaint to the Federal Trade Commission regarding the safety concerns of employers at the meat industry giant Tyson.[45] Such campaigns are organised by BBIPOC workers and activists who experience oppression at the intersection of race, gender and class.

Total liberation campaigns should focus on all forms of oppression and animal liberationists can campaign for the liberation of both workers and animals. These total liberation campaigns are particularly important for activists who combine animal liberation with a wider socialist or anarchist philosophy. Groups like the Anarchist Teapot and Food Not Bombs provide this solidarity by distributing vegan food at protest sites, environmental or peace camps, on picket lines and at benefit gigs.[46] Feminist animal sanctuaries highlight the intersecting oppression of gender and species by providing safe spaces for victims of domestic abuse and their companion animals.[47] Total liberation campaigns have also combined promotion of veganism with other initiatives focused around local communities growing their own food such as the Black Food Sovereignty Collective.[48]

44 Z. Z. McNeill, "COVID-19 Exacerbating Systemic Racism and Abuse in Animal Agriculture", *Sentient Media*, September 10, 2020, https://sentientmedia.org/covid-19-exacerbating-systemic-racism-and-abuse-in-animal-agriculture/

45 Ibid.

46 K. McHenry, *Hungry for Peace: How You Can Help End Poverty and War with Food Not Bombs* (Tucson: See Sharp Press, 2012).

47 C. J. Adams, L. Gruen, "Groundwork", in C. J. Adams, L. Gruen (eds.), *Ecofeminism: Feminist Intersections with Other Animals & The Earth* (London: Bloomsbury, 2014).

48 J. Molidor, "The Food System Is Built on White Supremacy", *Sentient Media*, October 6, 2020, https://sentientmedia.org/the-food-system-is-built-on-white-supremacy/

Towards Total Liberation Campaigns

Launching a truly intersectional solidarity campaign based on total liberation would involve approaching the trade unions that organize workers in these industries, asking about their concerns, genuinely listening and learning and slowly building trust and developing a campaign for human and animal rights. Such work has been carried out by Venceremos, a worker-based organization in Arkansas whose mission is to ensure the human rights of poultry workers. Venceremos have engaged in solidarity campaigns with animal advocates and other social justice groups, as can be seen in the Sentient Media discussion "Collaboration and Activism: Strength Through Alliances".[49] Venceremos and their allies believe that the struggle for social justice is a journey of many years and includes learning from mistakes and trying different strategies.[50] Venceremos believe that consumers and workers can unite to put pressure on the supply chain to change conditions for workers and animals. Venceremos explain that the majority of workers in the poultry industry in Arkansas are immigrants and refugees who are in a precarious position and that meat companies thrive on profiting from the exploitation of animals and the labour of humans.[51] Engaging in intersectional solidarity campaigns should be done whilst honestly stating that, as vegans, our ultimate aim is that animals should not be killed and exploited for food, but also that humans should not be exploited. This will clearly be a difficult and messy process, as slaughter-house workers are engaging in a practice that animal rights activists believe is fundamentally wrong.

The Food Empowerment Project promotes a sustainable world by high-lighting the abuse of animals and depletion of natural resources caused by capitalist agricultural practices, and promotes veganism, access to healthy food and farm workers' rights. The Food Empowerment Project argue that "every day, 'meat'-processing workers are knowingly exposed to serious safety hazards in their workplace… Slaughterhouses and 'meat'-processing facilities symbolize suffering and death for animals and exploitation for workers".[52] Of course, this is tied in with the argument that "we can choose not to support this cycle of exploitation and suffering by simply adopting a vegan lifestyle".[53]

---

49 Sentient Media, "Sentient Sessions: Collaboration and Activism: Strength Through Alliances", October 22, 2020, https://www.youtube.com/watch?v=UxQ1NOlS q2Q&t=4950s
50 Ibid.
51 Interview with Magaly Licolli.
52 Food Empowerment Project, "Slaughterhouse Workers", https://foodispower.org/ human-labor-slavery/slaughterhouse-workers/
53 Ibid.

Animal liberationists will continue to engage in diverse forms of direct action, but considering the class position of the targets of militant direct action reveals some complications. In particular, animal liberation activism contradicts the concept of total liberation if working-class employees are targeted because such actions do not focus on overarching systems of domination which include the marginalization, exploitation and oppression of dominated groups. Animal activists who coercively target workers might be relying on their marginalization because the police would be less likely to intervene if an undocumented worker (for instance) rather than a CEO is targeted. In this situation workers are also used instrumentally, and as a resource and a tactical pawn, because pressure on their own lives is designed to produce an unrelated outcome—benefits for animals, which is ultimately caused by putting pressure on the animal abusing company. Workers in animal abusing industries are often in precarious positions, where many slaughterhouses use cross-border, undocumented or otherwise precarious workers, and this may prevent such workers from securing support from their employers or the police. Indeed, it is likely that these workers will also face hostility, coercion or racism from the police and employers. Animal activists should not create a situation in which someone losing their job is seen as a successful protest outcome, because the workers' precarious position might make it easier for companies to dismiss workers than to increase their security measures. The animal protection movement has also sought the incarceration of individual slaughterhouse workers for abusing animals. Justin Marceau explains that "the very effort to end one 'systematic, institutionalized' form of oppression (mistreatment of animals) by resorting to another (incarcerating humans) would be farcical if it were not taken so seriously by the [animal rights] movement itself".[54] By promoting and upholding the racist criminal justice system, animal advocates ignore the oppression of humans and forego the chance to build solidarity alliances against all forms of oppression. Marceau explains that mainstream animal advocacy groups in the USA have supported "incarceration, deportation, or criminal registration, among other punitive outcomes" and this has had the effect of totally denying solidarity to BBIPOC activists because "there is not a safe harbour or zone of activism in which race or class are irrelevant to efforts to promote social justice".[55]

Building solidarity campaigns for total liberation will be a long and difficult processes, but by engaging with trade unions and supporting workers in their struggles, animal liberation activists can build solidarity campaigns

---

54 J. Marceau, *Beyond Cages*, p. 152.
55 Ibid, p. 166.

to resist the exploitation of animals, workers and the planet. As Magaly Licolli from Venceremos argues, there needs to be a deeper understanding that workers are victims of the food system, rather than oppressors, and that "these corporations [in the meat industry] and this economic system is not sustainable any more".[56] Solidarity campaigns bringing together workers and animal rights advocates will not be easy to build, the chances of victory may seem remote, but it is our best shot at creating a just and peaceful world.

References

C. J. Adams, L. Gruen, "Groundwork", in C. J. Adams, L. Gruen (eds.), *Ecofeminism: Feminist Intersections with Other Animals & The Earth* (London: Bloomsbury, 2014).

ALF Supporters' Group Newsletter, No. 6, August 1983.

Animal Aid, *Covid-19 Outbreaks in Slaughterhouses: Yet Another Reason to Opt for Cruelty-free Food*, June 26, 2020, https://www.animalaid.org.uk/covid-19-slaughte rhouses/

S. Best, *The Politics of Total Liberation: Revolution for the 21st Century* (Basingstoke: Palgrave Macmillan, 2014).

S. Best, A. J. Nocella II, "Behind the Mask: Uncovering the Animal Liberation Front", in S. Best, A. J. Nocella II (eds.), *Terrorists or Freedom Fighters? Reflections on the Liberation of Animals* (New York: Lantern Books, 2004).

S. Best, A. J. Nocella II, R. Kahn, C. Gigliotti, L. Kemmerer, "Introducing Critical Animal Studies", *Animal Liberation Philosophy and Policy Journal*, Vol. 5, No. 1 (2007), pp. 4–5.

A. Breeze Harper (ed.), *Sistah Vegan: Black Female Vegans Speak on Food, Identity, Health, and Society* (New York: Lantern Books, 2010).

A. Breeze Harper. "Veganism Should Always 'Trump' Intersectionality: Make Veganism Great [and White] Again!" May 21, 2016, http://www.sistahvegan. com/2016/05/21/veganism-should-always-trump-intersectionality-make-vegan ism-great-and-white-again/

K. Crenshaw, *On Intersectionality: Essential Writings* (New York: New Press, 2019).

M. Deckha, "Disturbing Images: Peta and the Feminist Ethics of Animal Advocacy", *Ethics and the Environment*, Vol. 13, No. 2 (Autumn 2008), pp. 35–76.

European Federation of Food Agriculture and Tourism Trade Unions, *Covid-19 Outbreaks in Slaughterhouses and Meat Processing Plants: State of Affairs and Demands for Action at EU Level* (EFFAT, September 7, 2020), https://effat.org/wp-content/ uploads/2020/09/Covid-19-outbreaks-in-slaughterhouses-and-meat-processing- plants-State-of-affairs-and-demands-for-action-at-EU-level-7.09.2020.pdf

56 Interview with Magaly Licolli.

J. Feliz, "Racialized Speciesism?", August 29, 2018, https://medium.com/@jd.feliz/rac ialized-speciesism-991eb3653ba0

J. Feliz Brueck, *Veganism in an Oppressive World: A Vegans-of-Colour Community Project* (Sanctuary, 2017).

Food Empowerment Project, Slaughterhouse Workers, https://foodispower.org/human-labor-slavery/slaughterhouse-workers/

U. Gordon, *Anarchy Alive!: Anti-authoritarian Politics from Practice to Theory* (London: Pluto Press, 2008).

A. Gough, "The Disturbing Link between Slaughterhouse Workers and PTSD", *Surge*, January 24, 2021, https://www.surgeactivism.org/articles/slaughterhouse-work ers-and-ptsd

D. Jensen, "Preface", in W. Churchill, M. Ryan, *Pacifism as Pathology: Reflections on the Role of Armed Struggle in North America* (Edinburgh: AK Press, 2007).

S. Ko, A. Ko, *Aphro-Ism: Essays on Pop Culture, Feminism and Black Veganism from Two Sisters* (New York: Lantern, 2017).

F. Lawrence, K. McVeigh, "'I'm not a slave, I just can't speak English' – Life in the Meat Industry', *Guardian*, March 13, 2010, https://www.theguardian.com/society/ 2010/mar/13/life-meat-industry-report-ehrc

T. Leenaert, "Slaughterhouse Workers: The Meat Industry's Other Victims", August 5, 2016, http://veganstrategist.org/2016/08/05/slaughterhouse-workers-the-meat-industrys-other-victims/

J. Marceau, *Beyond Cages: Animal Law and Criminal Punishment* (Cambridge: Cambridge University Press, 2019).

Z. Z. McNeill, "COVID-19 Exacerbating Systemic Racism and Abuse in Animal Agriculture", *Sentient Media*, September 10, 2020, https://sentientmedia.org/ covid-19-exacerbating-systemic-racism-and-abuse-in-animal-agriculture/

K. McHenry, *Hungry for Peace: How You Can Help End Poverty and War with Food Not Bombs* (Tucson: See Sharp Press, 2012).

E. McSweeney, H. Young, "'The whole system is rotten': Life Inside Europe's Meat Industry", *Guardian*, September 28, 2021, https://www.theguardian.com/envi ronment/2021/sep/28/the-whole-system-is-rotten-life-inside-europes-meat-industry

J. Molidor, "The Food System Is Built on White Supremacy", *Sentient Media*, October 6, 2020, https://sentientmedia.org/the-food-system-is-built-on-white-supremacy/

PETA, "PETA Germany's Holocaust Display Banned", March 27, 2009, https://www. peta.org/blog/peta-germanys-holocaust-display-banned/

K. Pevreall, Slaughterhouse Workers: The Forgotten Victims of the Meat Industry, *LiveKindly*, https://www.livekindly.co/slaughterhouse-workers-victims-meat-industry/

L. Pritchett, "Former Slaughterhouse Workers Will Be Trained to Make Vegan Meat", https://www.livekindly.co/former-slaughterhouse-workers-make-vegan-meat/

H. S. Salt, "Have Animals Rights?", *Human Review*, January 1908, Vol. 8, http://www.henrysalt.co.uk/bibliography/essays/have-animals-rights

M. Savage, *Social Class in the 21ˢᵗ Century* (London: Penguin Random House, 2015).

C. Sebastian McJetters, "The Prop of Black People in White Self Perceptions: Revisiting the Slavery Comparison", *Sistah Vegan*, December 28, 2015, http://sistahvegan.com/2015/12/28/the-prop-of-black-people-in-white-self-perceptions-revisiting-the-slavery-comparison-guest-post-christopher-sebastian-mcjetters/.

Sentient Media, "Sentient Sessions: Collaboration and Activism: Strength Through Alliances", October 22, 2020, https://www.youtube.com/watch?v=UxQ1NOlSq2Q&t=4950s

SHAC Newsletter, No. 42, July/August 2006.

Sistah Vegan, http://sistahvegan.com

A. Starotientskaya, "Latino Civil Rights Group Calls for Meat Boycott to Protect Workers from Covid 19", *Veg News*, May 1, 2020, https://vegnews.com/2020/5/latino-civil-rights-group-calls-for-meat-boycott-to-protect-workers-from-covid-19

D. Teather, "'Holocaust on a plate' Angers US Jews", *Guardian*, March 3, 2003, https://www.theguardian.com/media/2003/mar/03/advertising.marketingandpr

Vegans of Color, "About", https://vegansofcolor.wordpress.com/about/.

Vegan Society of Canada, "Strengthening Our Motivation: Compassion and Protecting the Health of Animal Agriculture Workers", February 6, 2019, https://www.vegancanada.org/news/article/2019/02/06/motivation-compassion-slaughterhouse-worker.html

An Essay on Total Liberation: Marcusean Insights for Catalyzing Transformation

Dan Fischer

A 2021 study found that 56% of young people across ten countries believed "humanity is doomed." The researchers rightly warned against narratives of "individualizing 'the problem' of climate anxiety, with suggestions that the best response is for the individual to 'take action.'" However, they followed with the equally misguided suggestion that "such action needs to be particularly taken by those in power."[1] Those of us influenced by Frankfurt School theorist Herbert Marcuse's analysis consider it unwise to rely on "those in power." The world capitalist system's so-called solutions—from nuclear power and geo-engineering to "regenerative ranching" and even industrial-scale renewables—not only fail to resolve the climate crisis but bring their own comparable existential threats to humanity, animals and the planet.[2]

Animal liberation campaigners have all the more reason to feel hopelessness, given the overwhelming human supremacism pervading global civilization. This is especially true in affluent countries such as the United States where only 6% of humans are vegetarian (compared to 14% worldwide) and

---

1 Elizabeth Marks, Caroline Hickman, Panu Petteri Pihkala, Susan Clayton, Eric Lewandowski, Elouise E. Mayall, Britt Wray, Catriona Mellor, and Lise Van Susteren, "Young People's Voices on Climate Anxiety, Government Betrayal and Moral Injury: A Global Phenomenon," *Social Science Research Network*, September 7, 2021.
2 *Hoodwinked in the Hothouse: Resist False Solutions to Climate Change*, 3rd edn, eds. Lucia Amorelli, Dylan Gibson, and Tamra Gilbertson (California: Community Printers, 2021).
"Grazed and Confused? New Report Evaluates the Climate Impact of Grazing Livestock," *University of Oxford*, October 3, 2017, https://www.oxfordmartin.ox.ac.uk/news/2017-news-grazed-and-confused/.

where per-capita meat consumption is about three times the global average. As Hailey Huget counsels in this volume, "you may feel as though there is no way out." Josh Harper, formerly of Stop Huntingdon Animal Cruelty has elaborated on the overwhelming sense despair experienced by animal liberationists:

> I mean, you reach this point when you're an animal rights activist where you are such a statistically insignificant part of the population. You know, where everywhere you go, people are wrapped in the skins of creatures that you consider your equals. And you walk in the store, and it's a fucking atrocity exhibit everywhere you turn. You reach this point where you feel like no one cares. You know? No one cares ... because there has never been a human holocaust in history that can compare to the number of animal lives taken in one year. I mean, there's nothing. I mean, we kill more animals every year—every single year—than humans have ever walked on this planet. If you were to chain up and kill every person who ever lived—every human who ever lived!—you would not equal the number of animals killed for food. In one, single, year.[3]

Today's situation resembles the bleak scenario Marcuse confronted in 1964s *One-Dimensional Man*, where he argued that industrialized society's masses have been so bought-off and brainwashed that their thought had become entirely "one-dimensional," or uncritical. "The critical theory of society," Marcuse dismally concluded, "possesses no concepts which could bridge the gap between the present and its future; holding no promise and showing no success, it remains negative."[4] Marxist-humanist Raya Dunayevskaya aptly criticized Marcuse for analyzing only official labor leadership and ignoring the "powerful oppositional voice" at the rank-and-file level.[5] Going further, fellow critical theorist Erich Fromm described Marcuse's view as non-revolutionary, since "revolution was never based on hopelessness, nor can it ever be."[6]

3 Hailey Huget, "Abolish the Meat Industry: A Roadmap for Transforming Animal Liberation from a Single-Issue Cause into a Mass Movement." In Zane McNeill (ed.), *Building Multispecies Resistance Against Exploitation: Stories from the Frontlines of Labor and Animal Rights*. Peter Lang, 2024.
   David Naguib Pellow, *Total Liberation: The Power and Promise of Animal Rights and the Radical Earth Movement* (Minneapolis: University of Minnesota Press, 2014), ch. 2.
4 Herbert Marcuse, *One-Dimensional Man* (Boston: Beacon, 1964). Retrieved from Marxists Internet Archive, https://www.marcuse.org/herbert/pubs/64onedim/odmcontents.html.
5 Raya Dunayevskaya, "Reason and Revolution vs Conformity and Technology," *The Activist*, 1964. Retrieved from Wisconsin Historical Society, https://content.wisconsinhistory.org/digital/collection/p15932coll2/id/4237.
6 Erich Fromm, *The Revolution of Hope* (New York: Harper & Row, 1968), 8–9.

Fortunately, an explosion of anti-racist and anti-colonial uprisings, sweeping from the Global South to the North at the time of *One-Dimensional Man*'s publication, sent Marcuse in a far more hopeful trajectory. Had *One-Dimensional Man* focused more on the world's unindustrialized areas, Marcuse might have already encountered greater possibilities for resistance, represented for example by Algeria's struggle against French colonialism. Writing from Algeria, Martinique psychoanalyst Frantz Fanon in 1961 theorized a "total liberation" that, encompassing social and psychological decolonization, "involves every facet of the personality."[7] When *One-Dimensional Man* was published, protests against white supremacism and the Vietnam War swept the United States where Marcuse lived. By 1968, many such liberatory struggles comprised a "worldwide eruption of new social movements."[8]

In 1969s *An Essay on Liberation*, which had the working title "Beyond One-Dimensional Man,"[9] Marcuse described these movements as a "Great Refusal" of domination and correctly predicted their lasting impact.[10] According to Black feminist scholar Angela Davis, his former student, Marcuse welcomed the 1960s movements as "much needed fresh air when the world was suffocating."[11] These struggles gave space to emerging anti-speciesist concerns, such as when French youths in May 1968 demanded the liberation of zoo animals.[12] During the subsequent decade, vegetarian lifestyles and philosophies spread substantially, and the formation of groups such as the United Kingdom's Animal Liberation Front and the United States' MOVE, spread militant tactics in order to sabotage animal exploitation.[13]

---

7 Frantz Fanon, *The Wretched of the Earth*, trans. Richard Philcox (New York: Grove Press, 2004), 233.

8 George Katsiaficas, *The Imagination of the New Left: A Global Analysis of 1968* (Cambridge: South End Press, 1987), 1.

9 Douglas Kellner, "Introduction: Radical Politics, Marcuse, and the New Left," in *Herbert Marcuse: The New Left and the 1960s*, ed. Douglas Kellner (London: Routledge, 2005), 22.

10 Herbert Marcuse, *An Essay on Liberation* (London: Penguin, 1969). Retrieved from Marxists Internet Archive, https://www.marxists.org/reference/archive/marcuse/works/1969/essay-liberation.htm.

11 Angela Davis, "Angela Davis on Protest, 1968, and Her Old Teacher, Herbert Marcuse," *LitHub*, April 3, 2019, https://lithub.com/angela-davis-on-protest-1968-and-her-old-teacher-herbert-marcuse/.

12 Katsiaficas, *The Imagination of the New Left*, 102.

13 Pellow, *Total Liberation*, ch. 1. Pellow notes that "Many MOVE members were vegetarians and staunch animal rights activists" and quotes the organization: "we will take immediate action to stop anyone from beating a dog, throwing stones at birds, or causing similar impositions on innocent life."

Pessimistic accounts of the possibility for transformation continue to be undermined by the eruption of uprisings in our times. Soon after social scientists declared an "end of history" in the 1990s, the Zapatistas launched a global justice movement shattering the neoliberal consensus. Just as the 2011 anarcho-nihilist pamphlet *Desert* announced the impossibility of world revolution, the Arab Spring and Occupy movements emerged. In April 2020, Frank B Wilderson III's acclaimed *Afropessimism* announced a ghastly choice between white supremacy and apocalypse.[14] One month later, Black youths and their accomplices launched the United States' largest uprisings in decades and helped bring the idea of police abolition into the mainstream.

Marcuse's trajectory demonstrates that even as we recognize the possibility of annihilation and the urgency it brings, we can transcend despair by organizing toward revolutionary alternatives.

A Place of Eros

The countercultural consciousness of the 1960s signified a resurgence of what Freud had labeled Eros—the life instinct—against a death-desiring society. As Marcuse's *Essay on Liberation* explained, young radicals eschewed ubiquitously-advertised "false needs" and instead sought truly "vital needs" including "the abolition of injustice and misery" and "to be freed from the administered comforts and the destructive productivity of the exploitative society, freed from smooth heteronomy." He envisioned "a society in which the abolition of poverty and toil terminates in a universe where the sensuous, the playful, the calm, and the beautiful become forms of existence." There would be an "aesthetic rather than repressive environment" with "parks and gardens rather than highways and parking lots." Even productive activities would become as playful and creative as painting or poetry. Our entire lives would resemble "the imagination, the beautiful, the dream."

Recognizing that a post-capitalist society could provide to each according to their true needs at a level "considerably lower than that of advanced capitalist productivity which is geared toward obscene affluence and waste",

---

14   See the following critiques of these pessimistic notions and texts.

     Mike Leach, "Chiapas: The End of 'the end of history'," *Green Left*, October 3, 1995. https://www.greenleft.org.au/content/chiapas-end-end-history.

     Huey Hewitt, "To Save the World," *Spectre Journal*, July 26, 2021, https://spectre journal.com/to-save-the-world/.

     John Warwick, "Desert: A Review Essay," *Organise!*, October 9, 2019, retrieved from The Anarchist Library, https://theanarchistlibrary.org/library/john-warwick-desert-a-review-essay.

Marcuse declared that "utopia" itself was possible. It no longer referred to "that which has 'no place'" (the literal meaning in ancient Greek) but rather to "that which is blocked from coming about by the power of the established societies." If such claims of abundance were already true in 1969, they have become even more true over the subsequent decades of increasing productivity along with an unconscionable wealth gap.

Accordingly, today's global movements often complement their necessary demands for reparations and demilitarization with radically anti-consumerist understandings of a good life. As documented in the 2019 collection *Pluriverse: A Post-Development Dictionary*, these ideas converge with concepts around the world including *buen vivir* (living well) across Latin America, *ubuntu* (humanness) in southern Africa and *swaraj* (self-rule) in South Asia.[15] Spearheaded by the world's poorer, Indigenous, Black and brown communities, along with some more privileged sectors challenging alienation, these struggles resist the capitalist imperative for endless economic growth. Instead they call for economic degrowth at the global level, especially in the Global North, and for alternatives to conventional development in the South.

Although these movements envision an end to consumerist society, they propose replacing it with what philosopher Kate Soper calls an "alternative hedonism" that finds meaning and happiness in stronger communities and more varied experiences. Their goal isn't private wealth but rather public affluence in the form of parks, libraries, cafeterias, free stores, gardens, theaters, free schools, museums, arcades, and makerspaces. Soper elaborates that alternative hedonism "might be enjoyed by both human and nonhuman animals" as delicious vegan food frees up land and ocean for wild critters to repopulate, and as sanctuaries provide a far better life for creatures rescued from animal experimentation and factory farms.[16]

By challenging anthropocentrism, such struggles echo Angela Davis's observation that "there is a connection between [...] the way we treat animals and the way we treat people who are at the bottom of the hierarchy."[17] This solidarity with nonhuman beings finds expression in 2010s historic

---

15 *Pluriverse: A Post-development Dictionary*, eds. Ashish Kothari, Ariel Salleh, Arturo Escobar, Federico Demaria and Alberto Acosta (New Delhi: Tulika Books, 2019).

16 Kate Soper, *Post-growth Living: For an Alternative Hedonism* (London: Verso, 2020), 135.

17 Herbert Marcuse, "Ecology and the Critique of Modern Society," *Capitalism and Nature* 3, no. 3 (September 1992): 33.
    Sista Vegan, "Angela Davis on Eating Chickens, Occupy, and Including Animals in Social Justice Initiative of the 99%," uploaded on February 24, 2012. Vimeo video, 3:37, https://vimeo.com/37361383.

Declaration of the Rights of Mother Earth, adopted by 35,000 grassroots campaigners gathered in Cochabamba, Bolivia, and by masses of people adopting vegetarian and vegan lifestyles, most widely in the Global South and in the North's communities of color.[18]

If such a radically ecological vision could shatter the hegemonic, "one-dimensional" worldview, then it would help address many of the typical objections to utopian, anarchistic visions. Answering "what's the incentive to work?" is not so daunting when a decrease in production enables a far shorter workweek of perhaps only ten hours of self-managed productive labor, plus a fair share of housework and caregiving. Marcuse's suggestion that we can rely on workers' intrinsic motivation, and "make the process of production a process of creation,"[19] does not seem so far-fetched if we only need to transform a small portion of today's workweek. The critical theorist wrote in 1969 that "the vast majority of the population" currently works in "unnecessary jobs" geared toward waste, repression, and manufactured needs. In 2018, anthropologist David Graeber confirmed with survey data that only twelve hours of industrialized countries' workweek are really productive.[20] An even shorter workweek, therefore, would be sufficient in an economy based on production for actual needs. With abundant free time, housework and elder care could be distributed more evenly across genders.

Answering "what about crime?," can be answered with reference to the stronger communities and wealth sharing enabled by global degrowth. Aside from disbanding the world's most violent institutions, particularly states and corporations, such a shift would help eliminate the massive inequalities, deprivation, and hyper-alienation that lead individuals to harm each other. Angela Davis and fellow Black liberationist Mumia Abu-Jamal point to Haudenosaunee (Iroquois) and Diné (Navajo) methods of community-based peacemaking and nonviolent sanctions facilitating repair and rehabilitation.[21] While such methods might have limited application in a sprawling society of strangers, they would be more practicable in a decentralized world based on Eros.

18 Laura Schleifer and Dan Fischer, "Animal Liberation from Below," *New Politics* Winter 2022 (New Politics Vol. XVIII No. 4, Whole Number 72).

19 Marcuse, "An Essay on Liberation."

20 David Graeber, *Bullshit Jobs: A Theory* (New York: Simon & Schuster, 2018).

21 Mumia Abu-Jamal and Angela Y. Davis, "Alternatives to the Present System of Capitalist Injustice," *Feminist Wire*, January 20, 2014, https://thefeministwire.com/2014/01/alternatives-to-the-present-system-of-capitalist-injustice/.

Catalyzing Many Creations

Around the turn of the 21st century, Mexican philosopher Gustavo Esteva summarized the emerging consensus of emancipatory struggles as "One no, and many yeses."[22] The "one no," a rejection of domination, paralleled the "Great Refusal" which Marcuse described:

> [N]o matter how great the distance between the middle-class revolt in the metropoles and the life-and-death struggle of the wretched of the earth— common to them is the depth of the Refusal. It makes them reject the rules of the game that is rigged against them, the ancient strategy of patience and persuasion, the reliance on the Good Will in the Establishment, its false and immoral comforts, its cruel affluence.

The "many yeses" referred to the creations of diverse horizontally-structured alternatives which form coalitions from below. In 1972s *Counter-Revolution and Revolt*, Marcuse advised militants to create "coun-terinstitutions," "popular assemblies," and councils "in the factories, offices, neighborhoods," as well as liberatory schools and imaginative art.[23]

Marcuse argued that small groups of people can become powerful "cata-lysts of transformation," affecting social change well beyond their local com-munities.[24] In the terminology of Marcuse's student George Katsiaficas, the 1960s movements sparked an "eros effect," meaning a "liberation of the life instincts" which enabled revolutionary sensibilities to spread worldwide.[25] Katsiaficas described the profound impact that such moments could have on multitudes of participants:

> Though secular, such moments metaphorically resemble the religious transfor-mation of the individual soul through the sacred baptism in the ocean of univer-sal life and love. The intergration of the sacred and the secular in such moments of 'political eros' (a term used by Herbert Marcuse) is an indication of the true potentiality of the human species.[26]

An especially inspiring potential catalyst today are Indigenous movements for land defense and cultural resurgence. Even in the face of settler-colonial genocide, Indigenous peoples have often delayed polluting infrastructure

---

22 Paul Kingsnorth, *One No, Many Yeses: A Journey to the Heart of the Global Resistance Movement* (London: Free Press, 2003).
23 Herbert Marcuse, *Counter-Revolution and Revolt* (Boston: Beacon Press, 1972).
24 Marcuse, *An Essay on Liberation*.
25 Katsiaficas, *The Imagination of the New Left*, 7, 10.
26 Katsiaficas, *The Imagination of the New Left*, 6.

while protecting the world's most intact landscapes.[27] With millennia of experience in stateless living, Indigenous societies have also been at the forefront of preserving what Marcuse terms the "anarchic element" of struggle.[28] It's no surprise, therefore, that their communities have played a key role in the alternative-creating movements of recent years.

The "many yeses" can also be seen in Sri Lanka's Sarvodaya villages, Brazil's Landless Workers Movement, South Africa's Abahlali baseMjondolo, Syria's Local Councils and Democratic Confederalists, North America's Zapatista, Cherán and Cooperation Jackson communes, and many like-minded projects worldwide affiliated with the Global Ecovillage, Transition Town, Right to the City and Symbiosis networks. Consistent with animal-liberationist goals, "Most ecovillages favour vegetarian, vegan, and organic cooking."[29]

By many accounts, participation in these movements offer a form of psychic liberation, cultivating what Marcuse called an "anti-repressive sensibility, allergic to domination."[30] By offering universal basic services that are unlikely to come from states, the mutual aid at the heart of such projects can be especially important as a means of survival during periods of unemployment and strike action. Moreover, as Lorenzo Kom'boa Ervin, a former Black Panther explains, mutual aid programs "inspire confidence in the revolutionary forces and expose the government as uncaring and incompetent."[31]

The liberatory experiments can also offer important means for community self-defense. Marcuse—in his 1965 essay "Repressive Tolerance"—advocated for militant intolerance of oppression, for the sake of "protecting [hu] man[ity] and animals from cruelty and aggression."[32] Toward these ends, Indigenous land defenders, Black Lives Matter protesters, anti-fascists, and the Animal and Earth Liberation Fronts engage in monkeywrenching, tire

---

27 Dallas Goldtooth, Saldamando, Alberto, and Kyle Gracey, "Indigenous Resistance Against Carbon," *Indigenous Environmental Network and Oil Change International*, August 2021, https://www.ienearth.org/wp-content/uploads/2021/09/Indigen ous-Resistance-Against-Carbon-2021.pdf.
  Julia E Fa et al., "Importance of Indigenous Peoples' Lands for the Conservation of Intact Forest Landscapes," *Frontiers in Ecology and the Environment* (2020): 135–140.
28 Marcuse, *An Essay on Liberation*.
29 Robert Hall, "The Ecovillage Experience, as an Evidence Base for National Wellbeing Strategies," *Intellectual Economics* 9 (2015): 37.
30 Marcuse, *An Essay on Liberation*.
31 Lorenzo Kom'boa Ervin, *Anarchism and the Black Revolution: The Definitive Edition* (London: Pluto Press, 2021).
32 Herbert Marcuse, "Repressive Tolerance," 1965, retrieved from https://www.marc use.org/herbert/publications/1960s/1965-repressive-tolerance-fulltext.html.

slashings, home demonstrations, arsons, and occasional physical confrontation. While following the alter-globalization movement's bedrock "respect for life,"[33] liberatory struggles commit to unwavering solidarity with peoples and anti-authoritarians defending the Earth's beings, cultures, land, water and air.

Refuse to Make the Stuff

While Marcuse emphasized the importance of participants well outside of the industrial proletariat, he maintained that "the working class is still the historical agent of revolution," thereby asserting an ongoing importance of struggle at the point of production and reproduction. Workplace organizing is all the more important given the ecological imperative to decrease and repurpose productive work. As the Industrial Workers of the World and Earth First! organizer Judi Bari emphasized, "It is only when the factory workers refuse to make the stuff, it is only when the loggers refuse to cut the ancient trees, that we can ever hope for real and lasting change."[34]

Uniting northern California's loggers and Earth First!ers against corporate deforestation, Bari's organizing became a central inspiration for the theory of green syndicalism, or horizontalist green unionizing. Seizing workplaces and establishing cooperatives, communities could decentrally coordinate with each other to contract and converge regional and global wealth, share sustainable technologies and dismantle oppression.

Green syndicalists build on green-unionizing efforts by Trade Unions for Energy Democracy and La Via Campesina. Trade Unions for Energy Democracy aligns trade union bodies on six continents in support of "a just transition to democratically accountable renewable energy systems."[35] Meanwhile, La Via Campesina, a network of tens of millions of small farmers in 88 countries, adopts a basically green-syndicalist approach of horizontal federation and direct action for local food sovereignty and climate justice. Based on La Via Campesina's belief that "we urgently need to reduce meat

---

33 Laurence Cox and Lesley Wood, "An Oral History of Peoples' Global Action," *Interface* 9, no. 1 (2017): 357–358.
34 Judi Bari, "Revolutionary Ecology," 1997, retrieved from http://www.judibari.org/revolutionary-ecology.html.
35 Trade Unions for Energy Democracy, "Why It's Important for Unions to Support TUED," retrieved March 11, 2023, https://www.tuedglobal.org/why-its-important-for-unions-to-support-tued.

consumption,"[36] and the mainstream scientific view that "grass-fed livestock are not a climate solution,"[37] peasant movements can ally with animal liberationists to resist large ranchers and factory farms, and to make plant-based diets and livelihoods more accessible to rural communities.

By organizing with fossil fuel and slaughterhouse workers, green syndicalists can help repurpose their workplaces toward restoring ecosystems, running animal sanctuaries and producing small-scale renewables. If hyperexploited[38] slaughterhouse workers went on strike with such demands, supported by solidarity funds, these workers would raise global consciousness and directly impede the entire meat industry. Slaughterhouses form a bottleneck in Brazil, the world's top killer of cows, and in the United States, the world's top killer of chickens. As the world briefly saw in the spring and summer of 2020, slaughterhouse shutdowns can keep supermarket shelves empty of meat. Moreover, as Huget notes in this volume, "a small handful of companies" produce "almost all of the meat products in the United States," providing a strategic focus for point-of-production organizing in the country with the world's highest per-capita meat consumption.[39]

Another focus for green organizers might be supporting employees of animal-rights and environmental nonprofits. Radicals rightly criticize these nonprofits for their reformist organization, but the employees themselves often tend to prefer bolder stances and actions.[40] A number of radicals and vegans get day jobs at such nonprofits, and the EF! network famously began when disgruntled Big Green employees quit in order to pursue a "no compromise" approach. Workers within these organizations continue to press for positive changes. For example, the Audubon Society workers' union is pushing for their employer to change its historic name, since Audubon was a slave owner.[41] Former and current employees of the Animal Legal Defense Fund have been urging changes that would make their workplace more equitable and more effective at protecting animals.[42]

---

36 La Via Campesina, "La Via Campesina in Action for Climate Justice," 2019, https://www.agroecology-europe.org/wp-content/uploads/2019/02/La-Via-Campesina-in-Action-for-Climate-Justice_volume_44_6_1.pdf.
37 "Grazed and confused?" *University of Oxford*.
38 See Marek Muller's "Violence Begets Violence" in the present volume.
39 Huget, "Abolish the Meat Industry."
40 Pellow, *Total Liberation*, ch. 1.
41 "Audubon Leadership Doubles Down on Racist Name," *The Bird Union*, March 15, 2023, https://www.birdunion.org/posts/NAS-keeps-racist-name-statement/.
42 Alexandra Martinez, "Former Animal Legal Defense Fund Staffers Accuse Organization of Transphobia, Union-busting, and More," *Prism*, June 26, 2023, https://prismreports.org/2023/06/26/animal-legal-defense-fund-toxic-workplace/.

In contrast to orthodox Marxist approaches, a green syndicalism would also recognize the role of houseworkers, peasants, and students as workers who reproduce the economy. Understanding students as apprentices for their future jobs, we can view the worldwide student climate strikes as significant economic disruptions. Young organizers such as Vanessa Nakate in Uganda and Ta'Kaiya Blaney in Canada have radicalized youths by explicitly rejecting capitalism and colonialism. If the right's fear and global union support are any indication, students' climate strikes could catalyze much broader unrest.[43]

Going further, a truly anti-anthropocentric or "deep-green"[44] syndicalism would recognize that many animals, too, belong to an expanded notion of the working class. In her chapter in this anthology, Catherine Oliver gives the example of chickens as laborers:

> Obviously, the chickens' labor extracted by humans is (at least) twofold: to grow big and fleshy for meat, a form of metabolic labor (Beldo, 2017), or to produce eggs at a rapid rate, a kind of reproductive or byproductive labor (Oliver, 2021).

Given what Davis calls "the horrendous conditions under which chickens are industrially bred," it's no surprise that chickens frequently engage in resistant behavior and have even escaped from farms and slaughterhouse-bound trucks.[45]

In fact, many animals worldwide resist domination and destruction. Poland's wild bison have sheltered a runaway cow, and Rwanda's gorillas have cooperate to dismantle poachers' traps.[46] An Australian parrot has removed anti-nesting spikes from windowsills, and South African elephants have released captive antelope.[47] A runaway goat in New Jersey has returned to rescue 75 other goats

---

43 Matthew Taylor, "Trade Unions around the World Support Global Climate Strike," *The Guardian*, September 19, 2019, https://www.theguardian.com/environment/2019/sep/19/trade-unions-around-the-world-support-global-climate-strike.

44 Val Plumwood describes "the critique of anthropocentrism or 'deep green theory" in *Feminism and the Mastery of Nature* (London: Routledge, 1993), 198. By using this term, I hope to avoid ceding it to the much newer network called Deep Green Resistance which has spread transphobic and authoritarian ideas.

45 "Real-life 'Chicken Run' for Stowaway Hen Using Lorry," *BBC*, June 17, 2018, https://www.bbc.com/news/uk-england-essex-44511686.
Sarat Colling, *Animal Resistance in the Capitalist Era* (East Lansing: Michigan State University Press, 2021), 9, 117–118.

46 Colling, *Animal Resistance*, 69.
Eben Diskin, "Young Gorillas Are Working Together to Destroy Poachers' Traps in Rwanda," *Matador Network*, June 5, 2018, https://matadornetwork.com/read/young-gorillas-working-together-destroy-poachers-traps-rwanda/.

47 Josh Taylor, "Chick Flick: Cockatoo Gives Anti-nesting Spikes the Bird in Viral Video," *The Guardian*, July 5, 2019, https://www.theguardian.com/environment/2019/jul/05/chick-flick-cockatoo-gives-anti-nesting-spikes-the-bird-in-viral-video.

and sheep from an auction house.[48] Dogs in Greece and Chile have participated in anti-austerity riots.[49] Whales have warned each other about whaling ships.[50] Since 2020, orcas have been attacking yachts in the strait of Gibraltar, a behavior that some scientists attribute to (industrial and upper-class) humans' attacks and invasions.[51] Forests have stubbornly regenerated, even in the wake of nuclear meltdown or generations of intensive farming.[52]

With these actions, nonhuman accomplices remind deep-green syndicalists that we aren't alone in struggling to decolonize and defend the planet. Observing life-promoting potentialities throughout the planet, Marcuse viewed "nature as an ally in the struggle" and declared "nature, too awaits the revolution!"[53]

Technology of Liberation

Revolutionary transformation is symbiotically linked to a widespread adoption of what Marcuse called "technology of liberation." Ecologically sustainable, decentralizing and labor-saving, liberatory technology could replace the Global North's fossil fuel-based infrastructure and offer the South an alternative to growth-centered development. For example, the 50 open-source, low-tech tools comprising the Global Village Construction Set, including an affordable 3D printer and sawmill, are being designed to cumulatively offer "a modern standard of living" at just "two hours of work per day."[54]

Fischer, "Let Nature Play."

48 Colling, *Animal Resistance*, 64.

49 "Riot Dog," *Wikimedia Foundation*, Last modified October 30, 2022, https://en.wikipedia.org/wiki/Riot_dog.
Colling, *Animal Resistance*, 115–117.

50 Philip Hoare, "Sperm Whales in 19th Century Shared Ship Attack Information," *The Guardian*, March 17, 2021, https://www.theguardian.com/environment/2021/mar/17/sperm-whales-in-19th-century-shared-ship-attack-information.

51 Cybele Knowles, "Boat-Sinking Orcas: Our New Folk Heroes," Earth First! Newswire, https://earthfirstjournal.news/2023/06/22/boat-sinking-orcas-our-new-folk-heroes/.

52 José M. Rey Benayas, "Rewilding: As Farmland and Villages Are Abandoned, Forests, Wolves and Bears Are Returning to Europe," *The Conversation*, July 2, 2019, https://theconversation.com/rewilding-as-farmland-and-villages-are-abandoned-forests-wolves-and-bears-are-returning-to-europe-119316.
Stuart Thompson, "How Plants Reclaimed Chernobyl's Poisoned Land," *BBC*, July 1, 2019, https://www.bbc.com/future/article/20190701-why-plants-survived-chernobyls-deadly-radiation.

53 Marcuse, *Counterrevolution and Revolt*.

54 "About factor e farm," *Open Source Ecology*, https://www.opensourceecology.org/about-factor-e-farm/.

Global degrowth would make possible a very fast transition toward small-scale renewable energy. The growth-based models say that achieving 100-% wind, water and solar energy will take decades, but they also purport that some 40% of today's energy consumption levels could be powered by wind, water and sunlight within just a few years.[55] If we relied only on that amount, and therefore achieved 100% green, renewable energy in under a decade, then that could be enough to converge the world's material living standards at a comfortable level, according to estimates by Joel Millward-Hopkins and co-authors and by Kris De Decker.[56] These studies suggest that the world can achieve living standards enjoyed today in the First World's voluntarily frugal countercultures where people reduce costs by sharing appliances, commutes, and often homes.

An example of liberatory technology is the multitude of knowledge-intensive small farming methods known as agroecology. Sustainably doubling yields in much of the Global South,[57] agroecology reduces labor in weeding and plowing and eliminates the application of herbicides and pesticides.[58] Cuba's farmers have found agroecological methods dramatically improve both per-hectare and per-hour productivity.[59] While adopting agroecology would require people in the North to devote more time to tending

"Machines: Global Village Construction Set," *Open Source Ecology*, https://www.opensourceecology.org/gvcs/.

55 Mark Jacobson, "Timeline and Land Area Required to Transition the All-Purpose End-Use Power of 143 Countries to 100 Percent Wind-Water-Solar and Five Reasons End-Use Demand Decreases 57.1 Percent Along the Way," December 20, 2019, https://web.stanford.edu/group/efmh/jacobson/Articles/I/TimelineDetailed.pdf.

56 Joel Millward-Hopkins, Julia K. Steinberger, Narasimha D. Rao, and Yannick Oswald, "Providing Decent Living with Minimum Energy: A Global Scenario," *Global Environmental Change* 65 (2020): 102168.
Kris De Decker, "How Much Energy Do We Need," *Low-Tech Magazine*, January 2018. https://solar.lowtechmagazine.com/2018/01/how-much-energy-do-we-need.html.

57 United Nations, "Eco-Farming Can Double Food Production in 10 Years, Says New UN Report," March 8, 2011, https://www.ohchr.org/en/press-releases/2011/03/eco-farming-can-double-food-production-10-years-says-new-un-report.

58 Miguel A. Altieri, "Applying Agroecology to Enhance the Productivity of Peasant Farming Systems in Latin America," *Environment Development and Sustainability* 1, no. 3 (1999), 197–217.

59 Peter Michael Rosset, Braulio Machín Sosa, Adilén María Roque Jaime, and Dana Rocío Ávila Lozano, "The Campesino-to-Campesino Agroecology Movement of ANAP in Cuba: Social Process Methodology in the Construction of Sustainable Peasant Agriculture and Food Sovereignty," *Journal of Peasant Studies* 38, 161–191.

farms and gardens, something that today's back-to-the-land and community-agriculture movements suggest would be welcomed by many people, the overwhelming majority of today's agricultural labor, which takes place off the farm in packing, transport and advertising, could be drastically reduced or eliminated in a decentralized food web.[60] Amir and Laila Kassim's 2021 edited collection *Rethinking Food and Agriculture* explores varieties of vegan agroecology that replace cattle manure with plant-based green manures and composted waste.[61]

Feeding the world population would be easier in a decentralized and mostly vegan world. Since the world's farmers already produce enough food to feed 12 to 14 billion human beings,[62] overwhelmingly without genetically modified crops,[63] feeding today's eight billion or 2050s expected 10 billion would be very achievable by giving harvests to humans rather than to livestock, and by reducing the spoilage caused by food's long-distance transportation. Plant-based farming will also be generally consistent with localizing food production. For example, veganism could make the United Kingdom completely food self-sufficient and would theoretically allow the United States to feed an additional 350 million people, which is more than the country's current population.[64]

Liberating land from animal agriculture and restoring it to wild grassland and forest, under Indigenous and local custodianship,[65] would sequester an estimated 800 billion tons of CO2 from the atmosphere, when including

60 By one estimate, off-farm labor accounted for some eighty-six percent of agricultural labor.
   Richard Levins and Richard Lewontin, *The Dialectical Biologist* (Cambridge: Harvard University Press, 1985), 211.

61 *Rethinking Food and Agriculture: New Ways Forward*, eds. Amir Kassam and Laila Kassam (Duxford: Woodhead Publishing, 2021).

62 International Assessment of Agricultural Knowledge, Science and Technology for Development, "Agriculture at a crossroads: IAASTD findings and recommendations for future farming," 2016, https://www.globalagriculture.org/fileadmin/files/weltagrarbericht/EnglishBrochure/BrochureIAASTD_en_web_small.pdf.

63 John Fagan, Michael Antoniou, and Claire Robinson, *GMO Myths and Truths* (Earth Open Source, 2014), 328.

64 Helen Harwitt and Matthew Hayek, "Eating Away at Climate Change with Negative Emissions," *Harvard Law School's Animal Law & Policy Program*, April 2019, https://animal.law.harvard.edu/wp-content/uploads/Eating-Away-at-Climate-Change-with-Negative-Emissions%E2%80%93%E2%80%93Harwatt-Hayek.pdf.

65 Somini Sengupta, Catrin Einhorn and Manuela Andreoni, "There's a Global Plan to Conserve Nature. Indigenous People Could Lead the Way," *New York Times*, March 11, 2021, https://www.nytimes.com/2021/03/11/climate/nature-conservation-30-percent.html.

above-ground and below-ground CO2.[66] Sustainable forestry practices could sequester another 600 billion.[67] Even after ocean outgassing, the combined drawdown would approach historical land-use emissions since the dawn of agriculture. Combined with a rapid energy transition, such measures bring radical climate and ecological targets within reach.[68]

Total Liberation from Compulsory Work

Today's "anti-work" movement protests the deep psychic violence involved in forcing people to work for a boss or in a market economy. Productive activity and distribution itself are not the problem, as people often enjoy and find fulfillment in creating, producing, and sharing. Yet as 2020's economic slowdown offered masses worldwide a temporary respite from alienated labor, there was awareness that, in the words of one journalistic account, "the bulk of today's jobs aren't necessary; instead, they enforce wage slavery and deprive workers of the full value of their output."[69] Examining Marx's 1844 manuscripts, Marcuse emphasized the importance of production being voluntary, self-managed, and imaginative:

> Labor in its true form is a medium for man's true self-fulfillment, for the full development of his potentialities; the conscious utilization of the forces of nature should take place for his satisfaction and enjoyment. In its current form, however, it cripples all human faculties and enjoins satisfaction.[70]

Likewise, the ruthless imposition of work on animals, plants, ecosystems, and the Earth intrudes on these beings' dignity, liberty, and health. Capitalists have called exploited ecosystems "working landscapes," exploited

66 Matthew Hayek, Helen Harwatt, William Ripple, and Nathaniel Mueller, "The Carbon Opportunity Cost of Animal-sourced Food Production on Land," *Nature Sustainability* 4 (2021), 21–24.

67 Kate Dooley, Doreen Stabinsky, Kelly Stone, Shefali Sharma, Teresa Anderson, Doug Gurian-Sherman, and Peter Riggs, "Missing Pathways to 1.5°C: The Role of the Land Sector in Ambitious Climate Action," *Climate Land Ambition and Rights Alliance*, https://www.iatp.org/documents/missing-pathways-15degc.

68 Dan Fischer, "Let Nature Play: A Possible Pathway of Total Liberation and Earth Restoration," *Green Theory & Praxis Journal* 14, no. 1 (2021), 8–29.

69 Brian O'Connor, "The Rise of the Anti-work Movement," *BBC*, January 27, 2022, https://www.bbc.com/worklife/article/20220126-the-rise-of-the-anti-work-movement.

70 Herbert Marcuse, *Reason and Revolution* (Oxford University Press, 1941), retrieved from Marxists Internet Archive, https://www.marxists.org/reference/archive/marcuse/works/reason/ch02-4.htm.

farm animals "labouring cattle," genetically modified crops "living factories" and extracted hydrocarbons "energy slaves." As Indigenous Environmental Network director Tom Goldtooth summarizes, the dominant worldview posits that "Mother Earth is a slave." These sorts of exploitation go well beyond, say, the mutually beneficial relationship between a blind human and a well-treated guide dog or between an organic gardener and dignified plants. Various Indigenous cultures and radical ecological movements alike intuit that the Earth willingly offers human communities the materials to their vital needs.[71] There is a difference, then, between sustainable use of the Earth's materials on one hand and the exploitative extraction and brutality characterizing capitalist production.

Combining the New Left's "refusal of work" and the green anarchists' reworking of Fanon's concept of "total liberation"—expanded to include the liberation of animals and the Earth—revolutionaries could propose a "Total Liberation from Compulsory Work." Drawing on the cell biologist and social theorist Barbara Ehrenreich's view of wild nature as fundamentally playful, a deep-green syndicalism would aim to eliminate compulsory work for humans, animals and ecosystems.

Emphasizing the inalienable right to relax and play, a deep-green syndicalism would share the Earth Liberation Front's solidarity with "the struggle of all species to be free"[72] and the Industrial Workers of the World's aim to "abolish the wage system, and live in harmony with the earth."[73] Insofar as we make demands, they might include: Abolish prisons, including zoos. Abolish torture, including experiments on animals. Abolish borders, including ecosystem-fragmenting highways. Abolish wars, including the war against Mother Earth. Free universal health care, including for animals.

Put aside the politicians' inadequate 1.5-degree Celsius and "Half Earth" targets, and instead strive for truly precautionary limits. Returning below 1 degree Celsius is necessary to protect island and coastal communities and to stay clear of catastrophic tipping points. Instead of protecting only half the Earth for wild nature, let's strive to protect at least 75%, allowing every species of plant to be covered by a communally preserved area and protecting the ocean's populations and biodiversity.[74]

Total liberation would not only protect human survival but would enable a life truly worth living. Humans should have abundant free time to hike with friends outdoors, to slowly travel the world by public buses and sail

71 Fischer, "Let Nature Play."
72 Earth Liberation Front, "Beltane, 1997," https://www.iiipublishing.com/elf.htm.
73 Industrial Workers of the World, https://www.iww.org/resources/constitution/.
74 See Fischer, "Let Nature Play."

boats, to be hobbyist cooks, graffitists, scientists, hip-hoppers, punk rockers, gardeners, philosophers and rewilders.

Drawing on Marcuse's vision of "miniskirts against the apparatchiks, rock 'n' roll against Soviet Realism," today's movements might take up the challenge of our establishment-friendly critics. A disparaging *New York Times* review of *An Essay on Liberation* mocked Marcuse's proposed utopia as a "sexy heaven on Earth."[75] At a time when scientists[76] and Indigenous prophecies[77] warn that the status quo could lead to an annihilation of biological life, or close, then the supposedly impossible alternative of utopia is an objective worthy of joyfully militant struggle.

Works Cited

Abu-Jamal, Mumia and Angela Y. Davis. "Alternatives to the Present Sstem of Capitalist Injustice." *Feminist Wire.* January 20, 2014, https://thefeministwire.com/2014/01/alternatives-to-the-present-system-of-capitalist-injustice/.

Altieri, Miguel A. "Applying Agroecology to Enhance the Productivity of Peasant Farming Systems in Latin America." *Environment Development and Sustainability* 1, no. 3 (1999), 197–217.

Amorelli, Lucia, Dylan Gibson, and Tamra Gilbertson, eds. *Hoodwinked in the Hothouse: Resist False Solutions to Climate Change*, 3rd edn. California: Community Printers, 2021.

Bari, Judi. "Revolutionary Ecology." 1997. Retrieved from http://www.judibari.org/revolutionary-ecology.html.

BBC. "Real-life 'Chicken Run' for Stowaway Hen Using Lorry." *BBC.* June 17, 2018. https://www.bbc.com/news/uk-england-essex-44511686.

Colling, Sarat. *Animal Resistance in the Capitalist Era.* East Lansing: Michigan State University Press, 2021.

Cox, Laurence and Lesley Wood. "An Oral History of Peoples' Global Action." *Interface* 9, no. 1 (2017), 357–358.

---

75 Sidney Hook, review of *An Essay on Liberation*, by Herbert Marcuse, *New York Times*, April 20, 1969, https://www.nytimes.com/1969/04/20/archives/an-essay-on-liberation-by-herbert-marcuse-91-pp-boston-the-beacon.html.

76 Giovanni Strona and Corey J. Bradshaw, "Co-extinctions Annihilate Planetary Life during Extreme Environmental Change," *Scientific Reports* 8, no. 1 (2018). https://doi.org/10.1038/s41598-018-35068-1.

77 Carol Jacobs, "Presentation to the United Nations July 18, 1985," *Akwesasne Notes*, 1995, retrieved from https://ratical.org/many_worlds/6Nations/PresentToUN.html.

Davis, Angela. "Angela Davis on Protest, 1968, and Her Old Teacher, Herbert Marcuse." *LitHub.* April 3, 2019, https://lithub.com/angela-davis-on-protest-1968-and-her-old-teacher-herbert-marcuse/.

De Decker, Kris. "How Much Energy Do We Need." *Low-Tech Magazine.* January 2018. https://solar.lowtechmagazine.com/2018/01/how-much-energy-do-we-need.html.

Diskin, Eben. "Young Gorillas Are Working Together to Destroy Poachers' Traps in Rwanda." *Matador Network.* June 5, 2018. https://matadornetwork.com/read/young-gorillas-working-together-destroy-poachers-traps-rwanda/.

Dooley, Kate, Doreen Stabinsky, Kelly Stone, Shefali Sharma, Teresa Anderson, Doug Gurian-Sherman, and Peter Riggs. "Missing Pathways to 1.5°C: The Role of the Land Sector in Ambitious Climate Action." *Climate Land Ambition and Rights Alliance,* https://www.iatp.org/documents/missing-pathways-15degc.

Dunayevskaya, Raya. "Reason and Revolution vs Conformity and Technology." *The Activist.* 1964. Retrieved from Wisconsin Historical Society, https://content.wisconsinhistory.org/digital/collection/p15932coll2/id/4237.

Earth Liberation Front. "Beltane, 1997." https://www.iiipublishing.com/elf.htm.

Ervin, Lorenzo Kom'boa. *Anarchism and the Black Revolution: The Definitive Edition.* London: Pluto Press, 2021.

Fa, Julia E., James E. M. Watson, Ian Leiper, Peter Potapov, Tom D. Evans, Neil D. Burgess, and Zsolt Molnár. "Importance of Indigenous Peoples' Lands for the Conservation of Intact Forest Landscapes." *Frontiers in Ecology and the Environment* (2020): 135–140.

Fagan, John, Michael Antoniou, and Claire Robinson. *GMO Myths and Truths.* Earth Open Source, 2014.

Fanon, Frantz. *The Wretched of the Earth.* Translated by Richard Philcox. New York: Grove Press, 2004.

Fischer, Dan. "Let Nature Play: A Possible Pathway of Total Liberation and Earth Restoration." *Green Theory & Praxis Journal* 14, no. 1 (2021), 7–29.

Fromm, Erich. *The Revolution of Hope.* New York: Harper & Row, 1968.

Goldtooth, Dallas, Saldamando, Alberto, and Kyle Gracey. "Indigenous Resistance Against Carbon." *Indigenous Environmental Network and Oil Change International.* August 2021. https://www.ienearth.org/wp-content/uploads/2021/09/Indigenous-Resistance-Against-Carbon-2021.pdf.

Graeber, David. *Bullshit Jobs: A Theory.* New York: Simon & Schuster, 2018.

Hall, Robert. "The Ecovillage Experience, as an Evidence Base for National Wellbeing Strategies." *Intellectual Economics* 9 (2015), 30–42.

Harwitt, Helen and Matthew Hayek. "Eating Away at Climate Change with Negative Emissions." *Harvard Law School's Animal Law & Policy Program,* April 2019. https://animal.law.harvard.edu/wp-content/uploads/Eating-Away-at-Climate-Change-with-Negative-Emissions%E2%80%93%E2%80%93Harwatt-Hayek.pdf.

Hayek, Matthew, Helen Harwatt, William Ripple, and Nathaniel Mueller. "The Carbon Opportunity Cost of Animal-sourced Food Production on Land." *Nature Sustainability* 4 (2021), 21–24.

Hewitt, Huey. "To Save the World." *Spectre Journal*. July 26, 2021. https://spectrejournal.com/to-save-the-world/.

Hoare, Philip. "Sperm Whales in 19th Century Shared Ship Attack Information." *The Guardian*, March 17, 2021. https://www.theguardian.com/environment/2021/mar/17/sperm-whales-in-19th-century-shared-ship-attack-information.

Hook, Sidney. Review of *An Essay on Liberation* by Herbert Marcuse. *New York Times*. April 20, 1969, https://www.nytimes.com/1969/04/20/archives/an-essay-on-liberation-by-herbert-marcuse-91-pp-boston-the-beacon.html.

Huget, Hailey. "Abolish the Meat Industry: A Roadmap for Transforming Animal Liberation from a Single-Issue Cause into a Mass Movement." In Zane McNeill (ed.), *Building Multispecies Resistance Against Exploitation: Stories from the Frontlines of Labor and Animal Rights*. Peter Lang, 2024..

Industrial Workers of the World, Constitution. Modified on January 1, 2022. https://www.iww.org/resources/constitution/.

International Assessment of Agricultural Knowledge, Science and Technology for Development. "Agriculture at a Crossroads: IAASTD Findings and Recommendations for Future Farming." 2016. https://www.globalagriculture.org/fileadmin/files/weltagrarbericht/EnglishBrochure/BrochureIAASTD_en_web_small.pdf.

Jacobs, Carol. "Presentation to the United Nations July 18, 1985." *Akwesasne Notes*. 1995. Retrieved from https://ratical.org/many_worlds/6Nations/PresentToUN.html.

Jacobson, Mark. "Timeline and Land Area Required to Transition the All-Purpose End-Use Power of 143 Countries to 100 Percent Wind-Water-Solar and Five Reasons End-Use Demand Decreases 57.1 Percent Along the Way." December 20, 2019. https://web.stanford.edu/group/efmh/jacobson/Articles/I/TimelineDetailed.pdf.

Kassam, Amir and Laila Kassam, eds. *Rethinking Food and Agriculture: New Ways Forward*. Duxford: Woodhead Publishing, 2021.

Katsiaficas, George. *The Imagination of the New Left: A Global Analysis of 1968*. Cambridge: South End Press, 1987.

Kellner, Douglas. "Introduction: Radical Politics, Marcuse, and the New Left." In Douglas Kellner (ed.), *Herbert Marcuse: The New Left and the 1960s*. London: Routledge, 2005.

Kingsnorth, Paul. *One No, Many Yeses: A Journey to the Heart of the Global Resistance Movement*. London: Free Press, 2003.

Knowles, Cybele. "Boat-Sinking Orcas: Our New Folk Heroes." Earth First! Newswire. https://earthfirstjournal.news/2023/06/22/boat-sinking-orcas-our-new-folk-heroes/.

Kothari, Ashish, Ariel Salleh, Arturo Escobar, Federico Demaria and Alberto Acosta, eds. *Pluriverse: A Post-development Dictionary*. New Delhi: Tulika Books, 2019.

La Via Campesina, "La Via Campesina in Action for Climate Justice," 2019, https://www.agroecology-europe.org/wp-content/uploads/2019/02/La-Via-Campesina-in-Action-for-Climate-Justice_volume_44_6_1.pdf.

Leach, Mike. "Chiapas: The end of 'the end of history'." *Green Left.* October 3, 1995. https://www.greenleft.org.au/content/chiapas-end-end-history.

Levins, Richard and Richard Lewontin. *The Dialectical Biologist.* Cambridge: Harvard University Press, 1985.

Marcuse, Herbert. *Reason and Revolution.* Oxford University Press, 1941. Retrieved from Marxists Internet Archive, https://www.marxists.org/reference/archive/marcuse/works/reason/ch02-4.htm

Marcuse, Herbert. *One-Dimensional Man.* Boston: Beacon, 1964. Retrieved from Marxists Internet Archive, https://www.marcuse.org/herbert/pubs/64onedim/odmcontents.html.

Marcuse, Herbert. "Repressive Tolerance," 1965, retrieved from https://www.marcuse.org/herbert/publications/1960s/1965-repressive-tolerance-fulltext.html

Marcuse, Herbert. *An Essay on Liberation.* London: Penguin, 1969. Retrieved from Marxists Internet Archive, https://www.marxists.org/reference/archive/marcuse/works/1969/essay-liberation.htm.

Marcuse, Herbert. *Counter-Revolution and Revolt.* Boston: Beacon Press, 1972.

Marcuse, Herbert. "Ecology and the Critique of Modern Society." *Capitalism and Nature* 3, no. 3, 29–48 (September 1992).

Marks, Elizabeth, Hickman, Caroline Hickman, Panu Petteri Pihkala, Susan Clayton, Eric Lewandowski, Elouise E. Mayall, Britt Wray, Catriona Mellor, and Lise Van Susteren. "Young People's Voices on Climate Anxiety, Government Betrayal and Moral Injury: A Global Phenomenon." *Social Science Research Network* (September 7, 2021), 863–873.

Martinez, Alexandra. "Former Animal Legal Defense Fund Staffers Accuse Organization of Transphobia, Union-busting, and More." *Prism* (June 26, 2023). https://prismreports.org/2023/06/26/animal-legal-defense-fund-toxic-workplace/.

Millward-Hopkins, Joel, Julia K. Steinberger, Narasimha D. Rao, and Yannick Oswald. "Providing Decent Living with Minimum Energy: A Global Scenario." *Global Environmental Change* 65 (2020): 102168.

Muller, Marek. "Violence Begets Violence." In Zane McNeill (ed.), *Building Multispecies Resistance Against Exploitation: Stories from the Frontlines of Labor and Animal Rights.* Peter Lang, 2024.

O'Connor, Brian. "The Rise of the Anti-work Movement." *BBC.* January 27, 2022, https://www.bbc.com/worklife/article/20220126-the-rise-of-the-anti-work-movement.

Open Source Ecology. "About Factor e Farm," *Open Source Ecology.* https://www.opensourceecology.org/about-factor-e-farm/.

Open Source Ecology. "Machines: Global Village Construction Set." *Open Source Ecology.* https://www.opensourceecology.org/gvcs/.

Pellow, David Naguib. *Total Liberation: The Power and Promise of Animal Rights and the Radical Earth Movement*. Minneapolis: University of Minnesota Press, 2014.

Plumwood, Val. *Feminism and the Mastery of Nature*. London: Routledge, 1993.

Rey Benayas, José M. "Rewilding: As Farmland and Villages Are Abandoned, Forests, Wolves and Bears Are Returning to Europe." *The Conversation*. July 2, 2019. https://theconversation.com/rewilding-as-farmland-and-villages-are-abandoned-forests-wolves-and-bears-are-returning-to-europe-119316.

Schleifer, Laura and Dan Fischer. "Animal Liberation from Below." *New Politics* Winter 2022 (New Politics Vol. XVIII No. 4, Whole Number 72), 14–26.

Sengupta, Somini, Catrin Einhorn and Manuela Andreoni. "There's a Global Plan to Conserve Nature. Indigenous People Could Lead the Way." *New York Times*. March 11, 2021. https://www.nytimes.com/2021/03/11/climate/nature-conservation-30-percent.html.

Sista, Vegan. "Angela Davis on Eating Chickens, Occupy, and Including Animals in Social Justice Initiative of the 99%." Uploaded February 24, 2012. Vimeo video, 3:37. https://vimeo.com/37361383.

Soper, Kate. *Post-growth Living: For an Alternative Hedonism*. London: Verso, 2020.

Strona, Giovanni, and Corey J. Bradshaw. "Co-extinctions Annihilate Planetary Life during Extreme Environmental Change." *Scientific Reports* 8, no. 1 (2018). https://doi.org/10.1038/s41598-018-35068-1.

Taylor, Josh. "Chick Flick: Cockatoo Gives Anti-nesting Spikes the Bird in Viral Video." *The Guardian*. July 5, 2019, https://www.theguardian.com/environment/2019/jul/05/chick-flick-cockatoo-gives-anti-nesting-spikes-the-bird-in-viral-video.

Taylor, Matthew. "Trade Unions around the World Support Global Climate Strike." *The Guardian*. September 19, 2019, https://www.theguardian.com/environment/2019/sep/19/trade-unions-around-the-world-support-global-climate-strike.

The Bird Union. "Audubon Leadership Doubles Down on Racist Name." March 15, 2023. https://www.birdunion.org/posts/NAS-keeps-racist-name-statement/.

Thompson, Stuart. "How Plants Reclaimed Chernobyl's Poisoned Land." *BBC*, July 1, 2019, https://www.bbc.com/future/article/20190701-why-plants-survived-chernobyls-deadly-radiation.

Trade Unions for Energy Democracy. "Why It's Important for Unions to Support TUED." Retrieved March 11, 2023, https://www.tuedglobal.org/why-its-important-for-unions-to-support-tued

United Nations. "Eco-Farming Can Double Food Production in 10 Years, Says New UN Report." March 8, 2011, https://www.ohchr.org/en/press-releases/2011/03/eco-farming-can-double-food-production-10-years-says-new-un-report.

University of Oxford. "Grazed and Confused? New Report Evaluates the Climate Impact of Grazing Livestock." October 3, 2017. https://www.oxfordmartin.ox.ac.uk/news/2017-news-grazed-and-confused/.

Warwick, John. "Desert: A Review Essay." *Organise!* October 9, 2019. Retrieved from The Anarchist Library, https://theanarchistlibrary.org/library/john-warwick-des ert-a-review-essay.

Wikimedia Foundation. "Riot Dog." *Wikipedia*, Last modified October 30, 2022, https://en.wikipedia.org/wiki/Riot_dog.

Concluding Thoughts

Nathan Poirier

It is an immense honor to be offered the chance to write a summary and conclusion in a book, especially one curated by Zane McNeill, someone I deeply respect and am inspired by. And it is an invitation I initially declined. Zane extended the offer for me to write this ending note at a time when I was besieged by multiple factors that seemed to conspire as one to make it unviable for me to produce writing that was worthy of such placement, at least within a reasonable timeframe. Having recently finished a PhD program, I was working part-time tutoring and adjunct teaching at a community college. My excellent and free graduate assistant health care ended with graduation, so I was scrambling to find (what turned out to be) much worse health insurance at a ridiculous cost. On top of that, through changing plans, I had to find a new primary care physician (PCP) who the system refused to allow me to see for three months. This also meant that I was not able to see the specialist doctors I had been seeing for two ongoing chronic health conditions until my new patient visit with my new PCP. During this wait, I had to pay for this insurance all the while, of course. But these experiences also came to motivate this writing.

There are at least two major issues at play here. One is obviously the atrocious state of healthcare in the "United States." The other factor is deeply related: labor. My part-time and low-paid, devoid-of-benefits work takes up much of my time which leaves me with little left to read, think, write, engage in activism, or shop for and set up health insurance. This is not to mention that in order to do things like doctor appointments, I have to take time off work which means losing out on income, further providing impetus to work more later on to make that money up, which is needed to pay the high costs of "healthcare." The other connection between health care and labor is that in the United States, health insurance is typically only provided (usually still at a cost) if one holds a full-time job (or is married to someone with a full-time job). This is one of the "perks" of employment that comes dangled at the end of forced, long-term, underpaid, demanding, and disciplining tasks—otherwise known as labor—designed to serve State-corporate-military interests. Despite this, Zane's invitation and all chapter authors of the present volume have left me feeling inspired to fight non/human worker oppression and to fight against work in general. This book has sparked much thought and emotion and it is a "labor of love" to share those impressions with you here. What follows are what I see as common threads that tie all contributions to this book together. This writing reflects what I interpret contributor calls for workplace organization, better pay, shorter hours, improved working conditions, legal protections, etc., as—an implicit call to abolish labor capitalism.

As the contributors to this collection show, labor exploitation constitutes multispecies violence and a violation of non/human social justice. For example, in the case of nonhuman laborers, bigger cages are "granted" to make human consumers feel better about purchasing animal products which are unhealthy and environmentally destructive. This harms not only those who consume these products but also all non/humans affected by habitat destruction and air/water/land pollution. This concession is also made to help improve animals' productivity because their bodies have already been pushed beyond limits by intensive confinement and unnatural (re)productive demands. Building from connections such as this, the collection of chapters in this book shows that animal rights are labor rights and vice versa. Contributors rightly push this connection to its ultimate and ideal conclusion: abolish all forced, coerced labor as such, along with capitalism in all its nefarious manifestations (racial, carceral, etc.). It is this theme that I read as the most profound of this book as a whole and the chapters within it.

This book focuses particularly on the intersection of non/human labor exploitation within the animal advocacy nonprofit sector. Such a focus is warranted because people who are involved in such labor tend to be more empathetic to non/human social justice causes and to understand these causes are connected. However, chapters in the second section of this book indicate that even this space is easily co-opted by the forces of racial and carceral capitalism. Such structures and ideologies potently and insidiously turn exploited groups against each other, each trying to push off their exploitation to another group. Infighting will not free anyone, but it will allow non/human labor to continue as oppressive. The focus on non/human labor exploitation and worker liberation is further justified when we consider, as authors of section 1 of this book do, that nonhuman animals can be considered laborers—both as producers of goods but also in their physical resistance to their own oppression.

In this case, the number of nonhuman laborers far outnumber human laborers by at least an order of magnitude. This also means that the atrocities leveled towards nonhuman laborers are also far more numerous than those towards human laborers. Labor struggles must take this into account. Where human labor is exploited, nonhumans are exploited in turn as a way to take (our human) frustrations out. The demeaning and meaningless laborious tasks humans are forced to perform leave us feeling powerless, so we take that anger out on those we are socially sanctioned to have power over, which often include nonhuman animals.

I have witnessed the negative effects of labor exploitation through my parents, my partner, and myself. Things like raises, bonuses, and promotions are frequently granted to those who exploit others the most or the most efficiently. They are not true incentives to vindicate all of the sacrifices we laborers go through (I don't intentionally mean to universalize here; I realize my labor at a community college is far different from the non/human labor of those, say, at a slaughterhouse). Such things "gifted" to us by employers simply seek to justify ongoing labor exploitation and to quell resistance. Such incentives are meant to keep us tired, passive, ignorant, and most of all bound to the employment/profit-making scheme. Therefore, at its very root, and intentionally by design, labor is inherently exploitative and promotes inequality, especially among social classes. But what is the cost of such "perks"? What do workers give up for fleeting monetary gain? How much do we get to actually live and how much do we decrease the quality and even the timespan of our lives due to direct or indirect consequences of our labor? The contributors to this volume see past all that and demand much more and much better. Another common tactic by the exploiting class is the promotion of a work/life balance. First, this places such responsibility on already exploited workers to sort out themselves without being given the proper time and space to think and work out such an arrangement (or, likely, to change a settled upon arrangement if feelings or circumstances change). Second, what if this balance comes out to, say, 25% work and 75% life? Will employers respect this decision? Of course not. The balance of work and life when propagated by employers is empty rhetoric. Perhaps unsurprisingly, some, like Jeff Bezos, have gone so far to encourage the two to become one, so that business and pleasure become conflated. It is neither acceptable to work to live nor live to work. We should be able to simply live well.

With the foregoing reflections on this text, recommendations of how to proceed seem clear enough. We must voice dissent, strike, unionize, sabotage our employers (and others'), loot and steal privately and collectively, deface property, work slower, disseminate "private," "classified," and "copyrighted" material, and burn office buildings and corporate headquarters down (although this is not the place and I am not the person to offer a primer on how to do this safely, many precautions must be taken in this act). Repurposing labor facilities into low-cost or free housing, free healthcare, or "free stores" is also a constructive direction to pursue. This goes for not only places of human employment but also the nonhuman exploitation factories such as factory farms, animal experimentation labs, and fur farms. As every chapter in this volume shows, where nonhumans are exploited, we are sure to find exploited humans within those industries as well. Because 99% of us are among the exploited working class (here I mean this term to refer to those of us who are employed rather than those who employ us, as opposed to its more common socioeconomic status reference), this necessitates and provides grounds for mass solidarity, not only between human factions but with nonhumans too. The Elite have constructed societies so that the only way to "fix" them is to abolish them, through force, as contributors to the third section of this book show and encourage us to do. All of these recommended actions should be done with structural change in mind. As is so apparent in the writings of Audre Lorde, we must keep a keen eye fixed on the Elite who constrain the conditions surrounding employment, and on social structures such as racial and carceral capitalism. This focus is abundantly present in the preceding chapters.

Those of us who can, should also work as little as possible. This could include those of us who are married to someone with health insurance. Or, for those for whom it is possible, potentially such as those who are provided free healthcare, as in every other "(over)developed" nation besides the U.S., should refuse to work full-time. On a larger scale, labor should also be reoriented towards necessary and meaningful acts such as care work and providing for community needs. In this, care must be taken to observe the boundaries of what is "needed" to not overrun environmental capacities or the abilities of the non/humans involved to avoid exploitation. In short, much less labor should be done on the whole—and this can become a full-fledged social movement as indeed it has been in past times. These all seem like natural take-aways and extensions of the chapters written by authors herein. It seems imperative we all think about how to implement such implications in our own lives, and how we can help make these issues become and stay political.

Another indirect thought comes to mind: readers (and laborers) should continue to think of new and different ways to resist their exploitation and disrupt their work—and to interfere with the exploitative labor of others. My first job was at an ACO Hardware. I would frequently damage products which then by protocol had to be sold at a heavily discounted price.

After damaging them, I then "fixed" them up, which usually left the product looking pretty undesirable. This "fixing" was a required part of my job if a product was noticed to be damaged. Altogether, this would not only waste my ACO's time but would, however marginally, decrease their profits. I would also routinely apply coupons already used by previous customers so that others could receive discounted items. After all, I did not have a stake in my employer's profits. Who among us does? In another job working housekeeping for my undergraduate college, I became particularly skilled at wasting time and avoiding the detection of my boss. When assigned to "trash run," which involved picking up bags of trash from about eight locations on (a very small) campus with a truck and throwing them in the college's main dumpster, I would routinely take 2+ hours to complete this when I was told it should easily be accomplished in twenty minutes. If employers will not grant us reasonable labor rights or the ability to do the "right" kind of labor, we should exercise our right not to work, while perhaps getting paid for it. All of the foregoing suggestions pick up on, fall in line with, and try to advance the prominent thread of animal resistance to labor, and resistance *as* labor that this book advances.

Lastly, despite all this talk of abolishing work, it must also be said that workers do need protection. This seems like an obvious corollary from the foregoing discussion. Indeed, many contributors assert this. Workers need legal protection to curb the rampant cruel intentions of employers who will always push the envelope as to how far they can exploit employees. Among other examples, the intertwined histories of child and nonhuman labor in the U.S. attests to this. Unless somehow protected against, there will be no absolutes in labor exploitation. Employers will be indifferent to the lives and working conditions of laborers, as indeed many are already. This is perhaps especially true in the case of nonhuman laborers who receive the fewest and weakest protections while often facing the harshest of conditions. This is why unionizing is still a powerful resistance tool even if it upholds the general system of work, employment, and wages. As laborers, we should take what we're given and demand the rest.

As with a previous volume *Vegan Entanglements: Dismantling Racial and Carceral Capitalism*, with the radical knowledge, experience, and insights from the volume you have just read—*Building Multispecies Resistance Against Exploitation: Stories from the Frontlines of Labor and Animal Rights*—Zane has again demonstrated their knack for connecting issues that are frequently kept separate. This book is a clarion call to make Covid's "great refusal" to labor in exploitative work conditions a multispecies mass liberation movement.

Notes on Contributors

Will Boisseau completed his doctorate at Loughborough University in 2015. His research focuses on the place of animal rights within the British left, particularly on the relationship between the anarchist/direct action and legislative wings of the movement. His work explores the class and gender issues influencing this relationship, the marginalization of animal rights in mainstream labour politics and a range of concepts including speciesism, total liberation, critical animal studies and intersectionality. Will is the Institute of Critical Animal Studies director of administration. Will is currently involved in trade union politics in the UK.

Dan Fischer is a middle- and Hebrew school teacher and a volunteer with Food Not Bombs, *New Politics*, and Promoting Enduring Peace. He can be reached at dfischer@riseup.net.

Hailey Huget is a labor organizer who also recently earned a PhD in Philosophy from Georgetown University, where they specialized in animal ethics.

Zane McNeill is a scholar-activist from West Virginia and has published edited collections with Lantern Publishing & Media, PM Press, University Press of Kentucky, and Routledge.

S. Marek Muller is an Assistant Professor of Communication at Texas State University. They study arguments pertaining to human/nonhuman animal liberation and the social constructions of humanity/animality.

Catherine Oliver is a geographer and lecturer in the Sociology of Climate Change at Lancaster University. Her research interests are animals (specifically birds), more-than-human studies, and veganism. Her recent projects include an ethnographic study of backyard chickens in London. Catherine is the author of two books, *Veganism, Archives and Animals* (Routledge, 2021) and *What's Veganism For?* (Bristol University Press, 2024).

Nathan Poirier, although hostile towards the academic industrial complex, has a PhD in sociology, with graduate specializations in (critical) animal studies and women's & gender studies. Nathan's dissertation analyzes and critiques in vitro meat from vegan and critical animal studies perspectives. Nathan co-edited the book Emerging New Voices in Critical Animal Studies: Vegan Studies for Total Liberation (2022). Nathan currently labors as a tutor at Lansing Community College.

Rajesh Reddy directs the Global Animal Law and Animal Law Advanced Degree Programs at the Center for Animal Law Studies at Lewis & Clark Law School. Outside of Lewis & Clark, he chairs the International Subcommittee of the Animal Law Section of the American Bar Association and serves as a board member for Minding Animals International. He has advanced human and nonhuman animal interests as part of his work for the Animal Legal Defense Fund and the Human Rights Law Network in New Delhi, India.

Kelly Shanahan is a recent law graduate from the University of Nebraska College of Law. In fall 2023, Kelly joined the asylum legal team at the Immigrant Legal Center in Lincoln, Nebraska. While at the University of Nebraska, she was a student attorney with the school's Immigration Clinic, representing undocumented individuals in various immigration matters. Kelly is a 2021 recipient of the Advancement of Animal Law award and is an advocate for creating a more intersectional field of law.

Drew Robert Winter is Managing Editor of the Political Animals section at the journal *Society & Animals*, co-founder of the Animal Politics Collective, and adjunct instructor in Anthropology and Sociology at Lansing Community College. He is interested in human-animal relationships within the context of infrastructures and cultural production, especially in Scandinavia. He received his PhD in Cultural Anthropology from Rice University in 2020, studying how cultural attitudes toward the meat industry inhibit climate policy in Denmark.

Ellyse Winter holds a PhD from the University of Toronto in Social Justice Education and Environmental Studies. Her research applies the intersecting fields of critical food studies, critical animal studies, and environmental justice to an examination of the changing landscape of food production and the possibilities for alternative foodways. In her work, Ellyse examines strategies for building solidarity or an alliance politics across various community groups and social justice movements. Ellyse also teaches in the Department of Sociology and Criminology at the University of Windsor and in the Environmental Sustainability Research Centre at Brock University.

RADICAL ANIMAL STUDIES AND TOTAL LIBERATION

Anthony J. Nocella II, S E R I E S E D I T O R

The **Radical Animal Studies and Total Liberation** book series branches out of Critical Animal Studies (a field co-founded by Anthony J. Nocella II) with the argument that criticism is not enough. Action must follow theory. This series demands that scholars are engaged with their subjects both theoretically and actively via radical, revolutionary, intersectional action for total liberation. Founded in anarchism, the series provides space for scholar-activists who challenge authoritarianism and oppression in their many daily forms. **Radical Animal Studies and Total Liberation** promotes accessible and inclusive scholarship that is based on personal narrative as well as traditional research, and is especially interested in the advancement of interwoven voices and perspectives from multiple radical, revolutionary social justice groups and movements such as Black Lives Matter, Idle No More, Earth First!, the Zapatistas, ADAPT, prison abolition, LGBTTQQIA rights, disability liberation, Earth Liberation Front, Animal Liberation Front, political prisoners, radical transnational feminism, environmental justice, food justice, youth justice, and Hip Hop activism.

To order other books in this series please contact our Customer Service Department:

PETERLANG@PRESSWAREHOUSE.COM (WITHIN THE U.S.)

ORDERS@PETERLANG.COM (OUTSIDE THE U.S.)

To find out more about the series or browse a full list of titles, please visit our website:

WWW.PETERLANG.COM